Political Forces
in
Argentina

POLITICAL FORCES IN ARGENTINA

Third Edition

PETER G. SNOW
and
LUIGI MANZETTI

 PRAEGER

Westport, Connecticut
London

Library of Congress Cataloging-in-Publication Data

Snow, Peter G.
Political forces in Argentina / Peter G. Snow and Luigi Manzetti.—
3rd ed.
    p. cm.
Includes bibliographical references (p.   ) and index.
ISBN 0–275–93384–9 (hc : alk. paper). — ISBN 0–275–93810–7 (pb :
alk. paper)
1. Pressure groups—Argentina. 2. Political parties—Argentina.
I. Manzetti, Luigi. II. Title.
JL2069.P7S6 1993
322'.0982—dc20   92–19595

British Library Cataloguing in Publication Data is available.

Library of Congress Catalog Card Number: 92–19595
ISBN: 0–275–93384–9 (HB)
      0–275–93810–7 (PB)

First published in 1993

Praeger Publishers, 88 Post Road West, Westport, CT 06881
An imprint of Greenwood Publishing Group, Inc.

Printed in the United States of America

The paper used in this book complies with the
Permanent Paper Standard issued by the National
Information Standards Organization (Z39.48–1984).

10 9 8 7 6 5 4 3 2 1

To Janice
and Carol

Contents

Tables

Abbreviations

AAA	Argentine Anticommunist Alliance
APF	Federal Popular Alliance
APR	Revolutionary Popular Alliance
CEA	Argentine Episcopal Conference
CFI	Federal Independent Confederation
CGE	General Economic Confederation
CGT	General Confederation of Labor
CGU	General Confederation of University Students
COA	Argentine Labor Confederation
CONADEP	National Commission on the Disappeared
DGFM	General Directorate of Military Manufacturing
ERP	People's Revolutionary Army
FAA	Argentine Agrarian Federation
FJL	Justicialist Liberation Front
FNP	National and Popular Front
FNPC	National Federation of Parties of the Center
FORA	Argentine Regional Labor Federation
FREJUPO	Justicialist Popular Front
FUA	Argentine University Federation
FUBA	University Federation of Buenos Aires
GAN	Great National Covenant
GOU	Group of United Officers

IAPI	Argentine Institute for the Promotion of Exchange
IMF	International Monetary Fund
JPI	Intransigent Party Youth
JUP	Peronist University Youth
MAS	Movement to Socialism
MID	Movement of Integration and Development
MODIN	Movement for Dignity and Independence
MRC	Movement for Renovation and Change
MUCS	Movement of Syndicalist Unity and Coordination
PAN	National Autonomist Party
PDC	Christian Democrat Party
PDP	Progressive Democrat Party
PI	Intransigent Party
PJ	Justicialist Party
PPC	Christian Popular Party
PRC	Christian Revolutionary Party
PRT	Worker's Revolutionary Party
PSA	Argentine Socialist Party
PSD	Democratic Socialist Party
PST	Worker's Socialist Party
SCAF	Supreme Council of the Armed Forces
SRA	Argentine Rural Society
UCD	Democratic Center Union
UCR	Radical Civic Union
UCRI	Intransigent Radical Civic Union
UCRP	People's Radical Civic Union
UDELPA	Union of the Argentine People
UIA	Argentine Industrial Union
UPAU	Union for a University Opening
USA	Argentine Syndical Union

Preface

The first edition of *Political Forces in Argentina* appeared two decades ago. Although a revised edition was published in 1979, the book has been badly out of date for some time now. This third edition incorporates not only the updating of each chapter but also many extensive revisions. Professor Manzetti co-authored the chapters on the Church and students.

Political Forces
in
Argentina

CHAPTER 1

Introduction

A surprising number of people in the United States continue to think of the nations of Latin America as small, sleepy, banana republics, populated by illiterate, poverty-stricken Indians who live in disease-ridden jungles. Such is not even an accurate picture of the nations of Central America and the Caribbean, much less of South America.

In Argentina one discovers not this stereotype, but a highly literate (94 percent) population, almost uniformly of European ancestry, inhabiting the world's eighth largest nation, virtually all of which lies within the temperate zone. Almost a third of these people live in metropolitan Buenos Aires, one of the world's largest and most cosmopolitan cities. Endowed with beautiful French-styled buildings of the turn of the century, a magnificent opera house, dozens of theaters and movie houses, myriads of excellent restaurants, and a very active cultural and artistic scene, Buenos Aires has long been regarded as the Paris of the Southern Hemisphere.

Even those persons living outside the city of Buenos Aires fail to conform to the stereotypical image that sees the vast majority as poor peasants working someone else's land. Certainly there are landless peasants in Argentina, but not nearly as many as might be expected. To begin with, almost three-fourths of the population outside Buenos Aires live in urban centers, by no means all small towns—at least nine of the cities of the interior have populations of over 250,000. The three largest might well be compared with cities in the United States. Rosario, quite similar in many ways to Pittsburgh, is a highly industrialized city of over a million people about 200 miles up the Paraná River from Buenos Aires. Córdoba, with about 1 million people, 450 miles northwest of the capital, is a very old cultural center where in recent years heavy industry has entered a traditional, almost colonial atmosphere—much as has been the case in Atlanta. Mendoza, a city of 610,000 people nestled against the foothills of the Andes, sparkles with the crisp orderliness of a mountain city such as Denver. Since Argentina differs in so many ways from the stereotypical image of Latin America, it is necessary to preface an analysis of the nation's major political forces with a few words about the nation itself, its people, and its history.

GEOGRAPHY

Argentina is about the same size as that part of the United States that lies east of the Mississippi River. Geographers usually divide the country into four general areas: Patagonia, the Andean region, the North, and the Pampas. The region south of the Colorado River, including the provinces of Santa Cruz, Chubut, Río Negro, and Neuquén, is usually referred to as Patagonia. This bleak and forbidding area contains more than a fourth of the national territory but less than 3 percent of the country's population. Prior to the 1860s it was populated only by a few Indians, but since that time it has been taken over by sheep ranches of enormous size. Wool is the main product of this cool, dry, and windy plateau, which cannot be farmed with any degree of success. While there are petroleum deposits near Comodoro Rivadavia and Plaza Huincal, and coal at Río Turbio, the great distance from the nation's population center and poor transportation facilities have discouraged their development.

In the Andean region of the northwest are the provinces of Jujuy, Salta, Catamarca, La Rioja, San Juan, Mendoza, and Tucumán. Except for the mountains in the extreme west, this is a high, dry plateau, a virtual desert in places. Like Patagonia, this region comprises about a fourth of the nation's land area; it has only a seventh of its population. The people are concentrated in a few small river valleys where irrigation makes possible the raising of sugarcane and several types of fruits. Mendoza is the center of the nation's wine production, and Argentina is one of the world's largest producers of wine. The small province of Tucumán is given over almost entirely to the growth and refining of sugar.

The northern provinces of Misiones, Corrientes, Formosa, Chaco, and Santiago del Estero make up a sixth of the national territory and a tenth of the population. This area may best be subdivided into the subtropical lowland plains of the Chaco and the Mesopotamian region lying between the Paraná and Uruguay rivers. In much of the Chaco, agriculture is virtually impossible, and the economy revolves around the production of wood products and tannin. Part of the area is suitable for grazing, and some cotton is grown near Resistencia. The northern part of the Mesopotamia, which is quite tropical in climate, produces a native tea called *yerba mate*, while livestock and grain production are dominant in the south.

Three-fourths of the Argentines live in the remaining region, the pampas (composed of the provinces Entre Ríos, Santa Fé, Córdoba, San Luis, La Pampa, and Buenos Aires), on about a third of the land. In the minds of many this is Argentina. The pampas is one of the world's largest and most fertile plains. It extends out from the nation's capital in a semicircle with a radius of about 500 miles. The southeastern section is devoted primarily to the production of livestock; a western belt is used mainly for alfalfa and wheat, and in the northwest corn and flax are the chief crops. The fourth section, surrounding the city of Buenos Aires, has been developed to supply the capital with fruit, vegetables, and dairy products. Traditionally, the pampas have produced 85 percent of the country's most important exports: livestock and cereals. It also has been the nation's industrial center. It accounts for about 90 percent of the national industrial product, 30 percent of which is concentrated in the city of Buenos Aires alone.

POPULATION

Argentina has about 32 million inhabitants. As is the case with most of the nations of this hemisphere, these people are distributed quite unevenly across the country. The Federal Capital alone has 3 million inhabitants; and with the twenty suburban cities included, the total nears 11 million, about a third of the entire population. The concentration does not stop there; the city and province of Buenos Aires together have virtually half the nation's population and, if the adjoining provinces of Santa Fé and Córdoba are added, the total reaches two-thirds. This means that twenty of the twenty-two provinces contain only a third of the population. Furthermore, the eleven most sparsely populated provinces, occupying 45 percent of the land area, have less than 10 percent of the population.

In terms of population growth, Argentina, with a yearly increase of 1.5 percent, is closer to the North American and Western European patterns than to that of Latin America. The number of people below the age of fifteen (30 percent) and the economically active population (37.3 percent) also resemble the trends experienced by developed rather than developing nations. Within Argentina the rate of population increase varies greatly from one area to another. The provinces of La Pampa and Santiago del Estero are actually declining in population, while in Buenos Aires, Chubut, Formosa, and Misiones the rate of increase exceeds 3 percent annually. In recent years the most striking increase has been in the suburbs of the Federal Capital, which now contain more than 7 million people.

This tremendous increase in the size of metropolitan Buenos Aires is part of an overall trend of urbanization in Argentina. The magnitude of this trend becomes apparent when one realizes that a hundred years ago the country was 75 percent rural; now it is over 86 percent urban. The fact that five out of six Argentines live in cities and towns of over 2,000 people is somewhat misleading, however, for only five of the provinces (Buenos Aires, Santa Fé, Córdoba, Entre Ríos, and Mendoza) are over 50 percent urban.

For many years now Argentina has been an almost completely "white" nation. The Indian population has constantly decreased, not just in terms of percentage but also in absolute numbers. Today there are probably no more than 100,000 Indians living in Argentina, and these are concentrated near the northwestern frontier, especially in Salta and Jujuy.

While most of the Indians were killed in the nineteenth century in order to push the frontier to the south, the *mestizos* (a mixture of Indian and European) were absorbed by waves of European immigration. Currently about 10 percent of the inhabitants are classified as *mestizo*, and these are concentrated in rural areas along the Andean and northeastern borders. There are virtually no blacks in Argentina. Although numerically significant at the time of independence, they were rapidly absorbed into the general population, until their number dropped to about 5,000.

One additional fact pertaining to the Argentine population needs mention: the large number of foreigners who reside in the country. The 1960 census classified 12.8 percent of the population as foreign. This is about the same percentage as shown by the first national census in 1869 but is down considerably from the high of 30.3 percent in 1914. These foreign-born come mainly from Italy (32 percent) and Spain (30 percent). The percentage is highest in the southernmost province, Santa Cruz, where two of every five inhabitants are foreigners, and lowest in Catamarca and La Rioja, where less than 2 percent of the population is foreign born. In the last two decades, because of the prolonged political instability and economic crisis, many Argentines have left their country. In 1980, of the 1.7 million Argentines estimated to live permanently abroad, 1,100,000 (64 percent) were located in the United States, 240,000 (14 percent) in Spain, and 170,000 (10 percent) in Canada.[1] Within the same period a new wave of immigrants came to the country, this time from bordering Latin American countries. Some 600,000 Chileans, 600,000 Paraguayans, 500,000 Bolivians, and 150,000 Uruguayans were reported to reside in Argentina, and many more were presumed to live in the country illegally.[2] The National Institute of Statistics (Instituto Nacional de Estadística y Censos—INDEC) reported that between 600,000 and 1 million foreign workers were in the country in 1990.

Unfortunately, while a large number of those Argentines who left were professionals or trained workers with some education, the newcomers were largely semiskilled workers or manual laborers. The trade-off has thus resulted in a net "brain drain" for the country.

SOCIAL AND ECONOMIC CLASSES

The 1980 national census (the 1990 census has been postponed for lack of funds) confirmed the trend toward urbanization begun at the turn of the

Table 1.1
Economically Active Population by Realm of Activity

	Total (in thousands)					Percentages			
	1947	1960	1970	1980		1947	1960	1970	1980
Agriculture[a]	1,646	1,457	1,411	1,306		26.3	19.5	15.9	13.1
Industry[b]	1,497	2,014	2,095	2,270		23.9	26.9	23.7	22.7
Service[c]	2,820	3,549	4,580	5,348		45.0	47.5	51.8	53.5
Construction	304	459	766	1,067		4.8	6.1	8.6	10.7
TOTAL	6,267	7,479	8,852	9,991		100.0	100.0	100.0	100.0

Source: National Censuses cited by José Nun, "Cambios en la estructura social de la Argentina,"
in *Ensayos sobre la transición democrática en la Argentina*, José Nun and Juan Carlos Portantiero
eds, (Buenos Aires: Puento Sur, 1987), p. 119.
[a]Agriculture, livestock, hunting, forestry, and fishing.
[b]Manufacturing industry, mining; electricity, gas, and water supply.
[c]Transport, commerce, domestic service, public administration, finance, and social services.

century, as agriculture provided the livelihood for only 13 percent of the
economically active population. Traditionally, in Argentina, as in most of
Latin America, the dominant characteristic of land tenure has been the
existence of a few huge estates and a large number of tiny subsistence plots,
with little in between. However, since 1947, large landowners, constituting
about 5 percent of the rural population, have seen their share of the total
land decline to 30 percent. Conversely, independent farmers, who often
used to be sharecroppers, have increased in number as their landowners have
preferred to sell them small plots of their estates because of taxes and, most
of all, freezes on land rents imposed by Peronist and Radical administrations.

As shown in Table 1.1, approximately 23 percent of the economically
active population in 1980 was engaged in the industrial sector of the economy,
with the largest number working in food processing, textiles, and metallurgical industries. Industrial employment rose steadily until the 1960s and
then began to decline after 1975. For instance, industrial workers in the
private sector accounted for 16 percent of the economically active population
in 1975 but ten years later only 10.5 percent.[3]

During the last two decades construction flourished to the point of com-
prising more than 10 percent of the economically active population, that is,

more than doubling the 1947 figure. However, it is reasonable to assume that today its share would be much smaller because of the deep recession that hit the country between 1988 and 1990, which hit this sector particularly hard. The nation's industrial establishments, the vast majority of which are very small, are heavily concentrated around the Federal Capital and to a lesser extent in the cities of Córdoba, Santa Fé, and Rosario. The remaining 53 percent of the population worked in the "tertiary" or "service" sector, which is composed mainly of public officials, state enterprise employees, and people engaged in commercial or service activities. It is this sector that is growing in relative size, while the percentage of the population engaged in agriculture and in the industrial sector has been declining. A major part of the growth of the tertiary sector is due to the increasing size of the bureaucracy, which in 1985 represented 18.4 percent of the economically active population. (Public employment jumped from 1.5 million in 1971 to 1.9 million in 1988.)[4] Furthermore, the rapid growth of the so-called "underground" or "informal" economy, that is, that part of the economy which escapes state taxation, regulation, and labor law controls, has contributed to this growth.

The often repeated myth of the lack of a middle class in Latin America simply is not the case in Argentina. While it is true that the upper class is extremely small (less than 1 percent of the population), the middle sectors amount to about 41 percent. Argentina for many decades had the largest and wealthiest middle class in Latin America. However, prolonged economic instability, which translated into inflation rates averaging 206 percent between 1975 and 1980, and 305 percent between 1980 and 1988, severely impaired the middle sectors' well-being and deeply affected their internal composition.[5] Between 1947 and 1980 the most affluent subgroups within the middle class (small businessmen, entrepreneurs, and professionals) shrank significantly while the least affluent groups (administrative and clerical personnel) increased. How does one explain this trend? In the view of Héctor Palomino, part of the reason rests on the fact that state sector employees, which traditionally have constituted the bulk of the middle classes, saw their purchasing power decline tremendously as the government kept salaries lagging behind the inflation rate in order to cut its deficit. In the private sector, white-collar workers in small- and medium-sized companies, whose production was geared toward the domestic market, suffered because of the liberalization policies pursued by the military government. While many businesses went bankrupt, those which survived had to cut operations and reduce salaries. In the agricultural sector something very similar occurred, as those employed by companies producing for the local economy saw their salaries plummet. Who then gained? Those professionals, self-employed, or salaried technicians possessing skills in high demand retained salaries close to international levels. Moreover, employees of agricultural, industrial, and service businesses exporting abroad fared quite well. Palomino contends that rather than a general decline of the middle classes, we should describe the transformation under way as an increasing "fragmentation" of the middle classes, with some groups linked to the service and export sectors emerging as the "new," dynamic middle. On the other hand, those employed in traditional economic activities, or the state, have seen their socioeconomic status deteriorate rapidly, a phenomenon, Palomino adds, that also has been observed in advanced industrial societies.[6] This is a crucial distinction but, altogether, it is undeniable that the beneficiaries of the economic transformation of the last fifteen years have been comparatively few. As a whole, the Argentine middle class is much worse off now than it was in the 1960s. Adding to the problem is the fact that most white-collar workers and professionals who identify with such a social class today make less than $300 a month. The question, then, is one of definition. If we regard the middle class as those people occupying an intermediate socioeconomic position between the wealthy and the working class, can these individuals still be categorized as middle class when they lack the economic means to make ends meet?

According to a 1980 sample, the working class made up about 54 percent of the economically active population. The percentage of skilled and unskilled salaried workers has diminished over time while that of self-employed manual workers has increased. This phenomenon finds an explanation in the profound crisis that affected the Argentine industrial sector between 1974 and 1985. The Census Bureau (INDEC) calculated that during this period workers in manufacturing dropped from 1,560,000 to 1,360,000. In percentage terms, William Smith estimated a decrease of 39.4 percent in the 1974–83 period and a further 5.2 percent decline between 1983 and 1988.[7] Many laid-off workers, as well as young people seeking their first jobs, turned to self-employment as an alternative. According to one study, 147,000 new jobs (usually independent employment) were created by services, construction, commerce, and transport.[8] Although self-employment helped soften the impact of the loss of jobs in manufacturing, it also fragmented and made more heterogeneous the composition of the working class. Self-employment is, in fact, characterized by low-paid, informal, nonunionized, and unstable jobs. A subsequent INDEC study concluded that in 1985, self-employed workers comprised 25 percent of the economically active population. Statistics published in early 1990 put the number of unemployed close to 3 million while of the 12.5 million holding a job almost 5 million were illegally employed. To have an idea how things have deteriorated in the last few years, suffice it to say that the new minimum wage approved in September 1990 was about $140 a month. Self-employment is heavily concentrated in the underground economy, which encompasses a wide range of activities from selling items on a street to small firms and cottage industries. The underground economy is a phenomenon that deserves some attention, as in the last two decades it has assumed profound socioeconomic implications. It is estimated that its output comprises as much as 60 percent (or $30 billion) of the official economy monitored by gross domestic product (GDP) indicators.[9] This may explain why manufacturing production has declined in recent years while electricity consumption for industrial purposes has increased. An example of the dimension it has reached in the last fifteen years can be seen in the Federal Capital and metropolitan Buenos Aires, where three out of five people are believed to make all or part of their income in this economic sector.[10] It is quite common for professionals and white- and blue-collar workers to hold two jobs, one of which is usually in the informal sector. In addition to self-employed workers, foreign immigrants tend to be heavily concentrated in this area of the economy.

INCOME DISTRIBUTION AND POVERTY

No systematic income distribution surveys have been carried out in Argentina since the 1960s. The few statistics on the subject matter usually cover only major urban areas and fewer income categories. Therefore caution should be used in taking them at face value. A World Bank study, using 1970 data, reported that the top 10 percent of the population had 35.5 percent of household income while the lowest 40 percent enjoyed only 14.1 percent of the total. A subsequent study found that by 1985 the top 10 percent had increased its share to 37 percent. The same study concluded that during the 1974–85 period the average household income had dropped by 20 percent in real terms, real wages by 37 percent; and the share of wages of the gross domestic product (GDP) from an average of 51 percent between 1970 and 1975 had fallen to 36 percent in the 1976–82 period.[11] Other sources using GDP shares come to more drastic conclusions. According to Smith, the GDP share of the wealthiest 10 percent, which was 39 percent in 1974, climbed to 44 percent in 1980 and 46 percent in 1988.[12] Although the incompleteness of these works makes comparisons difficult, a common trend appears clear: over time, income distribution has become increasingly skewed. Argentina, which has always thought of itself as a European outpost in Latin America, is becoming more and more like such unequal societies as Brazil, Peru, and Mexico, which it traditionally looked down upon. What can be concluded is that despite the constant enlargement of the middle sectors during the last several years, the class pyramid remains quite broad at the base and very narrow at the top.

Until 1939, Argentina enjoyed one of the world's highest standards of living and was reputed to have become a major economic power. However, the worsening of political and economic instability after World War II turned a promised land into a country of lost promises. While European and some Latin American nations began to develop at a fast pace in the second half of this century, Argentina went backward, experiencing what one sociologist has labeled "reversal of development."[13]

POLITICAL DEVELOPMENT

The area that is today Argentina was settled by two separate streams of colonization. The first, coming from Peru, entered from the northwest and founded the towns of Mendoza, San Luis, Tucumán, San Juan, Córdoba, and Santiago del Estero during the last half of the sixteenth century. The second, coming directly from Europe, settled in the Río de la Plata area. Throughout most of the colonial era the people of Buenos Aires and those of the interior lived quite separate existences. The interior developed primarily to provide food, livestock, and textiles for the mining areas in Peru, while Buenos Aires remained oriented toward Europe.

Prior to 1776, Argentina was a part of the Viceroyalty of Peru. It was of little importance to Spain, primarily because of its lack of precious metals. However, as the area increased in size and as the Portuguese in Brazil began to menace it, a new viceroyalty was created with its seat in Buenos Aires. Nevertheless, peninsular-born Spaniards continued to monopolize all the higher political offices, while those born in the New World were denied any influence in local political affairs.

In 1808, Spanish authority in the New World was weakened immeasurably by the French invasion of Spain and the overthrow of Ferdinand VII. Two years later, when the last vestiges of Spanish authority on the peninsula were gone, the lines of legitimate authority were at best blurred, and the New World viceroys found themselves in virtually untenable positions. On May 25, 1810, the Buenos Aires city council deposed the viceroy there and assumed control of the city. This was the beginning of the independence movement, although independence was not formally declared for another six years.

Between 1810 and 1819, the Argentines fought the Spanish, the Paraguayans, the Uruguayans, the Brazilians, and, most frequently, each other. A series of juntas, triumvirates, and supreme directors came and went without any success in the quest of national unification. However, by the beginning of 1819 the southern part of the continent was free from Spanish control.

Anarchy and *Caudillismo*

The first half-century of Argentina's national history was characterized by a bitter struggle between the interior provinces and Buenos Aires. The main issue in this conflict was the form of government to be established in the new nation. The political leaders of the interior, referring to themselves as Federalists, tended to equate federalism with democracy and liberty. They remembered the intense centralization of the colonial period and wanted no part of a continuance of the unitary system. They also recognized the economic and social differences among some of the provinces, especially between those of the interior and Buenos Aires, and felt that federalism was best suited to recognize these differences. On the other hand, the Unitarians of Buenos Aires were convinced that only a unitary system could weld the warring provinces into one united nation. They were afraid that if federalism were adopted, there would really be no nation.

In the realm of economics, the conflict revolved around the fact that the dominant source of income for the new nation was the import duties collected in Buenos Aires, which had the nation's only developed port. During and immediately after the war for independence, most of the interior provinces were in extremely bad shape economically. They were cut off from their traditional markets in Peru, and all their goods entering or leaving the country through the Río de la Plata estuary were taxed in Buenos Aires. The entire sum of this revenue went into the treasury of Buenos Aires.

In general terms, the Buenos Aires Unitarians wanted to form a strong national government, but one run by and for the people of Buenos Aires. To many of the political leaders of the interior, federalism meant only provincial autonomy and the right of the local *caudillo* (chief or boss) to exploit his own province as he saw fit.

These warring factions were first united by the Constitution of 1819, which was federal in form. Buenos Aires, however, refused to join this union and instead led its own independent life for the next seven years. Then in 1826, a new constitution created the United Provinces of the Río de Plata, which Buenos Aires was willing to join, since the government was to be unitary and a *porteño* (resident of the port of Buenos Aires), Bernardino Rivadavia, was to be the first president. Unfortunately, this attempt at national unification was also very short-lived. Rivadavia's attempt to impose a Unitarian pattern was greeted by rebellion on the part of the interior provinces. For the next several years Argentina was left without even a semblance of national government. What order existed was imposed by local *caudillos*.

The most famous of these *caudillos* was Juan Manual de Rosas, who first came to prominence when he volunteered his private army to restore order to anarchy-ridden Buenos Aires after the fall of Rivadavia. In 1829 the provincial legislature appointed him governor, but in 1833 he refused a second term and instead led a campaign against the Indians in the south. The return of anarchy, occasioned by Rosas's departure, led to his recall in 1835—this time with full dictatorial power. His dictatorship, frequently referred to today as the First Tyranny (the second allegedly being that of Juan Perón between 1946 and 1955), lasted until 1852. Although ostensibly the rule of the Federalists, Rosas's regime was basically a reaction against the liberalism of the 1810 revolution and a return to the old order of the colonial society. Rosas imprisoned or executed many of his political enemies; the fortunate ones were those who managed to escape into exile. He exercised rigid censorship over all means of communication and organized a secret police that is still infamous for its terror and assassinations. Rebellions by provincial *caudillos* were crushed ruthlessly as Rosas gained control over more and more of the interior. However, it was the *caudillo* of Entre Ríos, Justo José de Urquiza, who finally put an end to the Rosas dictatorship. In February 1852, Rosas's forces were defeated decisively by Urquiza at the historic battle of Caseros.

Soon after his victory on the battlefield, Urquiza met with other provincial governors, who agreed that a new constitution should be written immediately. Thus in November 1852, a constituent assembly met in Santa Fé, where it wrote the document that has served as Argentina's fundamental law to this day (except for the period between 1949 and 1955). Buenos Aires, however, boycotted the constitutional convention and refused to join the new nation. Thus once again there existed the spectacle of the country's largest and richest province acting as an independent nation.

Conflict between Buenos Aires and the government of the interior provinces increased until it came to renewed civil war in 1858 and again in 1861. In the latter year the forces of Buenos Aires, under the leadership of Bartolomé Mitre, defeated the provincial army of Urquiza at Pavón. After the adoption of relatively minor constitutional amendments, Buenos Aires agreed to join the union, and the next year Mitre became Argentina's first truly national president.

Political Stability and Economic Development

The inauguration of Mitre in 1862 marked the beginning of a new era in Argentina. For half a century the country had endured chaos and anarchy, interrupted only by the Rosas dictatorship; the next seven decades were characterized by peace and stability and by rapid economic and political development.

Mitre and the two presidents who succeeded him concentrated their efforts on pacification and the creation of the institutions of government. The Congress was moved from Paraná to Buenos Aires and began to meet regularly. A national judiciary was created and staffed with extremely competent people. The city of Buenos Aires was removed from the province of that name and converted into a federal district, much like Washington, D.C. And most important, general acceptance was gained for the existence of a single national government.

Beginning in 1880, emphasis was shifted from politics to economics. The next group of presidents set out to increase both the number of producers and production by importing Europeans as well as European capital. At this time there were barely 1.5 million Argentines occupying 1 million square miles. The vast majority of these people were rural, and most were engaged in subsistence agriculture. Agricultural exports and infrastructural development were accomplished primarily through British financing. This was most obvious in the case of the rail system, most of which was British and French owned until World War II. When Mitre took office, there were perhaps 2,000 miles of track; fifty years later there were 20,000. During the same period, the amount of cultivated land was increased from less than 1.5 million acres to more than 60 million, and the amount of land devoted to grazing was increased almost as dramatically.

Foreign investments continued unabated until the early 1900s. By 1910, they comprised 25 percent of the country's gross domestic product, of which about 65 percent was British. However, prior to the outbreak of World War I, British investors began to pull out of Argentina, slowly but steadily. In 1927, their share of foreign investments had dropped to 24 percent. Conversely, such a vacuum was partly filled by new capital from the United States, which in 1931 had reached 20 percent. The new foreign investments began to be concentrated in the export-import activities (shipping, banking, financing) and in the manufacturing industry linked to agricultural production, such as meat-packing houses, textiles, and beverages.

These and similar factors changed the nature of the Argentine economy from subsistence agriculture to that of a major exporter of primary products, and the change took place with amazing rapidity. By the time of World War I, Argentina was exporting 350,000 tons of beef and 5 million tons of cereals annually, most of which went to the United Kingdom. Between 1860 and 1930, Argentina had one of the fastest growing economies in the world. Carlos Díaz Alejandro estimated that the GDP averaged a yearly increase of at least 5 percent between 1864 and 1914 and a lower but still significant 3.5 percent between 1914 and 1930.[14]

During this same period, there were also important changes in the nature of Argentine society, largely as a result of massive immigration. Juan Bautista Alberdi, one of the fathers of the 1853 constitution, had said, "To govern is to populate," and this dictum was taken to heart by the country's nineteenth-century rulers. A concerted effort was made to attract Europeans to Argentina, an effort that was quite successful. Immigration began in the 1850s with little more than a trickle, but it increased at an astronomical rate during the next forty years: in 1870, 40,000 immigrants arrived; in 1885, 110,000; and in 1890, 200,000. Between 1869 and 1929, immigration was responsible for 60 percent of the nation's population growth.[15] However, most of these immigrants, unlike their counterparts in North America, did not become citizens. Many refused to become Argentine citizens to avoid the military service that was made mandatory after 1901. Others did not want to close the door on the option of returning home. The conservative governments dominated by the old elites did little or nothing to promote naturalization. As long as the newcomers did not become citizens, they were not eligible to vote, and as long as they could not vote, they could not alter the status quo upon which landowners, traders, and merchants thrived. As a result, by the time of World War I, less than 2 percent of the immigrant population had acquired citizenship.

Although the bulk of the populace attained a degree of economic well-being during this first conservative era (1862–1916), the average citizen was almost completely removed from the political process. The founding fathers of the Argentine Republic believed in a strict form of elitist democracy in which political and civil rights were two separate concepts. Political rights, such as voting and holding office, had to be restricted to an enlightened upper class who best appreciated their significance and who could translate them into good government. On the other hand, civil rights, meaning the ability to pursue the improvement of one's economic status, had to be enjoyed by the entire population in order to encourage the immigration of badly needed settlers.

Although the constitution was modeled upon that of the United States, the separation of powers among the presidency, the legislature, and the judiciary was ignored. The government machinery revolved around the person of the president. Elected for a six-year term (but without the possibility for a second consecutive term), the president had the authority to call for the implementation of a "state of siege" when internal strife threatened the constitutional government. The state of siege automatically suspended all constitutional rights and permitted the president to rule by decree, thus bypassing congressional approval. In the provinces (the equivalent of the states composing the United States) the legislatures were usually subservient to the governors, to whom most of their members owed their election. The governor was also quite influential in the selection of congressmen from his province. His legislature chose the members of the upper house of Congress, while he and the Conservative party had virtual control over the election machinery so that safe men were returned to the Chamber of Deputies. The governors were in turn almost the personal agents of the president. It was not difficult for him to keep them in line with the use—or just the threat—of his other meaningful constitutional power: the right to "intervene" in the provinces. Such a right in theory had to be used to maintain law and order or to repel foreign invasions, but in practice it worked to oust defiant governors and to replace them with government bureaucrats loyal to the president. The system was self-perpetuating, as the president and governors kept each other in office through the use of force and fraud.

Early in this first conservative era there were Federalist, Unitarian, National, and Autonomist parties, but all were essentially conservative organizations representing different sectors of the upper class—principally the large landowners of the interior provinces and the commercial and livestock elements of the city and province of Buenos Aires.

Between 1862 and 1880, Nationals and Autonomists argued over the site of the national capital. Those who wanted to make the city of Buenos Aires a federal district, thus forcing the province of Buenos Aires to find a new capital, formed the National party under the leadership of Mitre. Those who wanted Buenos Aires to remain the capital of the province of that name joined in the formation of the Autonomist party. With the creation of the federal district in 1880, there was no longer any reason for the existence of these parties, and they soon united to form the National Autonomist Party (PAN). At the time of its formation the PAN was the "official" party and the only one of importance. For a decade it ruled virtually unchallenged. However, more than the PAN, the organization that best embodied the interests of the elites, particularly those of Buenos Aires and the Pampean region, was the Argentine Rural Society (SRA). Formed in 1866, the SRA was a small but cohesive association of large landowners who would play an hegemonic role both in the realm of economics and politics until the mid-1940s.

This political system was perhaps appropriate for Argentina as long as its society was composed almost exclusively of a small landowning elite and a large, politically inarticulate mass; however, such ceased to be the case when the nation's social structure underwent fundamental alteration. The most important of the societal changes was the rapid formation of a middle class, a middle class composed largely of immigrants and their offspring. Of these new Argentines, Ysabel Rennie stated:

They took land, they opened small shops, they bought property, they saved their money. By the end of the century they were the most stable element in the community. . . . In commerce and industry foreigners outnumbered criollos three to one. . . . In medicine they outnumbered Argentine doctors five to one. They predominated in the communication industry, in transport, in whatever was not the care and feeding of cows and the harvesting of crops. They even went into agriculture, not as holders of enormous latifundia, but as small tenant farmers raising grain and fruits. . . . The immigrants were the middle class.[16]

It was this immigrant middle class that formed the base for Argentina's first nonaristocratic political party, the Radical Civic Union (UCR), which was founded in 1890. During its first forty years of existence this party was dominated by an enigmatic politician named Hipólito Yrigoyen. Convinced that UCR participation in elections supervised by the conservatives would serve only to place the party's stamp of approval on the inevitable electoral fraud, Yrigoyen saw to it that the Radicals boycotted all elections prior to 1912. Instead, they attempted to gain power by force, instigating unsuccessful rebellions in 1890, 1893, and 1905. Rather than nominating candidates and presenting electoral platforms, the UCR was content to denounce the oligarchic nature of the government and to insist that eventually it would be replaced by a "national renovation" directed by the Radicals.

For about half a century after the formation of the UCR, Argentina had what amounted to a two-party system. The conservatives (who adopted a multitude of different names during this period) were convinced that only the upper class was capable of governing. Restricted suffrage and/or fraudulent elections were a necessary evil as far as they were concerned, for otherwise the uninformed masses might gain political power and ruin the nation. Their Radical opponents, who represented a very nebulous liberalism, were opposed to the conservative regimes and in favor of change, but totally lacked a concrete program.

The original turning point in the fortunes of these parties came in 1911 with the enactment of a new election law that provided for universal and compulsory male suffrage, a secret ballot, permanent registration, and minority representation in Congress. Within four years, the honest administration of this law cost the conservatives their monopoly on political office.

In 1916, in what may have been the nation's first honest presidential election, Hipólito Yrigoyen became Argentina's first nonconservative chief executive. However, the Radicals, still lacking a definite program, had no idea how to put into effect the "national renovation" they had been promising for so long. The UCR retained executive power for fourteen years; but while the party did enact some fairly minor reforms, no fundamental changes were even attempted, and the economic power of the conservatives remained intact.

By 1916, the Radicals had lost their revolutionary zeal, and their goal was simply a recognition of the right of the middle class to participate fully in the economic, social, and political life of the country, or at least recognition of their right to a share of the spoils of office. During Yrigoyen's first term (1916–22) public employment increased substantially. The new jobs were dispensed to the members of the middle class, thus strengthening the UCR's electoral support from that social sector.

While in the opposition, Yrigoyen and the Radicals had exposed the corruption of the conservative administrations and their unrestrained use of electoral fraud. They had promised that Radicalism would, once in power, rule according to ethical and moral standards upon which democratic institutions were based. Yet after 1916, Yrigoyen and his followers seemed to practice what they had criticized in their despised predecessors, while adding their own hallmark. Yrigoyen himself instilled in his followers a cult of personality (*personalismo*) that downplayed the role of public institutions like Congress, the judiciary, the public administration, and political parties. More than at any time in Argentine history, Yrigoyen abused the presidential prerogative to intervene in the provinces. During his first term he deposed twenty conservative governors and replaced them with loyal Radicals. Moreover, setting a dangerous precedent, he also began to disrupt the armed forces' professionalism when he decided to reward those officers who had sided along with the Radicals during the revolts of the turn of the century. This angered many senior officers, who resented political intrusions in military affairs and eventually would become politicized themselves as they collaborated with anti-Radical lobbies later on.

The conservatives were willing to "share" power with Radicals, although certainly not on the basis of equality. They seem to have seen the provision in the new election law guaranteeing minority representation in Congress as a means of co-opting their middle-class opponents. What the conservatives were unwilling to do was to "relinquish" power to the Radicals, yet this is exactly what happened. Voter participation increased dramatically (from 190,000 in 1910 to 640,000 in 1912 and 1.46 million in 1928), and as it increased, so did the percentage of the vote obtained by the Radicals. By 1930 it was clear that the conservatives were quite unlikely to win any national elections in the foreseeable future. Although the policies adopted by the Radicals had not been particularly disadvantageous to the nation's elite, the large and growing Radical electorate meant that such disadvantageous policies were a definite possibility at any time in the future. Adding to the elite's and the military's misgivings was the increased level of popular support enjoyed by Yrigoyen in working-class neighborhoods of the Federal Capital. The institutions of liberal democracy that had served the elite so well in the past were now called into serious question.

Political Instability and Economic Decay

In September 1930, an economic crisis, ever-increasing corruption in the government, President Yrigoyen's senility, recognition by the conservatives that the rules of the political game had to be changed if they were to return to power, and widespread public disillusionment with the Radicals led to their overthrow and the establishment of Argentina's first military government.

The 1930 military coup marked the beginning of a new era in Argentina. The preceding seventy years had been characterized by a degree of political stability almost unknown in Latin America and by a level of economic development that led to the attainment of a standard of living superior to that of Southern Europe. The years since 1930, on the other hand, have been characterized by exactly the opposite: economic stagnation and an incredible degree of political instability.

Following the overthrow of Yrigoyen, the armed forces retained power for less than two years before returning control of the government to the conservatives by means of elections as fraudulent as those conducted before 1912. In fact, the period between 1932 and 1943 is frequently referred to as the Era of Patriotic Fraud. It was a regime supported by an electoral alliance of three conservative parties that claimed it was their patriotic duty to engage in electoral fraud, for otherwise the Radicals would hoodwink the immature voters, return to power, and once again lead the country down the road to ruin.

The social, economic, and political elite that governed Argentina between 1862 and 1916 was dedicated to national development. Such was decidedly not the case with the elite that governed following the 1930 coup. It did lead the country out of the depression and restore a degree of prosperity; however, it also saw to it that this prosperity was distributed even more inequitably than before. Argentina was run almost exclusively for the benefit of the landed aristocracy, the commercial and industrial elites of Buenos Aires, and foreign interests.

At about this time, there occurred a profound change in the character of the urban working class. Prior to World War I, 80 percent of the urban workers in the Federal Capital were recent immigrants, almost none of whom became naturalized citizens; but by World War II, they were largely recent migrants from the countryside and, to a lesser extent, the children of immigrants. Many of the migrants were from the poor northwest and were often of *mestizo* origin. During the 1930s and early 1940s there was a wave of migration to the cities of truly astonishing proportions. It has been estimated that in a single four-year period one out of every five rural dwellers moved into an urban center, most into greater Buenos Aires.[17] The devastating consequences of the Great Depression on the Argentine agricultural economy had much to do with this trend. Britain and other European countries cut substantially their food imports from Argentina. In turn, rural production, particularly cereals, dropped steeply. Between 1937 and 1947 the amount of land used for wheat and corn production dropped by 36.5 percent, with most of that land being put into pasture requiring less manpower.[18] This meant that a great many renters, sharecroppers, and day laborers were pushed out of the countryside. At the same time, the scarcity and high cost of European manufactured goods gave impetus to a disorganized but effective process of import substitution industrialization that centered primarily on the production of consumer goods. This process gained momentum in the second half of the 1930s and continued at a faster pace during World War II, as manufactured goods from overseas became even more scarce. In 1943, in what constituted a historic event, the industrial sector for the first time surpassed the agricultural one as the major contributor to the country's GDP.

The new industrial sector developed unevenly. In 1939, about 70 percent of manufacturing companies were located in greater Buenos Aires. In the late 1930s, 85 percent of these companies were small businesses employing ten or fewer workers, but 57 percent of the production was coming from 1.4 percent of the industrial establishments. Similarly, the larger corporations also employed three-fifths of the work force.[19] Additional discrepancies could be found in business organizations. In 1941, the Argentine Industrial Union (UIA), the largest entrepreneurial organization, represented only 3 percent of Argentine industrialists. Its members came almost exclusively from big corporations, while the vast majority of small and medium-sized businesses remained unorganized.

The European immigrants who came to Argentina at the turn of the century settled, for the most part, in Buenos Aires and other urban centers. Many had brought with them ideologies like socialism, anarchism, and syndicalism. The internal migrants, on the other hand, had grown up in environments where such ideologies had never been heard of. In the countryside, life was dominated by patron-client relationships in which loyalty and compliance to the will of the local landowner or rancher assured a meager but stable livelihood. For the rural migrants, life in the cities was quite different. More economic opportunities were available but, conversely, there was no patron to shelter them from the unpredictability of urban life. Trade unions were available almost exclusively to skilled workers. Many migrants found only occasional, part-time jobs, while the more fortunate could end up in small shops or larger industrial establishments where unionization was absent. Politically, however, the new urban working class differed from its earlier counterpart in at least one important way: its members were citizens and, hence, potential voters.

Unfortunately, the nation's political institutions were not equipped to handle large new groups of political participants. The structures, the programs, and the leaders of the existing political parties were not able (nor willing, perhaps) to offer anything of value to the working class. Until 1940, the Congress was dominated by the conservatives, who seemed totally unconcerned with the plight of the workers; for the next three years the Radicals used their congressional majority to harass the president and to prevent the enactment of any sort of program. The newcomers from the countryside received the attention only of Socialist and Communist union leaders. However, the highly ideological content of their political discourse prevented them from persuading many migrants to join them. The migrants were more inclined to look for a new *patrón* than to embrace Karl Marx's ideas. In the countryside they had been taught to follow individuals, not abstract ideals.

This was the scene in 1943, when the leaders of the armed forces again assumed the role of keeper of the national conscience and deposed the conservative government. The driving force behind the coup was the Group of United Officers (GOU), a secret association made up primarily of middle-grade officers that was as much pro-Axis as anti-Communist. In the military administration that followed the coup, power gradually came to be concentrated in the hands of one of the GOU's leaders, a colonel who was to dominate the course of Argentine politics for the next thirty years: Juan Domingo Perón.

Perón was the one military leader who appears to have seen the political potential of the labor movement. With the oligarchy and the Radicals rejecting his plans to create a new conservative alliance, he turned to the working class. He was content to accept a quite secondary position in the revolutionary government, that of secretary of labor, from which he began an active campaign for working-class support. He saw to it that wages were increased substantially and that existing ameliorative labor legislation was enforced, for the first time. He presided over the formation of new trade unions and the enormous expansion of existing unions that were friendly to him.

By mid-1945 Perón not only headed the Secretariat of Labor, but was also minister of war, head of the Postwar Council and vice-president. He was clearly in the process of becoming the real power behind the government of General Edelmiro Farrell when on October 9 he was arrested by a group of army officers who opposed both his political ambition and his prolabor policies. As soon as news of his arrest became public, labor demonstrations increased daily in size and vehemence. On October 17, hundreds of thousands of workers converged in the huge plaza in front of the government house to demand Perón's return. He was released and for the next decade was the master of Argentina.

In the presidential election of February 1946, Perón was the candidate of the hastily formed Argentine Labor party (Partido Laborista). Although opposed by a single candidate representing all the nation's traditional political parties, Perón won the election. In 1916, it was the newly emerging middle class that had been largely responsible for the election of Yrigoyen; thirty years later it was the new urban working class that could claim most of the credit for the election of Juan Perón. Within this urban working class, the migrants from the countryside played a crucial role in supporting Perón. Accustomed to a patron-client relationship, they seem to have been especially willing, even eager to follow the new *caudillo*.

While president, Perón continued to do a great deal for the working class, both psychologically and materially. Psychologically, he gave the working class an unprecedented sense of self-esteem and identity. He identified with them, using such symbolic gestures as taking his coat off and rolling up his sleeves during public speeches before large crowds. Such a gesture could hardly fool a sophisticated observer, but it caught the imagination of the workers, most of whom did not wear shirts and coats and were scornfully called by the upper classes *descamisados*, or shirtless ones. In their eyes Perón had become one of them. The cornerstone of Perón's rhetoric was justicialism, a vague catch-all ideal that in essence meant social justice in the form of a more equitable distribution of income and social services for previously neglected sectors of society: the workers, the lower middle class, the poor. Perón's rhetoric and symbolism also took a strong nationalistic twist. Nationalists of all walks of life had long regarded the foreign ownership of most utility and transportation companies an insult to Argentine sovereignty. To rally people around him and the flag, Perón nationalized telephones, tramways, telegraphs, subways, and shipping lines. The day Argentina purchased the British-owned railways was declared the Day of Economic Independence despite the fact that the price paid was several times higher than the real value of the assets. The nationalization campaign paid huge dividends in popularity but also contributed to drain the once-rich coffer of the national treasury. The nationalization policy scared off foreign companies. With their business activities increasingly restricted by a web of regulations, they began to leave the country. By 1955, foreign investments were only three-fifths what they had been in 1946. Another expression of Perón's

nationalism was his Third Position in foreign policy. It aimed at portraying
Argentina as a leader of the emerging nonaligned movement in the Third
World. In practical terms this meant playing an independent role in foreign
affairs and refusing to side with either the United States or the Soviet Union.
At a time when the cold war was in full swing, such a stand, while popular
at home, alienated the Truman administration which had been suspicious
of Perón's Fascist sympathies during World War II. Relations between the
United States and Argentina remained cold throughout Perón's first two terms
in office.

Economically, Perón gave great impetus to the successful import substitution industrialization process already under way. Cheap credit was granted
to medium- and small-sized businesses at rates below inflation. Yet the new
industries were primarily concentrated in the consumer goods sector, thus
leaving Argentina still highly dependent on the importation of capital equipment and strategic raw materials from abroad. To shelter the new industrial
activities from foreign competition, heavy tariff duties and import quotas
were established. The promotion of the industrial sector was funded primarily by drawing on the country's foreign reserves and by taxing agricultural
exports. The latter angered the landed oligarchy. While falling short of
promoting land reform or taxing their income, Perón attacked the vested
interests of the landed elites by depriving them of a substantial part of their
profits. To this end he created the Argentine Institute for the Promotion of
Exchange (IAPI), a state agency that acquired the monopoly over the exportation of beef and grain. Producers were forced to sell their production
at a fixed price to IAPI, which in turn sold it to foreign customers at a much
higher price. For instance, in 1948 IAPI paid fourteen pesos per ton for
sunflower seeds and sold them to the United States at 101.25 pesos.[20] An
additional measure that angered both landowners and farmers was the establishment of price controls on beef, other meats, and a variety of staples.
The whole rural sector felt it was victimized to subsidize an industrial economy that because of its high prices was incapable of exporting and paying
for its own purchases abroad. By the early 1950s, grain and beef producers
began to retaliate by reducing output to force Perón to make concessions.
In 1952, the whole economy fell into a recession, and the president had to
assure farmers better prices. Adding to the fiscal strain was the mushrooming
of the state sector. The public bureaucracy became an employment agency
for Peronist supporters, and corruption went with it hand in hand. Although
both conservative and Radical administrations had been marred by corruption
and clientelism, Perón carried these practices to new heights.

The process of unionization was also continued; wages and fringe benefits
were increased; and a modern social security system was created. To an
appreciable extent, there was a redistribution of income that favored the
workers. At least as important, in the long run, was the thorough politicization

of the working class, which came to realize its potential political strength. Nevertheless, the material benefits obtained by the workers during the Perón administration were essentially gifts from above rather than the result of pressure from below. The Peronist party (the name given the Labor party shortly after Perón's inauguration) functioned primarily as a vehicle for mobilizing working-class support for the regime; it did not, in fact, participate in the governing of Argentina. Perón himself always referred to Peronism as a movement of national opinion, not a party. In fact, he repeatedly stated his low opinion of politicians and party politics.

Although honestly elected in 1946 and reelected in 1951 (after amending the constitution), Perón moved steadily in the direction of authoritarian rule. Freedom of the press was virtually destroyed; the judiciary was purged, as were the universities; and opposition leaders were harassed, exiled, or imprisoned. Perón originally came to power with the support of the Church, the armed forces, and organized labor. By 1955, his labor support had declined somewhat, and the Church had moved completely into the opposition. Most important, an appreciable sector of the armed forces had decided that he must go.

In September 1955, Perón was deposed by the armed forces. In spite of the fact that there was some fighting involved (something rare in Argentine coups), it was relatively simple for the military to get rid of Perón; it was much more difficult to rid the country of Peronism. Perón was originally replaced by the leader of the September coup, General Eduardo Lonardi, who proclaimed his intention to adhere to the motto of Urquiza a century earlier: "Neither victors nor vanquished." Because of his unwillingness to take repressive measures against the Peronists, Lonardi remained in power only fifty days before a palace coup replaced him with General Pedro Aramburu.

For two and a half years General Aramburu presided over a provisional regime, labeled the Liberating Revolution, dedicated to destroying Peronism and returning the nation to civilian constitutional rule. As far as the former goal was concerned, there was almost complete lack of success. In fact, the extreme anti-Peronism of the Aramburu administration seems to have been counterproductive; that is, it served primarily to convince Perón's followers that they must remain united in support of their leader or see the political clock turned back to the pre-1943 period. Even the second goal met with only limited success. Elections were held and the country returned to civilian rule, but as far as the army was concerned, the wrong man won.

The 1958 elections were swept by the faction of the old UCR that called itself the Intransigent Radical Civic Union (UCRI). It leader, Arturo Frondizi, attained the presidency primarily through a bargain with Perón, who traded about 2 million votes for a promise of legality for his movement. This pact gave Frondizi the presidency, but it also cost him the ability to govern effectively. The anti-Peronist sector of the population, and especially the leaders of the armed forces, considered his election tainted and his administration illegitimate.

For four years President Frondizi made a concerted effort to accelerate the nation's rate of economic development and to integrate the Peronists back into the nation's political life. By 1962, his economic policies appeared to be in trouble, but it was his political maneuvers that by then cost him his job. Restored to a position of legal equality by Frondizi, the Peronist party emerged victorious in the congressional and gubernatorial elections of March 1962. This was the last straw as far as the anti-Peronist military leaders were concerned, and Frondizi was quickly deposed.

The interregnum between April 1962, when Arturo Frondizi was overthrown, and October 1963, when Arturo Illia was inaugurated, was characterized by a virtual civil war within the armed forces and another search for a means of transferring power to a civilian, constitutional government that was not tainted with Peronism. During this period an appreciable sector in the armed forces wanted to establish a military dictatorship whose primary function would be the elimination of Peronism once and for all; this sector was opposed by a much more moderate faction whose prime concern was the holding of elections and the removal of the armed forces from the political arena. It was the latter that came out on top; and, as a result, elections were held in July 1963, with the Peronists denied the right to nominate candidates for executive offices.

These elections were won by the People's Radical Civic Union (UCRP), the faction of the old UCR that had lost the 1958 election to Frondizi and his Intransigent Radicals. The new president was Arturo Illia, a mild-mannered country doctor who received only 26 percent of the popular vote. The three years of his administration were notable primarily for the lack of government action. In 1962, the military had deposed President Frondizi because it was in disagreement with the actions of his administration; in 1966, President Illia was deposed because he refused to act.

The Argentine Revolution

On the morning of June 28, 1966, General Julio Alsogaray walked into the office of President Arturo Illia and announced, "President Illia, sir, in the name of the armed forces, I demand that you leave this office." Power was transferred to retired general Juan Carlos Onganía, who was to be in charge of the Argentine Revolution, which in turn was to thoroughly revamp the political system. In his first public address after assuming the presidency Onganía said, "Argentina has completed a historic cycle."

The 1966 military coup came as a surprise to almost no one. By this time there was a general consensus that something had to be done, that fundamental changes in the political system had to be made. The coup had the approval, or at least the acquiescence, of all the nation's major political forces except the university students and the UCRP, the political party removed from power.

Onganía was left to decide what was to be done and what sort of political changes were to be made. The military junta responsible for the overthrow of President Illia immediately issued decrees dissolving Congress, the provincial legislatures, and municipal councils, removing from office all governors, mayors, and members of the national and provincial supreme courts, and disbanding all the nation's political parties. It then issued a manifesto entitled The Act of the Argentine Revolution, which was supposed to explain the causes of the coup and the goals of the new government, inaugurated Onganía as president, and dissolved itself.

The Act of the Argentine Revolution conferred upon Onganía all the powers normally held by a president, plus those delegated by the constitution to Congress (with the exception of the power to impeach federal judges), plus the power to appoint and remove provincial governors. In effect, the leaders of the armed forces gave Onganía the power to do whatever he felt necessary.

The new *caudillo* who was supposed to save Argentina from itself was virtually unknown to the civilian population before the September 1962 confrontation between *azules* and *colorados*. James Rowe said of him:

Of all the military men who have held the Argentine Presidency in recent years, Onganía is perhaps the most exclusively military in background and formation. General [José Félix] Uriburu was linked to the *estancieros* [large landowners] and the oligarchy; Colonel Perón built the CGT; General Aramburu had a wide circle of friends and supporters in the business and civilian world—but Onganía, who does not come from a prominent family, has few close associates outside the army. He is a soldier's soldier, "uncontaminated" by the connections that most important men have with the country's political and other elites. The uncommitted quality and his aloofness have no doubt enhanced the legendary character of his authority, but the plain fact is that Onganía assumed the presidency with very little being known about his political ideas or about his skill at convincing, as distinct from commanding.[21]

Onganía first attained prominence in September 1962, when he assumed leadership of the *azul* faction of the army; as soon as that group attained power, he was appointed to the position of commander-in-chief by President José María Guido. Throughout the remainder of the Guido administration, Onganía was clearly the dominant figure in Argentina. At any time during this period he could have deposed Guido and assumed the presidency; instead, he devoted all his efforts to seeing to it that elections were held and the government returned to civilian hands.

During the 1963 election campaign there were constant rumors that Onganía would become the presidential candidate of the National and Popular Front (FNP)—which would have been delighted to have him as its nominee.

Perhaps he decided not to run for fear of splitting the *azul* movement (some claim that all the *azul* leaders agreed in advance not to assume the presidency). Besides, his number-one goal at this time was to restore complete unity to the army, and becoming president would have forced him to retire from active duty before this could have been accomplished.

In the first two years of the Illia administration, Onganía remained in his post as commander-in-chief of the army, and it was generally assumed that he guaranteed Illia that there would be no military uprisings. Nevertheless, late in 1965 Illia virtually forced Onganía into retirement by appointing as secretary of war an active-duty general inferior to him in rank. Many feel that with the retirement of Onganía, Illia's days were numbered.

Onganía's assumption of the presidency seemed paradoxical to those who thought of him solely in terms of his celebrated Communiqué 150 and his insistence on elections in 1963. Still, his support of the 1966 coup (which probably would not have taken place had he opposed it) did not represent a complete repudiation of his earlier position. Onganía had always insisted that the army has functions that go well beyond that of guaranteeing national sovereignty and territorial integrity. In his speech at the Sixth Conference of American Armies in August 1964, he said that the armed forces must also "preserve the moral and spiritual values of the Western Christian world, assure public order and domestic peace, promote the general welfare, and sustain the application of the constitution."[22] And shortly before his retirement, he added that the military

cannot stay aloof from those emotional states that characterize the country and influence our conduct. We are not going to intervene to avoid small disasters. Small disasters are not our responsibility. On the other hand, we now have enough experience with intervention to avoid the wear and tear that, little by little, incapacitate us for our primary responsibility—that is, to intervene to avoid great disasters. Yes, when the conditions are appropriate, we shall intervene.[23]

Onganía's legalist position that the military must not govern was not at all the same thing as saying that the military must not decide who shall govern.

When Onganía took office, more was expected of him than of any president since Yrigoyen a full half-century earlier. The general public was not certain of exactly what to expect, but virtually everyone expected widespread changes—and changes for the better. Unfortunately, very little change of lasting value took place during the four years that Onganía was president. (The one major change that did occur was a dramatic increase in the level of political violence.) The lack of revolutionary change may be attributed, more than to anything else, to the failure to identify clearly the nation's major problems. A great deal of time was spent, instead, in attempting to decide what sort of government organization might be most capable of resolving undefined problems. Onganía put great emphasis on the achievement of law and order and economic stability. The latter task was given to Adalbert Krieger Vasena, a distinguished economist who earlier had served as economy minister under President Aramburu. While Krieger Vasena remained in office (from 1967 to mid-1969) Argentina experienced an economic stability that it has not achieved since then. By 1969, growth had resumed substantially, inflation had dropped to 7.3 (the lowest level since 1954), real wages and their share of the GDP were above the 1965 average, unemployment had fallen, and the budget deficit was brought down significantly. Unlike the 1964 Brazilian military government, whose stringent monetarist measures had induced a major recession, Krieger Vasena was able to successfully combine stabilization and growth without affecting employment levels. This was achieved by combining fiscal austerity and exchange and price controls with moderate monetary expansion, export promotion, and a balanced income policy.

On the political front, an attempt was made to deactivate many of the nation's major political forces, but the attempt was almost entirely unsuccessful. The nation's political parties were dissolved (as they had been dissolved before), yet the major parties, with all their defects, were not really destroyed, but rather forced into temporary hibernation; those parties taking part in the 1973 elections behaved in a manner almost indistinguishable from the behavior of those taking part in the 1963 elections. The organized labor movement was neither unified nor depoliticized; the cleavage between the official General Confederation of Labor (CGT) and the CGT of the Argentines was as deep as the former split between Peronists and Independents, and the followers of Raimundo Ongaro were every bit as politicized as had been the followers of Augusto Vandor. Student organizations were closed, yet student political activity during the last year of the Onganía administration may well have been at an all-time high, and certainly the students were engaged in violent activity to a greater degree than ever before. Even the Catholic church began to choose sides to an unusual degree. Within the armed forces, the *azul-colorado* cleavage of the early 1960s was virtually eliminated, but only to be replaced by a struggle between liberals and nationalists. And as was demonstrated by the military coup of June 8, 1970, which overthrew Onganía, the armed forces were not removed from the political arena. As a matter of fact, the higher echelons of the military, particularly the army commander-in-chief, General Alejandro Lanusse, became more and more frustrated with Onganía, who had removed the armed forces from actively participating in the decision-making process. Lanusse, who had personal ambitions to become president himself, feared along with his colleagues that Onganía could become an Argentine Franco. This could mean relegating the armed forces to a junior role for an extended period of time, something they were not willing to accept. In mid-1969 riots started in Córdoba (the Córdobazo) and several other cities of the interior, and urban guerrilla groups began to organize. In the aftermath of the Córdobazo, Krieger

Vasena resigned, and his departure coincided with a steady deterioration of the economic picture. By 1970, it was clear that Onganía was accomplishing very little, that the public acquiescence Onganía originally had enjoyed had eroded almost totally, and that the nation was experiencing a sustained level of political violence that was completely intolerable. In June 1970, Onganía was deposed by his former colleagues.

Political Violence

There had been guerrilla movements in Argentina prior to the Onganía administration, but they were all small and very short-lived. In 1959, twenty youths, mostly students, established a rural *foco* (center) in the poor, mountainous province of Tucumán, but all were captured within a few weeks. Three years later another small group established a *foco* in the neighboring province of Salta, but it too was quickly eliminated by the army. The first urban guerrilla organization was the Tacuara, which first attained prominence with a bank robbery in the federal capital in 1963; its leaders were soon captured, and little more was heard of it. For the remainder of the 1960s, guerrilla activities in Argentina were notable only by their absence.

The first guerrilla group to have an appreciable impact was the Montoneros formed in late 1969. (Montoneros is the label originally applied to the gauchos who fought in the war for independence, and later against the first national governments.) The ideology of this group was a rather curious blend of Catholicism, Marxism, and Peronism. Its original leaders were all militant Catholics. The founder, Fernando Abal Medina, was a leader of Acción Católica; and his successor, Mario Firmenich, was a leader of Catholic Student Youth. Each was heavily influenced by Juan García Elorrio, the editor of *Cristianismo y Revolución* and disciple of the Colombian guerrilla-priest Camilo Torres.[24]

The Montoneros were ardent Peronists. However, lacking any experience in the Peronist movement prior to the late 1960s, they tended to have an extremely naive view of both Perón and Peronism. "Starting, as they did, from the a priori assumption that the working class was the dominant force within Peronism, that, therefore, it was intrinsically revolutionary, it was logical that Perón as the sole leader and head of the movement should be considered the sole and authentic leader of the revolution."[25] They insisted, until after Perón's return to power, that their goals and his were identical.

The Montoneros first attracted attention in mid-1970, with the kidnapping, and later the execution, of former president Pedro Aramburu. A few weeks later they took over the small town of La Calera. This, and many of their other early actions, seem to have been designed primarily to attract public attention, to demonstrate that the Onganía government was unable to maintain order, and to gain popular support through daring actions that the working class might be expected to identify with.

The other major guerrilla organization active during the 1970s was the People's Revolutionary Army (Ejército Revolucionario del Pueblo, ERP), which was founded at the Fifth National Congress of the Worker's Revolutionary party (PRT) in June 1970. Although the PRT was a Trotskyite party, the ideology of the ERP went well beyond Trotskyism. Its leaders claimed to have taken from V. I. Lenin the idea of the vanguard party, from Trotsky the concept of permanent revolution, from Mao Zedong the idea of a party-army, and from Che Guevara the belief that the objective conditions for revolution can be created.[26] The ERP consistently denied the Montonero claim that Peronism was the political expression of the working class, insisting that Peronism contained within it the same basic class cleavage as Argentine society as a whole. They claimed that Peronist ideology served the interests of the bourgeoisie, and that the Argentine working class could never really attain power without the direction of a Marxist-Leninist party.

Like the Montoneros, the ERP first attracted attention by means of a series of kidnappings. In May 1971, its members kidnapped the British manager of Swift and Company; he was released only after 4,000 recently fired workers were rehired and $50,000 worth of food was distributed to the poor in the city of Rosario. Later kidnappings netted the organization enormous sums of money. The ERP reportedly received $5 million for the regional manager of Swissair and $14 million for the local head of Esso. The Montoneros reportedly received $60 million for two sons of a landowner/businessman.

The short-term goal of the Montoneros appears to have been to create the conditions under which Perón could return to power. Their guerrilla activities were designed to convince the armed forces that the only possibility of restoring order was a return to constitutional government—headed by Juan Domingo Perón. The ERP, on the other hand, seems to have believed that a high level of political violence would push the military government toward indiscriminate repression, which would increase popular dissatisfaction and eventually lead to a civil war, which, in turn, would result in the creation of a socialist state.

The Return of Perón

Onganía was replaced by a little-known intelligence officer, General Roberto Levingston, who was supposed to be a mere spokesman for the armed forces. When Levingston, like Onganía, showed no signs of moving toward elections, he was removed, after only eight months in office. Finally, in March 1971, the army commander-in-chief, General Alejandro Lanusse, assumed the presidency and announced that he would hold office only long enough to stop the violence and hold elections. In order to regain support for the regime, Lanusse ushered in a new political phase, the Great National Covenant (GAN). The GAN's short-term objective was to form an alliance among the military, anti-Peronist political parties, and business interest groups to fend off increasing economic instability. In the long run, the GAN was expected to be the point of departure for the creation of a conservative bloc that could endorse the presidential ambitions of Lanusse once the military decided to withdraw from power. In fact, the leaders of the armed forces decided that they had no choice but to hold elections and return to constitutional government. (There was evidently some hope that the return to constitutionalism would relieve the frustrations that were contributing to the violence, and also a feeling that even if this hope was not borne out, the armed forces would be relieved of responsibility for political events.) Lanusse's ambitions were quickly frustrated as the conservative bloc he had envisioned never materialized. It was obvious to all that if a newly elected government was to have any claim to legitimacy, the Peronist movement would have to be given complete electoral equality. Yet, since many military leaders were not at all enamored of the prospect of the Peronist government, changes were made in the election law to require a run-off election if no presidential candidate received an absolute majority of the popular vote. (There was general agreement that the Peronist candidate, whoever it might be, would receive a plurality of the vote but would be defeated in a run-off by a coalition of non-Peronist parties.) At the same time, a number of complicated maneuvers prevented Perón himself from being a candidate.

When the elections were held in March 1973, the Peronist candidate, Héctor Cámpora (whose campaign slogan had been "Cámpora to the presidency, Perón to power"), received 49.6 percent of the vote, more than double that of his nearest competitor. In clear violation of his own regulations, Lanusse decided that this was close enough to the required absolute majority, and the run-off was canceled. Upon Cámpora's inauguration all political prisoners (including many terrorists) received an amnesty, the universities were turned over to the far left, and in general the government took a vaguely leftist tint. However, after only fifty days in office Cámpora and his vice-president resigned, necessitating new elections—this time with Juan Perón a candidate.

The presidential election of September 1973 was almost a carbon copy of that held twenty-two years earlier: in each case Perón received 62 percent of the vote, and in each case he defeated Ricardo Balbín, the candidate of the Radicals. In 1951 he tried, unsuccessfully, to obtain the vice-presidential nomination for his second wife; in 1973 his third wife was his running mate.

Juan Perón, eighteen years and eighteen days after being forced into exile, once again became the president of the Argentine Republic. Now the government moved decidedly to the right. In the universities, the Marxist administrators were replaced with neofascists; several leftist governors were removed from office; and, most important, Perón openly sided with the relatively conservative labor sector of the Peronist movement against the leftist youth sector. During the 1973 election campaigns, the Montoneros devoted almost all their energy to the mobilization of support for Cámpora in March, and then for Perón in September. In this effort they were probably even more effective than the leaders of the labor movement. (The ERP, on the other hand, boycotted these elections, insisting that the election of a Peronist government would do nothing to further the cause of revolutionary socialism.)

With the return to power of Peronism, the Montoneros laid down their arms. They were greatly pleased with the short-lived Cámpora administration, whose amnesty decree freed a number of imprisoned Montoneros; however, they were rather quickly disillusioned by Perón when he returned to the presidency. Still, they publicly endorsed his claim that the first national goal must be the attainment of the true national sovereignty. The Montoneros saw this as merely the first step toward the creation of a socialist state, while Perón thought of an anti-imperialist state capitalism as the ultimate goal. Even after they realized this contradiction the Montoneros continued to support Perón, for as Mario Firmenich put it:

We have an ideological contradiction with Perón, but we also have a strategic coincidence. Perón is objectively an anti-imperialist revolutionary leader. It is stupid for us to fight with Perón over ideology. We will fight to the utmost for our conceptions, but if we lose we are not going to leave Peronism—it just wouldn't make the least bit of sense since we share the strategic project of Perón.[27]

As Perón consistently sided with the right wing of the movement against the left, the Montoneros found it increasingly difficult to continue to support his administration. The final break came at the time of the President's May Day speech (1974), when Perón and several Montoneros shouted insults at each other. At one point Perón railed against the "stupid and beardless youth who have infiltrated the movement and betrayed it." Although the Montoneros withdrew their active support of the government at this time, they did not resume terrorist activity as long as Perón lived.

While the Montoneros ceased their violent activities in 1973, the ERP did not. In fact, it seemed to be deliberately provoking Perón when, just two days after his election, members of the group assassinated the secretary general of the Peronist-dominated CGT. Their series of assassinations, kidnappings, and attacks on army bases was probably an attempt to drive Perón into the arms of the hardliners in the military and thus convince the workers that he was the right-winger they had always claimed.

The ERP opposition to the election of Perón, along with continuance of terrorism after his inauguration, allowed Perón to claim that the group was composed of anti-Argentine subversives attempting to overthrow the government of the people. Before 1973, the ERP had gained a degree of rapport with the working class, but as it openly attacked Perón, and was denounced by him, that rapport declined greatly. While the Montoneros refused to realize that Perón was not a revolutionary, the ERP failed to comprehend the degree to which the Argentine workers adored him.

By 1973, right-wing organizations were also engaged in kidnapping and assassination. The best known of these groups was the Argentine Anticommunist Alliance (AAA), which first gained attention in early 1974 when it released the names of several "Marxist subversives" who were marked for assassination. Among the early victims of the AAA were the lieutenant governor of Córdoba, a leader of the Movement of Third World Priests, a congressman, and a brother of ex-president Arturo Frondizi. It is widely believed that the AAA was organized by Perón's minister of social welfare, José López Rega, and financed through his ministry. It appears to have been staffed by military intelligence officers, off-duty policemen, and by veterans of the Algerian War who had fought for the Organisation de l'Armée Secrète. Not surprisingly, after the 1976 coup the AAA disappeared.

On July 1, 1974, Juan Domingo Perón died. For three decades he, more than any other individual, had shaped the destiny of Argentina. However, during his last term as president he was no more successful than had been his predecessors in attaining stability or prosperity. He was succeeded in the presidency by his widow, María Estela Martínez de Perón (more frequently referred to simply as Isabel). Although completely lacking in political experience, Isabel managed to hold the formal reins of power for almost two years. During this period, both the political and the economic situations continued to deteriorate, and at a seemingly ever-accelerating rate.

Soon after Isabel's inauguration, the Montoneros publicly announced that they had no choice but to resume clandestine activities because the government had been captured by the imperialists and oligarchs. Two months later they assassinated the head of the federal police (the official with primary responsibility for combating terrorism) and said that the ministers of labor and of social welfare would soon meet the same fate. At about the same time, the ERP established rural *focos* in the provinces of Catamarca and Tucumán. By 1975, AAA, ERP, and Montonero assassins were claiming a life once each eight hours. According to one report:

the most publicized of these murders have concerned prominent lawyers, politicians, liberal journalists, and so on, but those do not form the bulk of the victims. . . . The great majority are not in the least well known: rank and file trade unionists, community workers, priests, students, and teachers have all been included.[28]

Political violence was certainly not the only problem faced by the Perón administration. By the end of 1975 agricultural production declined dramatically, aggravating the already unfavorable balance on current accounts. Public finances got out of control, and the budget deficit in 1975 doubled the size of that of 1973. Political instability convinced many entrepreneurs to disinvest; this led to a major recession and high unemployment. Massive wage increases contributed to the outbreak of hyperinflation by early 1976. There were widespread stories of governmental corruption of staggering proportions, and the government appeared to be more and more in the hands of a cabinet member who claimed to be in regular contact with the angel Gabriel.

Throughout her last year in office Isabel was under a great deal of pressure to resign; this would have meant that the presiding officer of the Senate would have become provisional president, but only for long enough to call for new elections. When it became obvious that she would not resign, there was talk of impeachment, but this was never a serious possibility since it would have required the approval of the Peronist bloc in Congress. On March 23, 1976, she was deposed by the armed forces.

The Process of National Reorganization

After the overthrow of Isabel Perón, power was assumed by a junta of commanders-in-chief of the armed forces: General Jorge Videla, Admiral Emilio Massera, and Brigadier Orlando Agosti. The junta selected Videla to be the ad interim chief executive and eventually elected him as the new president in March 1979. Unlike the administration of the Argentine Revolution, which had been staffed largely by civilian technocrats, the Process of National Reorganization (or Proceso) was carried out almost exclusively by the armed forces; initially, within the cabinet, only the ministries of education and economics were entrusted to civilians.

This military government was considered at the time by a great many Argentines, including many military leaders, the nation's last chance. In previous crisis situations the prevalent attitude appeared to be "if this doesn't work, we can call on the military"; but now in 1976 if a purely military regime did not work, there was no one left to turn to.

The government devoted most of its energies to three basic objectives: improvement of the economy, the elimination of subversion, and the creation of a new institutional framework. While the armed forces took charge of the "dirty war" against terrorism, Videla appointed as new minister of the economy José Alfredo Martínez de Hoz—a member of one of the country's oldest and wealthiest oligarchic families. According to Adolfo Canitrot, the new minister

nurtured within the government the concept of a farsighted and remote authoritarianism, possessed of a morality and a discipline higher than that of a surrounding society made sick by years of mismanagement. In this way he both met the political objectives of a military government aimed at social transformation, and at the same time turned the interlude before political life was to be restored to his advantage, by steering the regime in a direction compatible with his own vision of conservative democracy.[29]

Between 1976 and 1980, Martínez de Hoz employed a series of neoconservative economic policies. In the first two years (1976–77), through the
assistance of the International Monetary Fund (IMF), Martínez de Hoz
carried out a fairly orthodox stabilization program that succeeded in reestab-
lishing a positive balance of payments and in beefing up the Central Bank
reserves which had been depleted by the Peronist administration. Inflation,
on the other hand, although declining substantially, proved much more
difficult to attack. This induced Martínez de Hoz in December 1978 to
switch to an expectation management approach to price stabilization based
upon an overvalued exchange rate. At the same time, the capital market was
deregulated, and many sectors of the economy were exposed to foreign
competition on the assumption that this would make local industry more
efficient and push prices down. The plan, instead of creating a new economic
order, led the country to bankruptcy. The combination of the overvalued
exchange rate and the elimination of most restrictions against the importation
of foreign capital made the purchase of U.S. dollars so cheap and easy as to
create the phenomenon that would soon be called the *plata dulce*, or "sweet
money." Wealthy Argentines, taking advantage of this artificially created
bonanza, bought billions of dollars but instead of investing them at home,
they deposited them in Uruguayan, U.S., or European banks. Conversely,
the high exchange rate was detrimental to the export sector and domestic
industry, which were left unprotected from cheap foreign goods. A large
number of small and medium-sized manufacturing producers, unable to compete with foreign companies, went out of business and took with them many
banking institutions that had overextended themselves. In March 1980, the
house of cards began to crack when the largest private bank, the Banco de
Intercambio Regional, went under when it was unable to collect bad loans.
Soon other banking institutions that had engaged in "easy lending" and
speculative operations followed suit, creating an unprecedented panic in the
financial markets of Buenos Aires. The Central Bank averted a run on the
banks by assuring depositors that their money would be returned. The rescue
operation cost taxpayers billions of dollars, but it was clear to all that the
worst was still to come, and capital flight began to gain momentum, with
wealthy Argentines transferring billions of dollars abroad. By early 1981, the
economic situation had deteriorated to the point that Martínez de Hoz had
fallen under the attack of most of his former supporters in the business
community. Some simple data are revealing of how things had deteriorated
so quickly. When Martínez de Hoz took office, there were 140 pesos to the
dollar; when he left office in early 1981, there were 2,300. During the 1976–
80 period the cost of living increased approximately 18,500 percent, and the
foreign debt tripled.[30] By 1981, the once proudly proclaimed high level of
foreign reserves was dwindling away, and so was the euphoria of the sweet
money.

The Dirty War

Although the economic objective had not been attained, the armed forces could claim that the elimination of terrorism had been achieved. By 1978, the ERP had virtually ceased to function, and little was heard from the Montoneros after 1980. This was accomplished, however, by means of unrestrained governmental violence. The 1976 coup was, to a large degree, a result of left-wing terrorism. The military was outraged when Cámpora, upon taking office, freed hundreds of terrorists, many of whom had been convicted of assassination. Equally important, they well knew that one of the main objectives of the ERP and the Montoneros was the destruction of the military as an institution. The response to left-wing terrorism by the leaders of the Proceso was almost diametrically opposed to that earlier employed by the leaders of the Argentine Revolution. In 1976, the nation's generals and admirals appear to have decided that the most effective means of combating antigovernment violence was the use of even greater violence. A retired general, often assumed to be the spokesman for the most extreme sector of the armed forces, was reported to have said, "First we will kill all the subversives; then we will kill their collaborators; then their sympathizers; then those who are indifferent; and finally we will kill all those who are timid."[31] A naval officer is reputed to have said that the number of subversives who would have to be killed was "about twenty thousand people; and their relatives, too—they must be eradicated—and also those who remember their names."[32]

The Videla administration engaged in an indiscriminate repression effort that had no equal in contemporary Latin American history. Even military regimes that ruled during roughly the same period paled, in terms of numbers, when compared to their Argentine counterparts. According to Alfred Stepan, "On a per capita basis, for every person who disappeared or died in official custody in Brazil, ten died in Uruguay, and over three hundred died in Argentina."[33]

Officially, the persons assassinated by the ERP and the Montoneros declined from about 1,500 in 1976 to perhaps 700 in 1977 and to 30 or so in 1978. However, the government itself, and/or segments of the armed forces beyond the control of the government, imprisoned without a trial thousands more.

The rationale behind the government's use of kidnapping, torture, and most often simple "disappearance" remains very much in dispute today. In fact, there are many who claim that these actions cannot be attributed to the government, that they were instead the acts of individual military members who were beyond the control of the president and the military junta. Such is the position of Jacobo Timerman, who was kidnapped and tortured by elements of the First Army Corps:

[Following the 1976 coup] military leaders hastily organized their personal domains, each one becoming a warlord in the zone under their control, whereupon the chaotic, anarchistic, irrational terrorism of the Left and of Fascist death squads gave way to intrinsic, systematized, rationally planned terrorism. Each officer of a military region had his own prisoners, prisons, and form of justice, and even the central power was unable to request the freedom of an individual when importuned by international pressure. Every individual whose freedom was solicited in the years 1976–78 by the central power, the Catholic Church, or some international organization immediately "disappeared."[34]

Timerman, and others who agree with him, may well be correct. Still, it seems unlikely that thousands of such acts could take place without at least the acquiescence of the president and/or the military junta. After all, it was Generals Videla and Roberto Viola who assigned to greater Buenos Aires, the area of the country with the greatest guerrilla activity, army officers most representative of the hard line: General (retired) Ibérico St. Jean as governor of Buenos Aires, Colonel Rámon Camps as chief of police for that province, and General Diego Suárez Masón as commander of the First Army Corps. Controversies aside, the reality is that thousands of innocent people died. In 1984 the National Commission on the Disappeared (CONADEP) appointed by President Raúl Alfonsín to investigate the facts reported that 8,060 people were still missing and presumably dead. The commission also stated that this was a conservative estimate. According to international human rights associations, the toll was much higher, ranging between 15,000 and 30,000. The social composition of the victims was also revealing of the military strategy. Blue-collar workers comprised 30.2 percent of the total; students, 21 percent; white-collar workers, 17.9 percent; professionals, 10.7 percent; teachers, 5.7 percent; self-employed and others, 5 percent; journalists, 1.6 percent; actors and performers, 1.3 percent; nuns and priests, 0.3 percent.[35]

While some of these people may have been subversive, the CONADEP report concluded that most of them were not. In reality, the great majority of the terrorists went into exile or preferred to die in combat operations rather than fall into the hands of the security forces, as they well knew that they would never come out alive anyway. The military employed the most vicious techniques of physical and psychological torture in what they themselves labeled as the "dirty war," implying that all means could be justified to achieve the end. Many of those who survived the torture were killed, their identity concealed, and their bodies buried in mass graves, or more simply dropped into the ocean. For the record they became *desaparecidos*. The climate of state terrorism that ensued, however, seemed to go well beyond the eradication of terrorism. Muting any kind of dissent, real or possible, and the regimentation of society appeared to be in the minds of the hard-line officers. No one was spared from the repression. Among the victims could be found pregnant women, elderly people, crippled individuals, and children. Some of the babies born in captivity were killed as well, while the more fortunate were either adopted by military officers or were sold abroad. Equally disturbing was the practice by the security forces of looting the homes of their victims and selling what was stolen for personal profit. What had been started as a holy war to preserve the values of Christianity and Western civilization had turned into a "business" of its own kind. Some of these activities were uncovered during the trials against military personnel that followed the collapse of the regime. Daniel Poneman described the case of a soldier during a cross-examination. The man denied having participated in antiterrorist activities but admitted having taken items "brought in" by other soldiers for which he had signed regular receipts.

"What rank did you have?" prosecutor Strassera inquired.

"I don't remember."

"Were your orders verbal or written?"

"Oral."

"To whom did you deliver the things brought in to you?"

"To the deposit."

"In whose charge?"

"Nobody's."[36]

In early 1981, General Videla was succeeded in the highest office by General Viola, the army commander. It was the first time that the Argentine military had transferred power in an institutionalized manner from one general to another. Some saw in this a consolidation of the regime, but it was not. In many ways, it was the beginning of the end for the latest military experiment. The armed forces had been successful in eliminating terrorism and destroying the institutions of participatory democracy. Yet, they proved equally incapable of creating new institutions that responded to the necessities of an authoritarian regime. After six years in power, military circles were still divided on what form their regime should take.

In the meantime, the economic situation was getting out of hand. With the dirty war over, the legitimacy of the government rested solely on its claim of superior economic performance with respect to civilian governments. By early 1981, such a claim no longer held true. Triple digit inflation, increasing business foreclosures, and rising unemployment drove people to the streets. In July and November of 1981, for the first time since the inception of the Proceso, some labor unions mounted mass rallies against the regime's policy. The granting of the Nobel Peace Price in 1980 to a Catholic activist, Adolfo Pérez Esquivel, and the support of international organizations and foreign governments, gave courage to a number of human rights groups, which began to organize rallies against the government.

Faced with mounting opposition, Viola began to explore the possibility of a relaxation of the authoritarian regime by hosting informal talks with former party leaders and moderate union bosses. His move was originally intended to diffuse criticism, but in the end it created the impression that the government was weak and lacked resolve. The civilian opposition interpreted Viola's initiative as a one-time opportunity to push the regime into holding elections. In July 1982, Ricardo Balbín's Radical Civic Union (UCR), Arturo Frondizi's Movement for Integration and Development (MID), and Oscar Alende's Intransigent party (PI) joined forces in a campaign for elections to be scheduled in 1984. This was the first time in a quarter-century that all the groups that came out of the old UCR agreed upon anything. Later on, these leaders included in their pact other political groups. The result was the creation of Multipartidaria, or multiparty alliance, a front uniting all the civilian opposition which was for the first time tolerated by the regime. The hard-line sectors of the armed forces also came to the conclusion that Viola was becoming too soft, but they reacted differently. General Leopoldo Galtieri, the new army commander, announced that the military was going to stay, and new elections were out of the question.

While these events were unfolding at a quick pace, the economy took a nosedive. The destabilizing effects of Martínez de Hoz's policies were inherited by his successor, Lorenzo Sigaut. Sigaut, in an eleventh-hour attempt, tried to avoid catastrophe by reverting to many earlier policies. Three successive devaluations depreciated the peso by 35 percent, and multiple exchange controls and import taxes were reimposed, but it was too little too late. Inflation and capital flight accelerated, unemployment increased, and the recession of the year before continued unabated.

The Multipartidaria's rejection of Viola's proposal for a military-civilian pact in November 1981 proved to be crucial. The following December, Viola, in precarious health, was deposed by a palace coup led by General Galtieri, who became the third president of the Proceso. Galtieri tried to give the impression of strong resolution and told his fellow Argentines "the period of words and promises is over, now is the time for firmness and action." In many ways, his rise to power was an attempt to return to the policies that had marked the early days of the Proceso. Roberto Alemann, an old-time advocate of free-market economics, was appointed as the new minister of the economy. Thus, economic policymaking took again a U-turn in less than a year. Alemann returned to the approach that had inspired Martínez de Hoz but added a new round of deflationary measures aimed at drastically reducing government outlays and consumption by salary and wage earners.

Despite Galtieri's attempt to portray himself as a tough leader, support for his administration began to erode even within the ranks of the armed forces. The nationalistic sectors of the officer corps, which had grudgingly accepted Martínez de Hoz's policies in 1976, openly questioned the return to an economic approach that had led the country to financial ruin. Others simply thought that with terrorism gone, the main task had been accomplished, and it was better for the military to retreat to the barracks when it could still bargain its exit from power with the civilian forces. Galtieri himself began to give contradictory signals. Rumors began to spread in early 1982 that the president was planning to seek an accord with right-wing political leaders and union bosses in order to form a conservative movement that could enable him to contest future elections.

It is within this context that in early April 1982, an Argentine task force took control of the Malvinas/Falklands, a small group of desolate islands in the South Atlantic that the British had taken away from Argentina in 1831. The two countries had carried on the dispute over jurisdication over the islands, which at the time of the invasion had a population of fewer than 2,000 Britons engaged primarily in fishing and sheep breeding, for a long time. Attempts to solve the dispute diplomatically had collapsed in the late 1970s, but nobody imagined that an invasion could ever take place. After all, Argentina was perhaps the Latin American country that historically had the strongest ties with the United Kingdom.

The reason why Galtieri decided to allow the invasion that the navy had been planning for years is still today a matter of controversy. Some believe that this military adventure was conceived as the last resort to rally popular support around a moribund regime. Others also note that the vast oil resources believed to be located in the area were also a motive behind the invasion.

Although virtually all Argentines were delighted at the "recuperation" of the islands, they were also totally disillusioned by the time the Argentine task force capitulated to the British on June 14. This rather ignominious defeat represented Galtieri's and the Proceso's political coffin. The conflicts existing before the war between the army on the one hand and air force and navy on the other exploded in a virulent way after the debacle. To save face, the junta, under mounting civilian pressure, set up a provisional government headed by retired General Reinaldo Bignone, whose only purpose was the holding of elections and the return to constitutional government. Despite a desperate attempt to negotiate its exit from power and secure immunity for the crimes committed during the dirty war, the military was unable to gain any concession from political parties. In fact, while in 1970 the armed forces could ascribe the failure of the Argentine Revolution to Onganía, in 1983 the demise of the Proceso had no culprit but the military. Aside from the defeat in the South Atlantic, most of the 1976 goals of the Proceso remained unfulfilled. Indeed, subversion was eradicated, but at such a high price that it tore society apart for many years to come. Both the institutionalization of a "stable, republican, and federal democracy" and its instrument, the "movement of national opinion," remained ill-defined declarations of intent. In the end, the policies of 1976–82 were essentially ad hoc responses to unfolding crises. Moreover, the regime never completely succeeded in eliminating opposition forces, particularly labor. On the economic front, the Proceso led the country to ruin. By 1983, national industry

was devastated by Martínez de Hoz's erratic policies. Many small and medium-sized manufacturers were wiped out, the banking system was crippled,
the foreign debt ballooned to US$45 billion, wages and salaries lost a third
of their 1975 purchasing power, unemployment and underemployment remained high, the budget deficit kept mushrooming, and the recession was
accompanied by galloping inflation (the peso reached 260,000 to the dollar).
The beneficiaries of the economic model chosen in 1976 were the local
conglomerates, some multinational corporations that increased their control
over key sectors of the national economy, and the financial speculators who
had exported abroad between US$20 and US$30 billion. The losers were
the middle and lower classes who saw their economic status worsen even
further.

The Alfonsín Administration

On October 30, 1983, Argentines went to the polls for the first time in
more than a decade, and to the amazement of most observers they chose as
their new president a Radical, Raúl Alfonsín. For the first time since the
party's formation in 1946, the Peronists lost a presidential election—and lost
decisively, as their presidential candidate, Italo Luder, received only 40
percent of the popular vote, while Alfonsín obtained 52 percent.

Alfonsín's was a stunning success that caught not only the Peronists but
even many Radicals unprepared. The president-elect had outlined many
policies during the electoral campaign, but some of them were still at the
design stage when he took office. To make things worse, there was little if
any collaboration from the Bignone administration to prepare the incoming
government for the challenges, and they were many.

To begin with, Alfonsín had promised to revitalize an economy that had
been depressed since the early 1980s. He also assured his people that he
would bring down inflation to tolerable levels by adopting stabilization measures whose cost would be equitably shared by everyone, not just by the
middle and working classes, as had been the case before. This, however,
appeared much easier to say than to do. In fact, when his administration
took office in December 1983, it faced a host of economic demands that had
been repressed during the Proceso. These demands now all surfaced at once,
forcing all economic groups to try to push the cost of economic austerity
onto other groups. Unions pressed for better wages and social services, price
controls, and a fairer income distribution, noting that the burden of Martínez
de Hoz's stabilization measures had fallen disproportionately upon them.
Industrial entrepreneurs asked for better prices, tax breaks, tariff protection,
and government subsidies. Agricultural producers demanded less tax on
primary exports and no price controls on foodstuffs. All these demands were
placed upon an administration that was money starved and burdened by a
huge foreign debt. In 1984, servicing just the interest on this debt cost

Argentina $6.5 billion. This equaled 24 percent of export earnings in that year but would climb to 61 percent in 1987.[37] What was also very disturbing was that a good part of this debt had been taken over by the last military administration from bankrupt private businesses. In 1987, the private sector shared less than 7 percent of the foreign debt, as opposed to 52 percent in 1975.[38] The nationalization of the private debt in 1983 had been dictated by the threat that foreign lenders would cut off Argentina from additional lending, which was desperately needed. Equally disturbing was the fact that a large part of the money borrowed abroad by private firms or individuals had not been invested in Argentina but abroad, particularly during the 1978–33 period. This phenomenon indicated a profound malaise that afflicted Argentine society, that is, the lack of confidence of its most affluent citizens in their economy and the officials in charge of it, regardless of whether those officials came to power through democratic means or a military coup. Such behavior finds a partial explanation in the staggering inflationary process that had affected Argentina since the mid-1970s. Using 1980 as a benchmark figure of 100, the consumer price index (CPI), an average of 3 in 1976, skyrocketed to 2,403 in 1983.

In the meantime, a serious decapitalization process affecting the industrial sector took place, as many domestic entrepreneurs began to go bankrupt in the late 1970s and early 1980s. The side effect of this situation was a socio-economic transformation of the working force. While in 1947 workers in manufacturing represented 15.8 percent of the economically active population, in 1980 they dropped to 12.7 percent. Within the same period, self-employed workers rose from 6.6 percent to 14.2 percent. Between 1973 and 1984, the thriving underground economy (in which self-employed are heavily represented) marked an increase of 8 percent in manufacturing companies with fewer than six employees. The opposite was true of companies with 200 or more workers, which suffered a 16 percent employment loss. This meant that traditional unionism, which had its strongholds in large manufacturing enterprises, saw its membership shrinking, and with it its ability to politically control the working class as it did in the heyday of Peronism. Self-employed and small business workers, in fact, were scarcely unionized and difficult to mobilize.

Yet, most of Alfonsín's attention during his campaign was geared around political issues related to the consolidation of democracy. He told his fellow citizens of the necessity to recreate a sense of confidence in the democratic institutions that had failed in the past and whose failure had led to a series of authoritarian experiments. He promised to reestablish the "rules of the game," which are the pillars of any democratic society but which had been abused or ridiculed in most of Argentina's history. This was a problem that both Frondizi and Illia had failed to resolve. In 1983, Alfonsín not only needed the support of his followers to set the tone for a new way of interpreting and practicing democracy but also had to obtain the collaboration of opposition parties and the skeptical economic interest groups (the CGT, the UIA, and the SRA, to name the most visible). In other words, he had to convince the opposition that the Radical administration would respect their rights and engage with them in a fair and constructive competition to solve socioeconomic problems. He also promised to make Congress a true forum for the discussion of national issues rather than the rubber stamp for executive decrees it traditionally had been. In this way, the Peronists and the minor parties could play a dynamic opposition role by keeping government action in line and occasionally come to bargains and negotiations with the Radicals where room for common agreement was possible. In so doing, the opposition in Congress would feel less estranged from the decision-making process, and by realizing its meaningful role, it would relinquish the old habit of petitioning the military when things did not go its way.

In order to create such a transformation, however, parties had to undergo a profound change. As we have seen, Argentine parties had traditionally been very polarized, ideologically weak, loosely organized at the national level, highly factionalized, and prone to openly favor their narrow constituency and the special interests linked to them at the expense of other sectors of the society. Their highly partisan nature prevented them from aggregating demands across different social sectors. The Peronists, for instance, were very closely associated with labor and the General Economic Confederation (CGE), the organization grouping small and medium-sized businesses (most of which were located outside Buenos Aires). The UCR, on the contrary, considered itself as the representative of the common citizen and refused to be compromised with specific interest groups whose demands it viewed as being selfish. Conservative parties, both in greater Buenos Aires and the provinces, were smaller and identified with even narrower interests, be they the upper class of the Federal Capital or the oligarchic families of the interior. This created a situation in which most socioeconomic groups felt alienated and remained generally unsupportive of the democratic system. As a consequence, the articulation of demands was dealt with in an ad hoc and discretionary manner that kept feeding the general sense of suspiciousness about the fairness of the system as a whole. In turn, most elected governments that needed interest groups' support, or at least compliance, in shaping socioeconomic policies found themselves captives of a situation that they had created. Parties then had to modernize themselves and convince interest groups that they (the interest groups) could pursue their goals through them and the institutional setting.

Alfonsín made a similar pledge regarding the judicial system. He promised to respect the independence of the judiciary and to abide by the rule of law which the Proceso had so openly disregarded. This meant delivering on the campaign promise that justice "without vengeance" would be accomplished and that those military men and terrorists guilty of human rights violations would be brought to justice. By the same token, the president promised to reform the armed forces and bring them, once and for all, under civilian control.

Finally, Alfonsín had to reform the statute regulating the internal organization of the unions and their rights before the state. Specifically, this meant the regulation of the right to strike, unions' internal elections, and control of unions' dues and welfare benefits. A modern country needed a responsive labor movement, but in Argentina, where the process for selecting delegates was open to manipulation by the outgoing leadership, unions remained under the control of union bosses often linked to rival Peronist factions. As a result, the CGT turned into the backbone of the Peronist party (PJ). The politicization of the CGT created enormous problems for any administration that was not Peronist, as unions could use their bargaining power, funds, and the unrestricted right to strike as very effective tools to severely limit the administration's policy options.

Having won an honest election by a clear margin, Alfonsín found his legitimacy not to be in question. The 52 percent of the popular vote gave him a clear mandate and strengthened his position in dealing with the opposition. Opinion polls showed that until 1988 Alfonsín's popularity among his compatriots was very high, perhaps second only to that of Perón. The president portrayed himself as a strong and charismatic politician, showing the kind of leadership most Argentines seem to prefer. On the other hand, he tried to act as a man above partisan lines who did his best to give an example to his fellow citizens on how to respect the rule of law and the rights of political adversaries.

Incrementalism was what characterized Alfonín's policy-making style. He knew that compromise and bargaining were necessary, but he tried to use them selectively, so that he could enforce his policy agenda as closely as possible to its original form. He also knew that the 52 percent of the popular vote gained in the presidential elections had come, for a good part, from constituencies outside the UCR and, if he wanted to retain such support, he had to design policies that could appeal to the broadest audience. It is in this light that we can explain his early policies, a bland mixture of nationalism, populism, and social democracy.

Unfortunately, one of the cornerstones of his reform program fell apart at the start. In March 1984, the administration suffered a decisive blow in Congress when a proposed bill curtailing union power was narrowly defeated. From then on, Alfonsín tried to persuade unions to adopt more conciliatory behavior by hosting talks, along with management, concerning a possible three-party agreement on socioeconomic policy. This would imply labor's compliance on key economic measures in return for concessions on wages, welfare benefits, and collective bargaining in contract negotiations. Yet it never happened. The problem was that collective bargaining meant different things to those involved. For Alfonsín's economists, working conditions and productivity had to be discussed ahead of wages, while the CGT wanted bargaining talks to be unrestricted and indexing to be automatic. Such positions remained far apart, and in response the CGT launched thirteen general strikes against the Radical administration, crippling the economy. To bypass the problem, the president resorted to ad hoc agreements with moderate sectors of the union movement, but to no avail; such accords fell apart relatively quickly.

Alfonsín suffered a second major setback in trying to deal with the "military problem." Initially, the president gave a chance to the armed forces to clean up its act. In February 1984, the Code of Military Justice was reformed, and with the support of the opposition, Congress passed a new law for the Defense of Democracy that sanctioned stiff penalties for attempted military coups. At the same time, the cases of human rights abuses were handed over to the Supreme Council of the Armed Forces (SCAF), the highest military court. After dragging its feet, the SCAF ruled that it was unable to reach a judgment, but it nonetheless believed that the "orders" issued by the juntas during the Proceso to combat terrorism were "unobjectionable." All cases were then transferred to civilian courts. In December 1985, Videla, Viola, and three other members of the first two juntas were sentenced to differing jail terms. Galtieri and the other members of the third junta were found not guilty but were tried and convicted by a military court for mismanagement of the war against Great Britain.

The drastic reduction of the armed forces budget and personnel, the retirement of most high-ranking officers deeply involved in the Proceso's policies, and the dismissal of military officers from state enterprises were all actions that the administration took as promised but they were carried out unevenly. Alfonsín, in fact, incurred strong military resistance to his policies as time went on. The combination of the proliferation of civilian lawsuits against junior officers, low salaries, lack of new equipment, and an unclear governmental policy about the armed forces' new mission all contributed to create unrest in the army. The result was three military uprisings between 1987 and 1988. Although the president was able to convince rebel officers to give up their arms on each occasion—and despite his denials—he was forced to make substantial concessions. Pay hikes were granted, but more important, two bills were passed in Congress that left only a handful of military officers liable to prosecution. Those who had voted for Alfonsín in 1983 in the belief that the rule of law would be finally upheld felt betrayed.

Prior to the elections, Alfonsín had stated that if elected, he would reverse the recessionary policies imposed by the military. Emphasis was going to be on economic growth and a tough stand on the renegotiation of the foreign debt with the International Monetary Fund and the foreign banks (by the end of 1983, Argentina had stopped interest payments to foreign lenders and had fallen into arrears). Alfonsín also ascribed part of the blame for the debt to foreign bankers and pledged that only the "legitimate debt" was going to be repaid. In practice this meant that the money borrowed for speculative operations (and which was eventually reinvested abroad) was not going to be returned.

Accordingly, once in office the president started by adopting a gradualist approach which simultaneously fostered economic growth, income distribution, and anti-inflationary policies. However, wage hikes and increased government spending to revitalize the economy turned out to be highly inflationary. Price controls were imposed to dampen inflation, but they turned out to be highly ineffective as producers began to withhold their goods and services in the official market while selling them at much higher prices in the booming black market. By mid-1984 inflation had doubled, thus compromising most of the government macroeconomic targets for the year.

Alfonsín at first tried to avoid pressure from the United States, the IMF, and international banks to renegotiate the debt by going to sympathetic European countries like France, Spain, and Italy to receive additional credit. The Europeans praised Alfonsín's efforts to bring democracy back to Argentina but, much to his disappointment, they also told him to honor Argentina's international commitments. Left with no option and with an economy on the verge of hyperinflation, the president approached the IMF, but slowly. He knew that changing his early nationalistic stand overnight would have caused a public outcry and stiff opposition even within the UCR, since going back to the IMF was equal to repudiating all he had stood for a few months earlier. Thus, negotiations with the IMF were prolonged so as to psychologically prepare the country. A tentative agreement was reached in September 1984 that translated into an standby loan the following December. Even then, it took about six months to enforce a serious stabilization plan. First, he fired his economic team, staffed with old-time Radicals that had opposed the IMF accord, and replaced it with younger technocrats not tied with the UCR. Then, he waited until the economic situation was so bad that very few would be opposed to the bitter medicine of economic stabilization. In mid-June 1985, with monthly inflation reaching 30 percent, the president and his minister of the economy, Juan Sourrouille, unveiled the details of a new economic package under the name of Austral Plan. The plan, which had received the seal of approval of the U.S. Federal Reserve and the IMF in the weeks previous to its announcement, aimed at breaking hyperinflation in the short run while paving the way for a series of "structural reforms" that would have modernized the Argentine economy and made it more efficient. The Austral Plan combined elements of economic orthodoxy dear to the IMF, such as the reduction of the fiscal deficit and a sharp devaluation, and less orthodox ones like the freezing of prices and wages. In addition, a new monetary unit, the austral, was created and its parity fixed at $1.25. The enactment of monetary reform by presidential decree openly violated the constitution, which prescribed that only Congress was entrusted with such power. However, Alfonsín argued that the surprise element was essential for the success of the plan and that a congressional debate would have defeated such a purpose. Regardless, resorting to executive powers to accomplish political ends broke the president's promise to revitalize the role of Congress and political parties. It seemed to all concerned that all major decisions were made behind the scenes again. This approach, perhaps dictated by necessity, unfortunately became more the rule than the exception later in Alfonsín's term, creating great disappointment among those who had seen in him the very personification of the democratic ideals.

But in the short term the gamble paid off. The Austral Plan was able to lower the inflation rate to an average of little more than 3 percent in the second half of 1985. The president's decision to go ahead with the bold measures of the Austral Plan, instead of political disaster as some Radical congressmen had feared, turned out to be a boost for the popularity of the president, who received approval ratings as high as 80 percent. The UCR was able to keep its absolute majority in the Chamber of Deputies in the first midterm elections of November 1985. On the other hand, the right-wing faction of the PJ (and its union allies) that had openly opposed the plan suffered its worst defeat ever. In brief, it looked as if economic austerity had succeeded in reinforcing support for the administration. Conversely, the opposition was forced on the defensive, leaving Alfonsín with greater room to maneuver. The UIA, the SRA, and many opposition leaders came out praising the administration policies.

However, when in March 1986 there was widespread desire for a return to economic growth rather than introducing the painful structural reforms that were an integral part of the Austral Plan, political considerations again prevailed over economic ones. Improvement of the economic picture lessened public concern, and with it the rationale behind the unilateral decision-making approach adopted by the administration in June of 1985. Alfonsín came increasingly under pressure to start a new phase, in which decisions would be taken in a more participatory fashion. A continuation of the discretionary policy-making style that marked the early stages of the shock treatment was perceived as an obstacle to social cooperation and the consolidation of democracy. The shock therapy had to be replaced by "mechanisms that would increase the transparency of public decisions and would allow the formulation of consensual economic interests."[39] Moreover, with the IMF agreement close to expiration, and with it the limits imposed on the administration's policies, it was now possible for the president to initiate a new phase. Accordingly, wage indexation (pleasing unions) was implemented, price freezes were phased out and accompanied by lax monetary policy (appealing to many businesses), and consultation with interest groups resumed again to the satisfaction of many.

Yet, Alfonsín's new expansionary policies did not work out. In February 1987, they caused a new surge in inflation and forced the government to institute a new four-month wage and price freeze. The new economic package failed to achieve its objectives. Once price and wage controls were lifted, inflation reappeared, reaching its highest peak just before a new round of congressional and gubernatorial elections.

Internecine squabbles within the cabinet diminished whatever credibility the administration's policies had retained from the successes of 1985. Sourrouille and his economic team were constantly attacked by the minister of labor, Carlos Alderete (a Peronist union leader who openly stated his loyalty to the labor movement and Peronism above that of the administration), who supported free collective bargaining between business and labor and expansionary policies. The administration's overture to moderate unions (of which Alderete was a representative), in an attempt to co-opt their support, failed when their leaders refused to comply with a decree establishing a wage-bargaining rule in August. The lack of decisiveness shown by the administration resulted in all parties concerned being alienated. Unions remained dissatisfied as wages still lagged behind inflation, while business and the public at large were increasingly frustrated at the government's inability to stick to its promise to halt inflation.

Prior to the September elections, Alfonsín appealed again to the voters, presenting the electoral context as a plebiscite on his administration's performance. He told people that a vote for his Radical candidates was a vote for democracy, something that the Peronists could not guarantee. However, by then people were tired of ethical discourses; they wanted to see tangible economic results. A long list of broken promises had created widespread disappointment among those who had voted for Alfonsín in 1983. The Peronists understood this and successfully turned the popular discontent to their advantage. The election results were a triumph for the PJ and equally disappointing for the UCR, which lost its majority in the Chamber of Deputies and the governorship of the most important province, Buenos Aires.

Right afterward, Alderete resigned, and the unions that had up to then engaged in talks with the government felt much safer openly joining the opposition. September 1987 marked the turning point of the Radical administration. From then on, the initiative switched steadily but decisively to the Peronists. Alfonsín himself, shocked by the electoral fiasco, felt that his fellow Argentines had abandoned him. It would take him several weeks to recover. For the remainder of 1987 and the first half of 1988, the president tried to strike ad hoc deals with Antonio Cafiero, who, having won the governorship of Buenos Aires, had taken control of the party apparatus of the PJ.

However, the Alfonsín-Cafiero collaboration ended abruptly in July 1988, when Cafiero lost the Peronist presidential primaries to the governor of La Rioja, Carlos Menem. Menem, who understood all too well that any association with the outgoing Radical administration was going to diminish his chances for the 1989 presidential elections, distanced himself as much as possible from Alfonsín. More to the point, he ran a campaign committed to old-fashioned Peronist themes: income distribution, state-led economic growth, and a moratorium on the foreign debt.

Left with no viable interlocutors within the opposition, and facing a further deterioration of the economy, Alfonsín and his economic team decided to play their last card. An agreement was made with the UIA granting industrialists a number of economic incentives in return for their respect of price guidelines to be set up by the government. The Spring Plan, launched in August, had also an important political twist. The upcoming presidential elections were scheduled in May 1989 although Alfonsín's term expired only in December of that year. The rationale behind this decision was simple. Sourrouille had predicted that the Spring Plan would be able to bring inflation to its lowest point in May. Setting the electoral contest at that time should give the Radical candidate for the presidency, Córdoba's governor Eduardo Angeloz, a good chance to win. Needless to say, the manipulation of the electoral agenda angered the Peronists and other opposition forces, thus further discrediting Alfonsín's image of being a genuine democrat. Yet, contrary to the government's expectations, the Spring Plan fell apart well before May. The SRA, left out of the negotiations, strongly resented the special treatment awarded to important industrial groups. In the eyes of the rural producers the Spring Plan represented just another attempt to force an income transfer from the agricultural to the manufacturing sector. Thus, the powerful SRA joined the CGT in denouncing an economic policy. In fact, the IMF had denied its own endorsement when Argentina suspended interest payments on the debt in April.

The crucial element for the success of the Spring Plan was the maintenance of a steady exchange rate. A stable exchange rate worked in two ways: it could avert financial speculations and give a psychological sense of security to investors. To make it happen, the Central Bank had to rely on a substantial amount of foreign reserves. A fresh $1 billion loan from the World Bank in September gave the administration some badly needed cash but, more importantly, the Central Bank needed agricultural exporters to keep cashing their profits in australs to attain a substantial level of foreign reserves. Nonetheless, these conditions failed to materialize. A combination of high fiscal deficit, business fear of a Peronist victory in May, and news that the IMF, the U.S. Treasury, and even the World Bank had serious misgivings about the durability of the plan doomed the whole scheme to failure. Exporters refused to cash their dollars into australs while firms, as well as wealthy individuals, started to purchase foreign currency with the expectation that a devaluation was imminent, and this is precisely what happened. In mid-February, massive purchases of dollars depleted the Central Bank's reserves and forced the government to devalue. The devaluation in itself failed to calm down the situation. The consumer price index jumped from 13 percent in February to 51 percent when Argentines went to the polls in mid-May.

In March, Angeloz asked a reluctant Alfonsín to fire the whole economic team in a last-minute effort to distance himself from the disastrous policies of the administration. Sourrouille and his collaborators were eventually replaced, but to no avail. Saddled with the debacle of the Spring Plan and five and a half years of ineffective economic policy making, Angeloz lost, polling only 37 percent of the popular vote as opposed to Menem's 47 percent.

In the weeks that followed the elections Alfonsín found himself under heavy criticism coming not only from the Peronists, the UIA, the SRA, and the unions but also by important groups within his own party that attributed to him the UCR's debacle at the polls. In the meantime skyrocketing inflation quickly eroded the meager income of many wage earners and shantytown dwellers. Food riots and widespread looting of grocery stores developed in Rosario and the poor districts of metropolitan Buenos Aires at the end of May. The government called for a thirty-day state of siege, and soup kitchens and other emergency measures were used to placate a hungry and angry population. By the time order was restored in June, 16 people had died in confrontations with the police, hundreds were injured, and over 2,000 were still under arrest. It was all the more tragic that such events could take place in one of the world's largest producers of foodstuffs. This also plainly showed how dramatic the socioeconomic situation had become in Argentina. These events gave the final blow to Alfonsín's prestige and his hopes to be the first president since 1928 to finish his term in office. Lacking the meaningful support necessary to enforce any policy agenda, the president agreed quite reluctantly to step down in July and allow Menem to take office six months early.

The rather inglorious demise of the Alfonsín administration could be ascribed to a variety of factors. First of all, the president himself created too many expectations that could not realistically be met. His failure to deliver on many of his campaign promises proved to be fatal. The military problem remained unresolved. On the other hand, the party system, Congress, and the judiciary remained relatively weak while the interest groups continued to exercise a substantial degree of political clout bypassing political institutions. The effectiveness of the public bureaucracy further deteriorated, and so did the provision of basic services. Alfonsín was unable to substantiate his political rhetoric with tangible and lasting socioeconomic improvements for the common citizen. Democracy had come, had brought greater freedom than ever before, but by 1989 had become associated with the worst economic depression ever experienced. The standards of living of the bulk of the population had deteriorated tremendously as the purchasing power of wages was at an all-time low, industrial production had plummeted, and the financial sector was on the brink of collapse. In the eyes of many common citizens democracy had once more resulted in political ineptness and economic mismanagement. Alfonsín's unwillingness or inability to take advantage of the early results of the Austral Plan to launch a major process of structural reforms via privatization of state enterprises and the deregulation of the economy (which his economists had advised) was the critical juncture of his administration. In part, this shortcoming could be explained by the stiff opposition both in the business and labor sectors that saw in such reforms a threat to their vested interests. However, it is not unlikely that Alfonsín's personal inclination for a strong welfare state influenced his decision.

To be fair, not all that went wrong was the president's fault. The foreign debt was not created by him, yet his assumption that macroeconomic problems could be solved "politically" proved to be wrong. Alfonsín had the merit of reinserting Argentina in the international community after having being an outcast for its human rights violations and military adventurism during the Proceso. Ties were strengthened with traditional regional rivals like Brazil through the signing of treaties aimed at the economic integration of the two countries. Additionally, an old territorial dispute over three small deserted islands along the Beagle Channel that had almost led to a war with Chile in 1978 was peacefully solved through papal mediation. Relations were also improved with the United States and the European Economic Community although no progress was made toward a compromise with the United Kingdom over the Malvinas/Falklands. Domestically, the president was instrumental in having Congress pass new legislation legalizing divorce, a National Food Plan was created to provide food stamps for low-income families, and some attempt was made to reform university curricula and revamp primary education. Most of all, Alfonsín could claim that no matter what his failure, a minimum climate of tolerance and public contestation had been established in Argentina.

The Menem Administration

When, on July 8, 1989, Carlos Menem took office, Argentina was in the midst of runaway inflation and social turmoil. Thus, if his predecessor's attempts had focused on the consolidation of the democratic regime, economics became the paramount concern of the new Peronist administration.

During his campaign, Menem had promised a return to the policies reminiscent of the glorious days of Peronism, among them, a moratorium on the foreign debt, a massive wage increase, and a "productive revolution," meaning the creation of more jobs through state intervention in the economy. In reality, Menem offered few specific programs, but he kept repeating over and over again, "Follow me!"

In many ways, Menem was the archetypical provincial *caudillo*, and despite the fact that he had been supported by Peronist union bosses, he had very little in common with them. This became plain shortly after he assumed the presidency. In fact, Menem quickly allied himself with traditional enemies of Peronism: big business and the political right of the Federal Capital. Accordingly, he started to do just the opposite of what he had promised.

In economics, instead of a massive wage increase and union participation in the decision-making process through a social pact, the president accepted a plan presented to him by Argentina's largest agro-exporting conglomerate, Bunge & Born. (The plan was inspired by the ideas of U.S. economist Lawrence Klein.) It contemplated yet another series of anti-inflationary policies followed by a series of measures aimed at restructuring the state sector. The Bunge & Born economists were handed the ministry of the economy. The plan seemed to succeed in the first three months of its implementation, but the opposition of some cabinet members and important economic groups to the enormous political clout acquired by Bunge & Born led to a climate of uncertainty that peaked just before Christmas, when there was a new outburst of high inflation. As a result, the Bunge & Born people had to go, but instead of diminishing, the harshness of the anti-inflationary measures stepped up. In fact, between December 1989 and February 1991, a newly appointed minister of economy, Antonio Erman González, launched seven stabilization plans. One of his first measures was to confiscate $4 billion of fixed-term domestic bonds yielding high returns to investors. Instead of paying the interests on these bonds, which were due shortly, the government turned them into ten-year dollar-dominated bonds. The move had a number of intended effects. It practically eliminated the government domestic debt, took away from circulation a substantial amount of local currency (thus reducing the inflation effect), and in turn forced people to sell their dollars as the austral became much harder to find.

Under González's tenure the administration embarked on a sweeping campaign to privatize state enterprises. In the 1940s Perón had personified what has been called state interventionism by nationalizing companies, overregulating the economy, creating government-owned enterprises under monopolistic conditions, and overstaffing the public bureaucracy. Forty years later, Menem, claiming to be Perón's heir, began to privatize, disinvest, and deregulate at a speed that had no equal in Latin America, save perhaps for the authoritarian regime of General Augusto Pinochet in Chile. A new act, the State Reform Law, was passed by Congress allowing the government to put up for sale most of the 400 state enterprises. Foreign investors, once looked at with suspicion, were now actively sought to create new job opportunities and bring modern technology. By the end of 1990, the government had sold to the private sector around $7 billion, most of which was in the form of debt equity papers, and had shed 64,000 employees.

Moreover, the complex web of state subsidies, tax breaks, export promotions, and the like that had favored some industrial and agricultural sectors through taxpayer money were for the most part suspended. Finally, substantial cutbacks were enforced to trim the national bureaucracy, and salaries of state employees were purposely left lagging behind the inflation rate.

In February 1991, González was forced to resign as inflation picked up again. He was replaced by Domingo Cavallo, who, although one of the country's best-known economists, had until then occupied the position of minister of foreign affairs. The following month Cavallo announced what constituted the tenth stabilization plan in a little more than two years; yet this proved to be the most dramatic. Cavallo practically enforced what was a "dollar standard" type of economic regime. The austral was made fully convertible with foreign currencies by fixing its rate to 10,000 australs per $1. This measure forced the government to live up to its own means. From then on, it could no longer be possible to run deficits by "printing" money, which had been done in the past and which was, incidentally, one of the greatest sources of inflation. The plan was an instant success, and by December the inflation rate had dropped to 0.6 percent, the smallest monthly increase in three decades. Much to Cavallo's credit, the economic package, unlike the Austral Plan, was passed by Congress. Additional cuts in the state bureaucracy and in social services, coupled with the revenues from recently privatized companies, allowed the government to produce a fiscal surplus. Equally important was the fact that the Congress approved the budget for the incoming year, a rarity in Argentina.

All these measures, as expected, aroused widespread opposition from many socioeconomic sectors. Big business, which had benefited from easy credit and fat government contracts, tried to fight back, but with little success. The big losers, however, were the unions. Menem used their finances and organizational network in his presidential bid but, once in office, quickly proceeded to emasculate their power. In fact, more than opposition parties, unions represented the greatest stumbling block to the achievement of his conservative economic agenda. First, the president created an internal split within labor that led to the formation of two rival CGTs. Then he sided consistently with that part of the CGT that endorsed his policies and rewarded it by granting both posts in the new administration to some of its leaders and access to federal money. To those unionists that opposed him, like CGT General Secretary Saúl Ubaldini, Menem used a carrot-and-stick approach. He kept talking to them while proceeding toward their political isolation. With unionism deeply divided, Menem began to enact measures leading to the restriction of the right to strike and the use of social security funds that had proved impossible under Alfonsín.

With respect to the military, the president acted swiftly to put the problem to rest. In late 1989, Menem issued presidential pardons which released from prisons all the officers that were still serving jail terms for human rights violations, including Videla, Viola, and Massera. At the same time, he proved capable of retaining the loyalty of the bulk of the armed forces when in late 1990 he crushed a coup attempt organized by many of the same officers that had revolted against Alfonsín.

Despite his controversial policies, Menem encountered little opposition.

The Radicals, still deeply divided after their 1989 defeat, were not able to propose a concrete alternative plan of action. The more moderate wing of the party headed by Angeloz was, in general, supportive of Menem's policies, restricting its criticism to the means chosen to carry them out. Alfonsín, on the other hand, kept reproposing the old redistributional, welfare program without giving any specifics.

The political Right, on the other hand, had campaigned strongly in favor of the presidential policies during the 1989 campaign. Many of its most prominent leaders were appointed by Menem to important posts in his administration. Ironically, the Right, while seeing its policies implemented, soon found itself completely co-opted by the presidential initiatives. Thus, its freedom of maneuvering declined sharply, and so did its appeal among conservative voters.

In foreign policy, Menem reversed many of Alfonsín's initiatives to make Argentina a leader of the Third World movement. In fact, contrary to the long Argentine tradition of exercising an independent role in foreign affairs, Menem put Argentina squarely within the U.S. camp. As a result, strong ties with the Bush administration were pursued relentlessly as a means to bring Argentina a step closer to the "Club" of the developed nations. Unlike most of its neighbors, Argentina sent a small naval squad to enforce the blockade against Iraq in 1990. The Menem administration also backed U.S. foreign policy on most issues, ranging from the fight against drug smuggling to the condemnation of Castro's regime in Cuba. It was hoped that this would allow the country to receive a privileged status in renegotiating its foreign debt under the Brady Plan. Such a status, granted only to Mexico, could have helped Argentina to slash as much as 35 percent of its debt. Better relations with the United States also meant the establishment of a positive image that could encourage foreign investment. Menem also was able to reestablish diplomatic ties with Great Britain, which was regarded as a precondition to improvement of commercial ties with the European Economic Community.

The popularity of the president went up and down, following macro-economic trends. In February 1991, the future of the Menem administration appeared dubious to many. Facing a new inflationary surge and marred by a series of scandals that had forced most of Menem's original ministers and close associates to resign, the administration seemed in disarray. Yet, the surprising economic turnaround after March that resulted from Cavallo's "dollar standard" proved to pay high political dividends. With inflation and unemployment declining and foreign investments pouring into the country and setting on fire a bullish stock market, there were plenty of signs that an economic recovery could be just around the corner. In September 1991, facing a weak and divided opposition, Menem's PJ scored a clear victory in the midterm congressional and gubernatorial elections, capturing a near majority in the Chamber of Deputies and retaining control of key governorships,

among them that of Buenos Aires. As 1992 ended, Menem could claim that
the majority of Argentines were supportive of his policies.

NOTES

(Unless otherwise noted, translations here and elsewhere from Spanish sources are
done by the authors.)

1. Juan Carlos Zuccotti, *La emigración argentina contemporanea* (Buenos Aires: Plus
Ultra, 1986), pp. 53–54.

2. Ibid., p. 83.

3. Fundación de Investigaciones Económicas Latinoamericanas (FIEL): *El fracaso del estatismo* (Buenos Aires: Sudamericana-Planeta, 1987), p. 568.

4. World Bank, *Argentina: Reforms for Price Stability and Growth* (Washington, DC:
World Bank, 1990), p. 148.

5. José María Fanelli and Omar Chisari, "Restricciones al crecimiento y distribución del ingreso: el caso argentino" (Paper presented at the Fifteenth Latin American Studies Association Congress, Miami, December 3–6, 1989), p. 5.

6. Héctor Palomino, "Reflecciones sobre la evolución de las clases medias en la
Argentina," *El Bimestre*, no. 43 (1989): 12–13.

7. William Smith, "Democracy and Distributional Conflict in Argentina: Constraints on Macroeconomic Policymaking during the Alfonsín Government," in *Latin
American and Caribbean Contemporary Record*, vol. 8: 1988–89, ed. James Malloy and
Eduardo Gamarra (New York: Holmes and Meier, forthcoming), Table 10 and Graph
5.

8. Juan Villareal, "Changes in Argentine Society," in *From Military Rule to Liberal
Democracy*, ed. Monica Peralta Ramos and Carlos Waisman (Boulder, CO: Westview
Press, 1987), p. 84. Villareal cites *El mercado de trabajo en Argentina* (Buenos Aires:
Ministerio de Trabajo. Dirección Nacional de Políticas y Programas Laborales, 1980),
p. 43.

9. *New York Times*, 23 January, 1989, p. 1.

10. Manuel Mora y Araujo et al., *Investigación sobre la economía informal: area
sociopolítica* (Buenos Aires: IDEC, 1987).

11. World Bank, *Argentina: Social Sectors in Crisis* (Washington, DC: World Bank,
1988), p. 1.

12. William Smith, "Democracy," note 80.

13. Carlos Waisman, *Reversal of Development in Argentina: Postwar Counterrevolutionary Policies and Their Structural Consequences* (Princeton, NJ: Princeton University
Press, 1987).

14. Carlos F. Díaz Alejandro, *Essays on the Economic History of the Argentine Republic*
(New Haven, CT: Yale University Press, 1970), pp. 2–8.

15. David Rock, *Politics in Argentina, 1890–1930: The Rise and Fall of Radicalism*
(London: Cambridge University Press, 1975), p. 11.

16. Ysabel Rennie, *The Argentine Republic* (New York: Macmillan, 1954), p. 166.

17. Díaz Alejandro, *Essays*, p. 95.

18. Gino Germani, "El surgimiento del Peronismo: el rol de los obreros y de los
inmigrantes internos," *Desarrollo Económico* 13 (1973): 479.

19. Monica Peralta Ramos, *The Political Economy of Argentina* (Boulder, CO: Westview Press, 1992), pp. 21–22.

20. Ibid., p. 27.

21. James W. Rowe, "Onganía's Argentina: The First Four Months," *AUFS Reports* 12, no. 8 (November 1966): 2.

22. Quoted in José Manuel Saravia, *Hacia la salida* (Buenos Aires: Emecé, 1968), p. 36.

23. *Confirmado* 1, no. 23, 7 October 1965, p. 11.

24. Donald C. Hodges, *Argentina, 1943–1976: The National Revolution and Resistance* (Albuquerque: University of New Mexico Press, 1976), p. 54.

25. Daniel James, "The Peronist Left, 1955–1975," *Journal of Latin American Studies* 8, no. 2 (November 1976): 284.

26. James Kohl and John Litt, *Urban Guerrilla Warfare in Latin America* (Cambridge, MA: MIT Press, 1974), p. 391.

27. Quoted in James, "The Peronist Left," p. 289.

28. *Latin America Political Report* 9, no. 22 (June 6, 1975): 172.

29. Adolfo Canitrot, "Discipline as the Central Objective of Economic Policy: An Essay on the Economic Programme of the Argentine Government since 1976," *World Development* 8 (1980): 916.

30. Inter-American Development Bank, *Economic and Social Progress in Latin America* (Washington, DC: Inter-American Development Bank, 1981), p. 12.

31. *Latin America Political Report* 11, no. 16 (April 29, 1977), p. 125.

32. Jacobo Timerman, *Prisoner without a Name, Cell without a Number* (New York: Alfred A. Knopf, 1981), p. 50.

33. Alfred Stepan, *Rethinking Military Politics: Brazil and the Southern Cone* (Princeton, NJ: Princeton University Press, 1988), p. 69.

34. Timerman, *Prisoner without a Name*, pp. 26–27.

35. Argentine National Commission on the Disappeared, *Nunca Más* (New York: Farrar Straus Giroux, 1986), p. 448.

36. Daniel Poneman, *Argentina: Democracy on Trial* (New York: Paragon, 1987), p. 97

37. World Bank, *World Tables* (Washington, DC: World Bank, 1989).

38. Ibid.

39. Juan Carlos Torre, "Entre la economía y la política. Los dilemas de la transición democrática en América Latina," (Unpublished paper, Buenos Aires, Instituto Torcuato Di Tella, p. 9).

CHAPTER 2

The Political Party System

Historically, parties have played a major role in the political development of the nation. At the same time, however, they must assume a major share of the blame for the chronic instability that has plagued Argentina since 1930.

THE MAJOR PARTIES AND THEIR PROGRAMS

After the overthrow of Perón in 1955, an incredible number of political parties were formed in Argentina. At least 150 separate parties took part in the elections held during the following decade; however, only three of them had sufficient popular support to have any real chance of attaining power at the polls. These were the Peronists, who were outlawed by the revolutionary government in 1955, and the Radicals, who in 1957 split into two separate parties. Throughout its history Radicalism has been subject to bitter intra-party disputes. Before 1955 the conflict was basically between the conservative and liberal wings of the party; however, by the time of the fall of Perón the latter was firmly in control, and the basis of conflict shifted from ideology to personalities and electoral strategy. In 1957, those who wanted to seek Peronist support for the presidential candidacy of Arturo Frondizi formed the Intransigent Radical Civic Union (UCRI), while those opposed both to the candidacy of Frondizi and to an electoral alliance with Peronism formed the People's Radical Civic Union (UCRP) under the leadership of Ricardo Balbín.

Frondizi and the New Radicals

The original UCRI, and later the sector of it that formed the Movement of Integration and Development (MID), departed from both the tactics and the program of the old UCR. The direction of this change may be described in terms of the two words constantly repeated by this group: integration and development.

Integration was an attempt to reincorporate Peronism into national political life, preferably by attracting individual Peronists to the banner of the UCRI. The first step was to obtain Peronist support for UCRI candidates in the 1958 elections. An appeal was made both to local Peronist leaders and to Perón himself, then in exile in Caracas. During the election campaign, *frondicistas* (followers of Frondizi) stressed the UCRI economic program and its similarity to the general goals of Peronism. One Peronist leader said of the Intransigent Radicals, "Their discourses, their pronouncements, their postulates, their declarations, their watchwords sustained and even repeated in essence the principles of our doctrine."[1] He also claimed that Frondizi met several times with Peronist leaders to explain his program and to show how it was basically the program of Peronism.

Throughout the 1958 election campaign UCRI leaders were in constant contact with Peronists, both those still in the country and those in exile in Chile, Uruguay, and Venezuela. Some even visited Perón in Caracas. One of those making this trip was Rogelio Frigerio, Frondizi's most trusted adviser. It is generally assumed that Frigerio took with him a copy of an agreement, signed in advance by Frondizi, whose terms included a promise to legalize the Peronist movement in return for the support of that group in the 1958 elections. Frondizi to this day denies that such an agreement was ever made; however, shortly before the election Perón sent word to Argentina that all his followers were to vote for UCRI candidates. A comparison of the results of the 1958 election with those of 1957 and 1960 (when Peronists cast blank ballots) indicates that the vast majority of the Peronists did indeed vote for Frondizi and the other UCRI candidates and quite probably supplied the margin of victory for the new Radicals.

After his election Frondizi continued to woo the Peronists. The labor sector of the movement was appealed to by means of a general amnesty for local Peronist leaders and a new labor statute that allowed the Peronists to regain control of the CGT. This policy was not immediately successful, and within six months of his inauguration Frondizi was faced with a wave of Peronist-led strikes, many of which became quite violent. By November 1958, the president was forced to resort to the application of a state of siege in order to remain in control of the situation; as the tempo of violence increased, the army had to be used.

In spite of its quite limited success, the integration policy was continued throughout the Frondizi administration (1958–62). As the 1962 elections approached, the UCRI stepped up its campaign for Peronist support. Party publications became even more pro-Peronist. One spoke with pride of Peronist support in 1958, and in comparing the two movements said "they have identical national views."[2] The UCRI tried to play both ends against the middle. At the same time that Peronist support for UCRI candidates was being sought, the Peronists were allowed to nominate their own candidates for the first time since 1955, and the *frondicistas* appealed to the anti-Peronist sector of the electorate as the only real alternative to a return to Peronist dictatorship. The UCRI leaders evidently believed they could win with the support of either the Peronists or a large sector of the anti-Peronists. This maneuver backfired, however, when the Peronists obtained almost a third of the total vote, outpolling the Intransigent Radicals by about 700,000 votes; they gained control of nine of the nation's twenty-two provinces, including all-important Buenos Aires. This Peronist election victory marked the beginning of the end for Frondizi, who was deposed by the armed forces just eleven days later.

The integration policy was continued by the new Radicals even after they were removed from office. During the 1963 election campaign they joined the Peronists in the formation of a National and Popular Front (FNP), which tried to present a single presidential candidate. When at the last moment the provisional government announced that all votes cast for the FNP candidate would be voided, Frondizi joined with Perón in asking their followers to cast blank ballots in protest. Once again, in 1973, there was a formal alliance between the *frondicistas* and Peronists, this time in the victorious Justicialist Liberation Front (FJL).

The economic counterpart of integration was *desarrollismo*, or developmentalism, which was both a diagnosis of Argentina's economic problems and a prescription for recovery. The diagnosis began with the assumption that the "old" economic system worked reasonably well until about the time of World War I. Before that time Argentina produced enough agricultural goods to feed its small population and had a surplus to export, at prices high enough to pay for imported industrial goods. This system was said to have broken down for a number of reasons; as the Argentine population grew and became more prosperous, it consumed more and more of the goods formerly exported; the prices of industrial goods increased far more rapidly than did the prices of agricultural products, and agricultural productivity could not be increased fast enough to take care of the difference. Added to this was the fact that the beginnings of industrialization brought increased migration from rural to urban areas, causing increased demand for industrial goods that agricultural exports could no longer pay for; and thus an inflationary spiral set in.

This interpretation of the past, plus the definition of underdevelopment as "the incapacity to finance economic growth with the produce of foreign trade,"[3] led to the assumption that a permanent cure could be effected only by radical structural change. The change advocated was total industrialization based on the creation of heavy industry. The role to be played by the government in the process of industrialization was summarized in five points: (1) stimulation of domestic savings; (2) encouragement of foreign investment; (3) establishment of a system of investment priorities; (4) development of fiscal and monetary policies in accordance with developmental necessities; and (5) a foreign policy that would open new markets.[4]

Implementation of *desarrollismo* signified a major departure from the economic nationalism long advocated by the Radicals. The UCR had consistently opposed foreign imperialism and had advocated strong government intervention in the economy, while Frondizi's economic policies included free convertibility of the peso, loans from the IMF, and the granting of petroleum concessions to foreign oil companies. In addition to being a political liability, *desarrollismo* was less than a complete success from an economic point of view. While some progress was made in the area of industrialization—the production of steel was increased dramatically, and the nation became virtually self-sufficient in petroleum products—the cost of living increased 300 percent and the value of the peso declined from 28 to 140 to the dollar.

Between 1963 and 1966, Frondizi and his followers consistently attacked the Illia government for its failure to continue the drive toward industrialization. The *frondicistas* backed the 1966 revolution at least in part because of their belief (or perhaps their hope) that General Onganía's economic policies would be more to their liking. Likewise, their support of the administrations of Juan and Isabel Perón was conditioned upon their adoption of developmental economic policies.

Illia and the Old Radicals

While the UCRI had a single acknowledged leader and a relatively coherent program, the UCRP was for some time handicapped by its heterogeneous composition and the lack of a party leader. In 1957 it was assumed that the Intransigent Radicals were the former left wing of the UCR, the personal followers of Frondizi, and those who opposed the military government of General Pedro Aramburu. The People's Radicals were felt to have come from the right wing of the old party, those who opposed the presidential candidacy of Frondizi and who were quite anti-Peronist. However, because of the economic policies adopted by Frondizi and the general shift to the left by the UCRP, the two parties virtually switched positions, at least in the eyes of the general public. By 1960, the UCRP was claiming to be the nationalistic segment of Argentine radicalism.

It was this nationalism, in addition to the old UCR concept of intransigence, that were the hallmarks of the People's Radicals. The UCRP attacked the economic policies of the Frondizi administration at every opportunity.

It denounced the petroleum concessions as a sellout to foreign imperialism, claimed that the president was allowing the IMF to dictate the nation's financial policy, and labeled intervention in the CGT as a return to Peronism.

This nationalistic posture was retained by the UCRP after it gained power in 1963. In the election campaign of that year, the party placed a great deal of emphasis upon a promise to cancel the 1958 petroleum concessions, and indeed one of the first official actions of President Arturo Illia was the signing of an executive decree to this effect. Also, as had been promised, no new agreements were negotiated with the IMF. Illia's foreign policy was nationalistic to some extent, as it involved the establishment of economic relationships with several communist states and the identification of Argentina with the developing nations of Asia and Africa, while at the same time supporting the Western world in almost all security questions.

The other major characteristic of the Illia administration, and of the old Radicals in general, was what the founders of the UCR referred to as intransigence. In practice, intransigence meant opposition to electoral alliances, coalition governments, or any relationship with other political groups that might endanger the purity of the Radical ideals. In 1958, while the *frondicistas* were bargaining for the electoral support of the Peronists, the People's Radicals went to the polls alone. And in 1963, the UCRP was the only major party that consistently refused to take part in the creation of a National and Popular Front. Even though Illia attained the presidency with only 26 percent of the popular vote, thus necessitating the support of several other parties in the electoral college, all major administrative positions were given to UCRP members. And in spite of the fact that the party obtained only 72 of the 192 seats in the lower house of Congress, it refused even to consider the formation of a legislative coalition.

While intransigence cost Illia and the old Radicals a good deal of potential political support, nationalism was evidently not the most advantageous of economic postures. One example of this was the large foreign debt, which was constantly aggravated by an unfavorable balance of payments. After the cancellation of foreign concessions in November 1963, Argentine petroleum production declined appreciably, and the Illia administration had to use about $100 million a year of its precious hard currency to import oil. Much of this problem could probably have been avoided by the granting of new petroleum concessions, but the UCRP was trapped within its own rhetoric, for such an act would almost certainly have had dire political consequences.

The question of which group was the "real" Radicals was further complicated in 1963, when the UCRI split into two separate parties, but it was largely resolved by the time of the 1973 elections, when only one political party included the term Radical in its name. The followers of Frondizi reorganized as the Movement of Integration and Development, while the more nationalistic, and somewhat leftist, Intransigent Radicals remained in the UCRI under the leadership of Oscar Alende. When political parties were legalized prior to the 1973 elections, the *frondicistas* in the MID joined the Peronists and several minor parties in the formation of the Justicialist Liberation Front (FJL). Alende's followers reorganized as the Intransigent party (PI) and then joined with the Revolutionary Christians and the Communists to form the Revolutionary Popular Alliance. The traditional Radicals in the UCRP dropped the word *People* and once again became the Radical Civic Union with Ricardo Balbín as their undisputed leader.

The early 1970s marked a fundamental change in the Argentine political scenario. Radicalism and Peronism came to historical reconciliation after nearly a quarter-century of bitter and often intransigent opposition against one another. This rapprochement was marked by The Hour of the People, an accord between Perón and Balbín that practically sanctioned the end of hostilities between the country's two largest political movements. The two leaders recognized the legitimacy of each other's political demands and the necessity to moderate the rhetoric and content of the political discourse. This also implied that, from then on, both Peronists and Radicals would engage in loyal opposition. The Hour of the People also sanctioned the end of General Lanusse's attempt to control the transition process in a way that would support the interests of the military. Once deadly enemies, Perón and Balbín created a very close relationship, which continued after the Peronist triumph in the presidential elections of 1973. While recognizing the Peronist hegemony, Balbín was now consulted on major policy decisions. All this came to an end with Perón's death. The 1976 coup then abruptly aborted the brief interlude of intraparty collaboration, and party politics was officially outlawed.

The Rise of Alfonsín

The disintegration of the military regime in early 1981 gave Balbín the opportunity to unite under his leadership the political opposition into what became the Multipartidaria (Multiparty). His sudden death a few months afterward, however, left the Radicals leaderless. After defeating Fernando de La Rua, one of Balbín's lieutenants, in the Radical primaries in 1983, Raúl Alfonsín emerged as the UCR's candidate for the upcoming presidential elections. Alfonsín had tried to gain the Radical nomination back in 1973, but he and his faction, the Movement for Renovation and Change (MRC), had been soundly defeated by Balbín. Between the late 1960s and early 1980s, Alfonsín and the MRC represented the left wing of the UCR. Alfonsín liked (and still does) to portray himself as a social democrat, but with a Latin American twist which places heavy reliance on personal charisma. By the time he became president, he had moderated many of his earlier nationalist stands attacking foreign investments and U.S. foreign policy. Yet Alfonsín made no secret of his antipathy for the Argentine upper class that preferred to spend its money abroad rather than investing it at home. His concept of social democracy was based upon a reorganization of the welfare state created by Perón, but one that avoided the excesses of the latter. In fact, it called for the rationalization of the state bureaucracy and government enterprises in order to make them more efficient. In Alfonsín's view, the central government was to retain the leading role over the private sector in order to promote economic growth and development goals and avoid the greediness of freewheeling capitalism observed during the military regime. In this way, he hoped to achieve a more equitable distribution of income and also to give the lower classes a better standard of living and economic opportunities. Alfonsín also gave new meaning to the old Radical themes like the respect for individual freedoms and justice. During the 1983 presidential campaign he made his own issues such things as human rights and greater openness and honesty in government action. In other words, Alfonsín made the question of "democracy" and what that concept may entail the cornerstone of his appeal to the voters. It worked, and so did his allegations (never proven) of a Peronist-military pact that would guarantee to the armed forces impunity for the murders of the dirty war.

Until mid-1987, Alfonsín remained a very popular president. His election had marked the first time a Radical had won since 1928 in a honest electoral contest. Postelection survey studies clearly showed that Alfonsín's electoral support cut across class lines. According to one report, the vote was distributed as follows: 30 percent UCR traditional voters, 20 percent conservative voters, 12 percent Peronist defectors, 4 percent left-wing voters, and 34 percent new voters. Interestingly enough, Alfonsín's electoral coalition was strongly skewed toward the center-right, although he portrayed himself as a social democrat.[5]

With Alfonsín as president, the Radicals began to fill up the squares and rally hundreds of thousands of people, a type of mobilization that had been the exclusive monopoly of Peronism since its appearance in 1946. His great personal appeal, reinforced by the success of the Austral Plan in late 1985, helped the UCR retain its control over the Chamber of Deputies in that year's midterm elections. In the months that followed, his supporters began to talk of Alfonsinismo. In their eyes, Alfonsinismo was the nation's Third Historical Movement, referring explicitly to Yrigoyen and Perón's political movements that had dominated Argentine politics in different decades. The euphoria, however, disappeared right after defeat in the 1987 midterm congressional and gubernatorial elections. As the administration's policies started to unravel, so did the president's grip on the UCR. A year later, the Radical presidential primaries were won by Governor Eduardo Angeloz of Córdoba. Angeloz was a moderate, old-fashioned Radical who did not share Alfonsín's social democratic viewpoint or rhetoric. In point of fact, Angeloz's campaign proposed free-market economic policies and privatization plans, which were in open contrast with Alfonsín's ideas.

After defeat in the 1989 presidential elections, the UCR fell into disarray.

On the one hand, Alfonsín, who still chaired the party's national committee, engaged in an all-out negative campaign against the neoconservative policies of the Menem administration. In addition, his advocacy of a social democratic, welfare-minded policy platform that he had been unable to implement while in office seemed to be out of step with the public mood. On the other hand, the leaders of the moderate wing of the party, Angeloz and Fernando de La Rua (the minority leader in the Chamber of Deputies), were in general agreement with most of Menem's reforms but disagreed on the way they were being carried out. The polarization of the party and the incapacity to put forward a viable alternative to Menem's plans undermined the appeal of the UCR. In the 1991 midterm elections the party was able to capture five provincial governorships but suffered a further loss of votes at the congressional level, polling only 28 percent of the total vote, which represented only three-fifths of what it had obtained in the 1983 elections. The biggest loser was Alfonsín, as many candidates close to him failed to be reelected. Shortly afterward, Alfonsín, completely discredited, resigned from the party's highest post. By 1992, the UCR was in a deep crisis of both ideas and leadership.

The Peronists

Although prevented from entering elections between 1955 and 1962, Peronism refused to disappear from the political scene or to be absorbed by other parties. Casting blank ballots in 1957 and 1960 and supporting Frondizi and the UCRI in 1958, the movement flourished in the underground opposition and retained the constant support of a great sector of the Argentine populace. When given nearly complete legality in 1962 and 1965, Peronism demonstrated that it was still the nation's largest political party, thus leading directly or indirectly to the military coups that removed Presidents Frondizi and Illia.

Between 1946 and 1955, Peronism was essentially an alliance of three distinct social groups: the industrial working class centered in the Federal Capital and its suburbs, the middle class in the provinces of the interior, and the new industrialist groups that had prospered during the war but needed protection thereafter.[6] During the late 1950s appreciable segments of the last two groups, especially the industrialists, were won over by Frondizi and the new Radicals. However, the integration policy was quite unsuccessful in gaining the support of the urban working class.

During the period from 1955 to 1970 the Peronist movement was split into two main sectors: a "hard-line" syndicalist group centered in metropolitan Buenos Aires, and a "soft-line" or neo-Peronist group whose strength was concentrated in several of the interior provinces. The hard-line group, headed by José Alonso, was by far the more important in terms of numbers. Its leaders dominated the CGT and its vast financial resources. This group advocated little more than a return to the good old days of 1946–55. Playing an essentially negative role in the political system, it was vehemently opposed to both the Frondizi and the Illia administrations and was overjoyed at the fall of each, in spite of the fact that neither military coup was immediately to its own advantage. Typical of the tactics of this group was the Plan de Lucha, or Battle Plan, of May and June 1964, which included general strikes and the occupation of factories by workers. While its avowed purpose was a demonstration of opposition to the economic policies of the Illia government, it seems clear that the real goal of the Battle Plan was to invite a military coup by showing the armed forces that Illia could not maintain order.

The neo-Peronists of the interior provinces were a quite different group. Without strong ties to the CGT, this sector of the movement was essentially a very loose alliance of virtually autonomous provincial parties, most of which were more willing than their syndicalist counterparts to work within the system. The neo-Peronists showed a degree of independence from Perón, even to the extent that some of their leaders spoke of a "Peronism without Perón." In the 1963 elections most of the neo-Peronist organizations refused to follow Perón's order to cast blank ballots. Instead, they nominated their own candidates and obtained sufficient votes to elect two governors, gain control of five provincial legislatures, and win sixteen seats in the lower house of Congress. The neo-Peronist victories in the 1963 and 1965 congressional elections marked a critical juncture in union behavior. After 1964 Augusto Vandor, the powerful leader of the Metallurgical Workers Union (Unión Obrera Metalúrgica, UOM) and the "62 organizations" (the Peronist branch of unionism), slowly abandoned the stiff opposition of the Plan de Lucha for a more pragmatic stance. Vandor began to work for a Peronism without Perón leading to the creation of labor-based political party that could gain simultaneously the support of provincial neo-Peronists and the tolerance of the military because of its disengagement from Perón's leadership. Indeed, a working relationship quickly developed between the military-supported Onganía regime and Vandor after 1966. This provoked a split within the labor movement, as those intransigent unionists loyal to Perón challenged the UOM leader's project, which ended prematurely with Vandor's assassination in 1969.

The neo-Peronists lacked the class consciousness of the hard-line group. In many provinces the neo-Peronist movement was more personalist than ideological, and the personality involved in some instances was the local political leader, not Juan Perón. It is not surprising to find that the neo-Peronist parties were strongest in the least developed provinces (such as Chaco, Neuquén, Río Negro, Salta, and Santiago del Estero), where *caudillismo* still plays an important role in the political process.

By the time of the 1973 elections, the syndicalists and neo-Peronists were largely reunited in their support of the candidacies of Cámpora and then Perón. However, by this time the Peronist movement was suffering from a different sort of cleavage: the relatively conservative bloc made up by trade union leaders and the former neo-Peronists against the quite radical youth sector. About the only thing these two groups had in common was the desire to see Perón returned to power. To most union leaders a Peronist election victory was primarily a means of attaining greater political power and raising the standard of living for rank-and-file union members; to the Peronist youth, Perón's return to power was to be the beginning of a socialist revolution.

The bitterness of the labor-youth cleavage became apparent to all on the day Perón returned from exile. Hundreds of thousands of Argentines made their way to Ezeiza International Airport to cheer his return. However, shortly before his plane was scheduled to land, a gun battle broke out between the labor and the youth sectors. Twenty people were killed and hundreds wounded, leaving no doubt about the degree to which each side would go to impose its brand of Peronism. In the aftermath of Perón's death the Montoneros went underground, leaving the battle for the control of the movement to the archconservatives headed by social welfare minister José López Rega and the union bosses led by the new UOM leader, Lorenzo Miguel. The internal struggle finally ended in mid-1975 with the departure of López Rega from the cabinet. Miguel and labor came finally to control the Peronist movement, but it was a pyrrhic victory, as in the meantime the country had fallen into such chaos as to trigger a new military takeover.

The years of the authoritarian regime only hid the profound crisis that affected Peronism after Perón's death. The internal contradictions of the movement came bluntly to the open when the last military administration allowed political parties to compete in honest elections in 1983. Much of the responsibility for the state of confusion that marked Peronism in that period had to do with Perón himself. While aging, the old leader had steadfastly refused to name a successor, or even a second in command. In his last public speech Perón stated, "My only heir is the people." One manifestation of his desire to retain control over his movement was that until 1973 Peronist candidates for major offices were selected by Perón himself. Peronism did have a formal party organization, said to reach into each town, county, and province, but it was not a political party like the Radical or the conservative party. Perón himself said that the Peronist party functioned for only a few days prior to election and that as soon as the votes were counted, it disappeared. Such a pattern was surely his intention, and he did his utmost to ensure that the structures in place did not usurp his influence. However, such an effort was futile. Structures emerge and gradually take hold. In this case, however, Peronist party organizations competed with Peronist union organizations and Peronist government organizations. The party structure remained fragmented and weak—and Perón seemed more than content with this arrangement. Consequently, after his death, Peronism had neither a unifying belief system, nor a coherent organizational structure, nor a leader.

It is within this scenario that Peronism went into the 1983 elections. For the first time there was some controversy over the nomination of candidates. Since Perón had not selected a successor, Peronism lacked an obvious presidential candidate. Italo Luder appears to have been selected largely because he was a compromise candidate. In reality, Lorenzo Miguel, the powerful union boss, soon became the gray eminence behind the scenes. He was the man who masterminded Luder's selection. To Miguel, Luder appeared a man of prestige (he had been acting president in 1975 while Isabel Perón was ill), but one who could be easily manipulated because he lacked a personal base of support. This was most convenient because the union movement was perceived by large sectors of the public opinion as having heavy responsibility for the chaos that occurred during the Isabel Perón administration. Furthermore, while many rank-and-file workers had been a prominent target of the Proceso repression efforts, many union bosses actively collaborated with the military regime.

Unfortunately for Miguel, Luder, an upper-middle-class intellectual, was completely lacking in the sort of personal appeal Peronists were accustomed to. That was especially evident in comparison with his dynamic Radical opponent, Alfonsín.

The Peronist candidate that seems most to have appealed to voter emotions was Herminio Iglesias, mayor of the archetypical working-class city of Avellaneda from 1973 to 1976; in 1983 he ran for governor of the province of Buenos Aires, the second most powerful office in the Argentine political system. Iglesias, regularly accused of being a labor racketeer, based his 1983 campaign almost exclusively upon demagoguery. At a Peronist rally in downtown Buenos Aires on the last day of the campaign, almost 2 million people watched in person and several million more on television as Iglesias burned a coffin draped with Radical colors. For many Argentines Iglesias represented the violent past of Peronism that they wanted desperately to forget.

Carlos Grosso, a Peronist elected to the Chamber of Deputies from the Federal Capital, said of the party's campaign errors, "One of the major causes of our electoral losses was the fact that we kept considering societal options that no longer correspond to reality."[7] This is an important point, for the Peronist campaign did seem to ignore the enormous changes that had taken place in Argentina since Perón's first election in 1946. For example, in 1947 only 18 percent of the residents of the Federal Capital owned their homes; in 1980 that number was 68 percent.[8]

Emphasis upon the past instead of the present almost certainly was a mistake, but it may not have been uniformly disadvantageous. In Greater Buenos Aires the Peronists lost all the suburban counties abutting the Federal Capital, except La Matanza and the residential counties of San Isidro, San Fernando, Tigre, and Quilmes, but they won in the "second industrial belt," that is, those counties once removed from the capital where there had been spectacular demographic growth between 1973 and 1983 as a consequence of continued migration from the interior. In 1983, Peronism fared best in those sections of Greater Buenos Aires that most closely resembled the areas of its greatest success in 1946: counties with the largest number of migrants. The product moment correlation between 1970–80 demographic growth and the 1983 Peronist vote was +.771; the correlation between demographic growth and the 1973–83 change in the Peronist vote was +.949.[9]

After the 1983 elections, divisions within Peronism seemed to multiply daily. One faction insisted that the electoral debacle was a result of not realizing that the movement still had a single leader: María Estela Martínez de Perón. However, Isabel had returned to Spain and appeared uninterested in the internecine conflicts within the movement her husband had founded. The trade union movement, still overwhelmingly Peronist, at least in principle, was as badly divided as the political sector. And though no longer a major force, there remained an extreme Left within Peronism. Former Montoneros, now calling themselves Revolutionary Peronists, again became an organized faction within the Peronist party (now actually the Justicialist party). Divisions within Peronism were epitomized by the fact that in 1987 the twenty Peronist senators were divided into eight formal blocs, four of which had a single member.

Shortly after the 1983 electoral defeat a group of moderate Peronist politicians, calling themselves Renovators, set out to convert Peronism into a modern political party, democratically organized, with a definite program. In the congressional elections of 1985 their candidates competed with other Peronist candidates in several parts of the country. In the province of Buenos Aires the Renovators' slate of candidates overwhelmed the Orthodox slate, loyal to Miguel and Iglesias, by a margin of almost three to one. Iglesias was unable to carry even his own voting box.

In these elections the Peronists lost seven seats in the Chamber of Deputies as their share of the popular vote dropped under 35 percent. The result greatly improved the position of the Renovators and allowed one of their leaders to gain control of the party in the all-important province of Buenos Aires. Two years later, in the far more important gubernatorial elections, an at least partially "renovated" Peronism gained control of a majority of the nation's provinces. Antonio Cafiero was elected governor of Buenos Aires, giving him a great advantage over his competitors for the presidential nomination in 1989.

Union leaders, who dominated the Peronist movement after 1955, saw in the Renovators a threat to their continued domination. In the congressional debate of a new organization bill that President Alfonsín claimed would lead to greater union democracy, one Peronist deputy, himself a union leader, said, "if the union movement is split, Peronism is also split. . . . The political movement rests upon us; we are its backbone."[10]

The most important of the Renovators' renovations was the establishment of a national party primary for the selection of presidential candidates. In spite of his control of the party apparatus and the support of all but one

Peronist governor, Cafiero's nomination was challenged by Carlos Saúl Menem, *caudillo* of the poor province of La Rioja. Menem had been one of the founding fathers of the Renovators, but as the latter came under Cafiero's influence, he thought that his presidential ambitions were best served by allying himself with some of the old union bosses who had grown extremely resentful of the secondary role in which the Renovators had confined them.

On July 9, 1988, Peronist rank and file had a voice for the first time in the selection of their presidential candidate. Menem received 53 percent of the vote against Cafiero's 46 percent. He rolled up huge majorities in the poorer western provinces and in the poorer counties surrounding the Federal Capital, while losing to Cafiero in the more developed areas of the country. Less than half of the 4 million Peronist party members cast a ballot. The marginal sectors of society, cut off from the benefits of social welfare for the most part, were those that had most suffered the effects of the economic recession. Uninterested in Cafiero's appeals to strengthen democracy and show patience with hard recipes of economic stabilization, which sounded very much like what Alfonsín had preached for five years with no tangible results, these marginal people found in Menem's populist rhetoric based upon a "bread and jobs for all" message what they wanted to hear. Thus, they became Menem's strongest supporters and were crucial in helping the La Rioja governor defeat the Peronist electoral machine controlled by Cafiero. In the mid-1940s Perón understood and turned to his advantage the plea of the workers. In 1988, Menem run as an outsider, an antiestablishment leader whose messianic and charismatic style struck a chord with the core constituency of Peronism.

The policy U-turn that Menem adopted once elected was a watershed for the Peronist movement. After promising a new dose of old-fashioned economic nationalism and income redistribution, Menem implemented a draconian austerity program with the support of the Argentine political Right and the backing of domestic big business and the international financial community. Many union bosses, along with the Justicialist Party left wing, tried to mount stern opposition to the president's policies, but to no avail. Quite adroitly, Menem took advantage of the divisions existing within the Peronist movement and isolated his critics. By 1990, the president consolidated his control over the PJ apparatus that had opposed him in 1988 and, like Perón before him, reduced the party to a marginal role.

After Peronism's resounding electoral defeats in 1983 and 1985, one might have suspected that the party might not long outlive its founder. However, given the fact that Peronism in 1992 had a majority of the seats in both houses of Congress and control of the majority of the provinces, in addition to the presidency, it seems more likely that this once-charismatic movement has now become fully institutionalized. As President Menem himself put it, "Peronism of today is not the Peronism of 1946, nor even the Peronism of the 1973–1976 period."[11] Menem's Peronism is indeed very different, so much so that some have began to talk of Menemismo as a new political movement that is making a clear break with the past. Whether or not Menemism is going to be an ephemeral political phenomenon like Alfonsín's Third Historical Movement it is too early to say. Certainly, like Perón, Menem is a conservative, but his base of support is quite different. The labor sector seems to have lost most of its political clout in Menem's coalition to the advantage of longtime foes of Peronism: the political right of Buenos Aires and big domestic and foreign capital. The explanation for Menem's turnaround may not be so difficult. Elected in the midst of the country's worst economic crisis, Menem quickly realized that the key to economic recovery was in the hands of the private sector. Accordingly, such policies as economic deregulation, privatization, and the drastic reduction of the state bureaucracy were essential incentives to persuade private corporations to invest again. Within the scheme, unions constituted an obstacle and had to be emasculated both politically and economically. By itself this is a historic departure from the old Peronism. If this new coalition lasts, it will have enormous consequences for the political and economic development of the country in the next few years.

MINOR PARTIES

Although completely dominant on the political scene before 1916 and again between 1930 and 1943, the Conservative party disintegrated rapidly during the first Peronist era. Between 1943 and 1955 only three of its members were elected to Congress. Never more than a loose alliance of autonomous provincial parties, Argentine conservatism after 1955 was further divided in its views toward Peronism. The most vehemently anti-Peronist conservative parties formed a National Federation of Parties of the Center (FNPC), while a much smaller group, which openly appealed for the electoral support of the outlawed Peronists, reorganized as the Popular Conservatives. Although almost completely ineffectual on the national level after 1955, the local parties in the provinces of Mendoza (Democrats), Corrientes (Liberals), and San Luis (Liberal Democrats) enjoyed appreciable electoral success. In 1973, a great deal of time and money was expended in the effort to create a new, modern conservative party—New Force. Although this party may well have spent more campaign money than all its opponents combined, its presidential candidate received only 2 percent of the total vote. Several of the provincial conservative parties refused to relinquish their separate identities by joining New Force and instead affiliated with the new Federal Popular Alliance, which managed to obtain almost 15 percent of the vote for its 1973 presidential candidate, Francisco Manrique.

Another of the nation's traditional parties that survived the first Peronist era was the Progressive Democrat party (PDP). A moderate, somewhat anticlerical party originally meant to voice the interests of the small farmers of the interior provinces, it soon came to appeal primarily to intellectuals and professionals in Santa Fé. Dying a not-so-slow death, the PDP gained a new lease on life in 1963 with the nomination of Pedro Aramburu as its presidential candidate. The party survived the 1976–83 period and as late as 1987 had two representatives in the Chamber of Deputies. In 1989, the PDP joined the Centrist Alliance, an electoral coalition of provincial conservative parties and the Democratic Center Union (UCD) of Buenos Aires.

In 1963, Aramburu was also backed by a new party formed solely to support his candidacy, the Union of the Argentine People (UDELPA). This was clearly a personalistic party with little ideological content. During the 1963 campaign Aramburu refused to espouse a definite program. Realizing that many Argentines looked upon him as a strong man who could bring order to the chaotic political scene, he was quite willing to run as a sort of Argentine Charles de Gaulle. Following the assassination of Aramburu in 1969, UDELPA virtually disintegrated. In 1973, two of its former leaders were vice-presidential candidates, one for New Force and the other for the Federal Popular Alliance (APF).

The political right of Buenos Aires reorganized in the early 1980s under the name of Democratic Center Union (UCD). Its founder, Alvaro Alsogaray, had been for a long time a supporter of free-market economics. Despite having the chance first in 1958 and again in 1962 to apply his ideas as minister of the economy, Alsogaray never succeeded in achieving what he preached. A man of strong convictions, Alsogaray had supported the 1966 and 1976 coups (he was himself a retired military officer and brother of one of the highest ranking generals who deposed Illia) and had publicly condoned the dirty war crimes. Because of these facts, many have disputed his democratic credentials. From 1983 on, Alsogaray and his cronies, including his daughter María Julia Alsogaray, devoted their effort to create a conservative party that could appeal to the middle- and upper-middle-class and military circles that, in the past, saw in the coup the easy way out of a political stalemate. His creed was the deregulation of the economy, the privatization of the state enterprises, the opening up of the economy to foreign competition and investors. "Rolling back the state" epitomized Alsogaray's political agenda. This Argentine version of Reaganomics made the UCD one of the most ideologically minded parties in contemporary politics.

Alsogaray's message found strong support in the Federal Capital but failed to convince conservative voters beyond the province of Buenos Aires. In 1987, the UCD became the third largest party in the country with a delegation of ten representatives in the Chamber of Deputies. However, Alsogaray's attempt to create a conservative bloc through an alliance with regional conservative parties failed miserably. In the 1989 presidential elections Alsogaray's Centrist Alliance polled only 6 percent of the vote. Other conservative parties grouped around the Federal Independent Confederation (CFI) preferred to back the presidential ambitions of the Radical candidate.

Many were the reasons for the UCD's inability to make the "great leap forward." First was Alsogaray's abrasive style and his tendency to treat the party like the exclusive domain of his family and personal friends. This was particularly disturbing among the younger cohorts of the UCD, who wanted to create a modern, democratic conservative party. Second, Alsogaray's elitist vision of politics clashed with the attempt by some maverick party members, like Buenos Aires councilwoman Adelina D'Alessio de Viola, to broaden the UCD's base by reaching out to lower social strata. Last, many conservative leaders in the provinces opposed economic liberalism. Their goal was to preserve the political status quo and protect the local economies from the very competition that Alsogaray wanted to unleash.

After the 1989 elections, several members of the party, including the Alsogarays and D'Alessio de Viola, joined the Menem administration in different governmental posts. Most of the UCD's policy proposals were actually implemented by Menem. While this could be a vindication in the eyes of many party rank and file, in the long run it cost the UCD its political agenda. By 1992, the Peronist administration had completely co-opted the UCD, whose leadership had become extremely divided and incapable of recreating an identity of its own.

In 1955, Argentina's first important Catholic party was formed—the Christian Democrat party (PDC). Originally a right-center party, much like its Italian counterpart of the same name, its early platforms stressed the need for a strengthening of Congress vis-à-vis the president, the adoption of a system of proportional representation for the selection of congressmen, and the right of private organizations to operate educational facilities. In 1960, the party began to move to the left in an attempt to gain the support of the more moderate sector of the Peronist movement. Many of the original members of the party left at this time, claiming the PDC was beginning to advocate a program more similar to that of the Peronism of 1946–55 than to that offered by the contemporary Peronists. When political parties were granted legality again in 1972, two parties of essentially Christian democratic principles were formed. The Christian Popular party (PPC) joined the Peronists and *frondicistas* in the Justicialist Liberation Front (FJL or Frejuli), while the Christian Revolutionary party (PRC) joined the Intransigent party and the Communists in the Revolutionary Popular Alliance (APR). During the 1983–89 period, the Christian Democrats remained a party of ideas, of center-left orientation, but with negligible electoral strength. Both in 1987 and in 1989, they made alliances with the PJ that enabled them to elect three deputies to the lower house in the latter year.

The Socialist party, which gained some strength during the 1930s, lost most of it between 1942 and 1962 (during which time it did not elect a single congressman). From the time of its formation early in this century, the Socialist party commanded a great deal of respect. It was one of the very few parties completely removed from the many scandals the nation witnessed, and the caliber of its leadership, which included men such as Juan B. Justo, Alfredo Palacios, and Nicolas Repetto, was as high as that of any Argentine party. Argentine socialism has always been more moderate than its counterparts in other Latin American nations, and this proved to be to its detriment between 1943 and 1955, when Peronism won over most of the unskilled and semiskilled labor vote. In 1959, the socialists split into two separate parties, one retaining the original Argentine Socialist party (PSA) label, and the other calling itself the Democratic Socialist party (PSD). The former, primarily the left wing of the old party, which was willing to negotiate with Peronism, virtually ceased to exist during the late 1960s. The bitterly anti-Peronist PSD was so moderate that it was socialist in name only. In 1973 its presidential candidate, Américo Ghioldi, received only 1 percent of the vote.

The return to democracy in 1983 saw a flourishing of many new political parties, as well as the decline of old ones like MID. Within the left, two new Trotskyite parties emerged in the 1980s, the Workers party (PO) and the Movement toward Socialism (MAS). MAS, the Communist party, and other minor left-wing groups formed the United Left Front in 1989; this coalition received only 2.4 percent of the presidential vote and won only one seat in the lower house. This coalition dissolved prior to the 1991 mid-term elections.

The socialists experienced an unexpected return of popularity when in 1990 the Socialist Alliance won the election for the mayor of Rosario, the country's second largest city. Nonetheless, the favorable result seemed to be more a vote of no confidence on Menem's policies rather than a long lasting party realignment. In 1991, Socialist Unity, another grouping of less radical socialist and reformist parties, gained three seats in the Chamber of Deputies. The reorganized Intransigent party, after a further drift to the left that helped it to score some impressive gains in the 1985 congressional elections, mostly at the expense of the Peronists, suffered a serious setback in 1987. After a severe internal split, the PI joined the Justicialist Popular Front (FREJUPO) in 1989 only to leave it again a year later.

A number of factors account for the Left's lack of success. First, factionalism, more than capitalism or imperialism, seems to be its worst enemy. In 1989, there were as many as five different center-left and leftist tickets for the congressional elections; combined, they polled only 6.1 percent of the total vote and obtained only one seat in the Chamber of Deputies. Among ups and downs the electoral performance of the left averaged a meager 6.8 percent in the Chamber of Deputies elections during the 1983–89 period. To complicate things, most of the left-wing support comes from urban centers, where the number of votes necessary to elect a representative is much greater than in rural areas. For example, in 1989 it took 573,583 votes for the United Left Front to get a representative, as compared to 48,596 for the Neuquén Popular Movement. This prevents the Left from translating its votes into greater congressional representation. Last, the more radical leftist parties are still tied to a class analysis that finds little response in a society like Argentina, which is more receptive to populist than to doctrinaire rhetoric. As a matter of fact, the Communist party, PO, and MAS have received their greatest support among intellectuals, university students, and a small number of blue- and white-collar workers while most workers have remained loyal to Peronism.

Provincial parties saw their congressional vote strengthening over time as their share of congressional seats rose steadily, reaching their peak in 1991. There is little doubt that like the smaller national parties, provincial ones fared much better in midterm elections, when polarization between Radicals and Peronists played a smaller role in voting decisions. Of the many provincial parties, in 1989 only six captured seats in the Lower House. Four did so through electoral alliances with the UCD and FREJUPO (the Peronist-led alliance), while the Neuquén Popular Movement and Tucumán Republican Force won seats without alliances. In 1991, former Colonel Aldo Rico, who had staged two military rebellions against the Alfonsín administration, made his electoral debut, heading a right-wing populist movement, the Movement for Dignity and Independence (MODIN) that captured 10 percent of the vote in the province of Buenos Aires. The revival of provincial parties in 1989, apart from such long-standing factors as *caudillismo* and clientelism, may be explained by the profound socioeconomic crisis that hit the interior of the country much more severely than greater Buenos Aires. The sense of disillusion with both Radicalism and Peronism may also have convinced many to vote for provincial lists.

COMPOSITION OF PARTY ELITES

It has long been assumed that the conservative parties, always representing the interests of the nation's aristocracy, have received the bulk of their votes from the large landowners; that the interests of this group consistently have been opposed by the Radical parties, who received their electoral support from the urban middle classes; and that later Peronist parties championed the cause of, and have been supported at the polls by, the industrial workers. Yet contrary to the popular myth, it now appears that prior to the 1943 revolution there was very little difference among the social backgrounds of the leaders of Argentina's major political parties and also that correlations between social class and voting behavior were quite insignificant. In their study of candidates for major elective offices in 1916, Ezequiel Gallo and Silvia Sigal concluded that "as far as occupation, nationality and education are concerned, the Radicals do not differ in any way from their Conservative counterparts."[12] In each case the vast majority of the candidates came from the well-educated upper and upper-middle class. The same was true of the

Table 2.1
Social Background of Party Leaders, 1936–1961 (in Percentage)

	Well-to-do Bourgeoisie	Dependent Middle Class	Working Class	N
Progressive Democrats	100	0	0	43
Conservatives	97	3	0	39
Christian Democrats	95	5	0	22
Radicals	90	10	0	53
Socialists	62	36	2	52
Peronists	63	5	32	79

Source: José Luis de Imaz, *Los que mandan* (Buenos Aires: Editorial Universitaria de Buenos Aires, 1964), p. 192.

members of the national committees of these parties, almost all of whom were recruited from the economically privileged classes.

The popular view of the Radicals of this period as representatives of the urban middle class who consistently opposed the interests of the landowning aristocracy is refuted by the actions of Radical congressmen. For example, Peter Smith showed that between 1916 and 1930, while the Radicals were in control of the national government, there were presented in Congress ninety bills that clearly were favorable to the interests of livestock producers; 60 percent of these bills were introduced by Radicals, 29 percent by Conservatives, and the remaining 11 percent by Progressive Democrats and Socialists.[13]

This picture changed a great deal after the rise of Peronism, and it now appears that since the mid-1940s there have been substantial differences in the social composition of Argentina's major political parties—at least between the Peronists on the one hand and the non-Peronists on the other. As far as party leaders are concerned, this difference may be seen in the class structure of the various national committees. In the quarter-century between 1936 and 1961, over 90 percent of the Radical, Conservative, and Progressive Democrat national committee members were from the upper or upper-middle class, while the small remainder was uniformly from the lower-middle class; in contrast, over a third of the Socialists came from the lower-middle class, and almost a third of the Peronists were lower class in origin (see Table 2.1).

Additional differences in party leadership may be seen in Table 2.2, which gives the primary occupation of Argentine congressmen serving in 1890 (when the Conservatives ruled unchallenged); in 1916 (the first year in which a large number of Radicals were elected); in 1946 (the first year of Peronist domination); and in 1963 (the first time since 1946 that Conservatives, Radicals, and Peronists were all represented in Congress). In 1916, the differ-

Table 2.2
Occupation of Argentine Deputies, 1890, 1916, 1946, and 1963 (in Percentage)

	1890	1916		1946		1963		
	Conservative	Conservative	UCR	UCR	Peronist	Peronist	Conservative	UCR
Lawyers	65	66	57	51	32	48	50	43
Doctors	10	10	13	18	9	15	12	19
Other professions	4	7	7	15	9	23	6	24
Landowners	8	15	23	10	12	8	20	9
Teachers	4	2	0	3	2	0	5	5
Military	9	0	0	3	3	0	0	0
Employees	0	0	0	0	17	0	0	0
Workers	0	0	0	0	17	0	0	0
Other	0	0	0	0	0	6	12	0
N	78	59	44	39	106	16	47	21

Sources: Darío Cantón, *El Parlamento Argentino en épocas de cambio: 1890, 1916, y 1945* (Buenos Aires: Editorial del Instituto [Torcuato Di Tella], 1966), pp. 40, 55–56; and Peter G. Snow, "El Político Argentino," *Revista Española de Opinión Pública*, no. 6 (October–December, 1966), pp. 135–50 (for 1963 data).

ences in occupation between Conservative and Radical congressmen were relatively insignificant. Members of the liberal professions dominated both delegations; however, about one and a half times as many Radicals as Conservatives were landowners (just the opposite of what the popular myth would lead one to expect). In the 1946 Congress, the differences between Radicals and Peronists were far greater. Over half of the Radical congressmen were lawyers, and 84 percent were members of the liberal professions; less than a third of the Peronists were lawyers, and only half of them were professionals of any type. More important, 17 percent of the Peronist congressmen were classified as white-collar workers (*empleados*) and another 17 percent as blue-collar workers (*obreros*); none of the Radicals fell into these categories.

In 1963, the differences were less striking. The combined percentages of lawyers and doctors in the Radical, Conservative, and Peronist delegations were almost exactly the same; however, while most of the remaining Peronist congressmen were landowners, the bulk of the remaining Radicals and Conservatives were members of other liberal professions. The disproportionate number of landowners among the Peronists in 1963 can probably be explained by the fact that only the neo-Peronist parties of the interior took part in the 1963 congressional elections; the labor-dominated sector of the movement

Table 2.3
Occupation of Argentine Deputies, 1983–1989 (in Percentage)

	1983			1985			1987			1989		
	UCR	PJ	Other	UCR	PJ	Other	UCR	PJ	Other	UCR	PJ	Other
Lawyers	43	17	57	49	26	50	51	31	45	58	28	50
Doctors	12	4	7	9	7	21	11	9	16	13	8	5
Professionals	12	10	14	14	13	8	8	14	11	7	15	8
Landowners	1	4	7	1	4	0	2	1	3	1	0	2
Teachers	3	4	0	1	6	0	2	9	8	1	10	5
Entrepreneurs	4	4	0	4	2	4	2	6	2	2	6	5
Employees	6	24	0	5	23	0	7	19	2	3	16	2
Union leaders	0	2	0	0	2	0	0	0	0	0	2	0
Merchants	8	13	7	14	13	4	10	7	5	7	6	8
Other	11	18	8	3	4	13	7	4	8	8	9	15
N	129	111	14	130	101	24	113	103	38	90	124	40

Source: Calculated from Liliana de Riz and Eduardo Feldman, Guía del Parlamento Argentino (Buenos Aires: Fundación Friedrich Ebert, 1989).

cast blank ballots in protest of the government ban on Peronist candidates for executive office.

The class composition of the Chamber of Deputies during the 1983–89 period shows some continuity, but also a few marked differences from the 1963 data (see Table 2.3). In terms of continuity, the membership of the UCR and particularly that of the minor parties remained dominated by lawyers. The liberal professions (including lawyers and doctors) as a whole comprised roughly 71 percent of the Radicals and 73 percent of the minor parties across the period. However, this has not been the case of the Peronists, among whom lawyers have at best represented 31 percent of the total and the liberal professions only 45 percent. The reason for the more diversified membership of the PJ and its changes over time is attributable, in part, to the internal struggles within the party, described previously, which significantly altered the candidates' selection process. The main difference with the past has been a larger representation of teachers, employees, and merchants across parties; these made up a consistent subgroup of the PJ contingent. Landowners have been much fewer in number; entrepreneurs made their appearance, although their contribution has remained small and unstable across time and parties. An explanation for this greater diversification may rest on the fact that both Radicals and Peronists have made an attempt to appeal to different socioeconomic sectors in order to broaden their electoral support. In all likelihood, this has been reinforced by a greater degree of popular involvement and political activism during the 1980s than in the past.

THE MAJOR DEFECTS OF THE PARTY SYSTEM

The Argentine political party system has been susceptible to indictment on a large number of counts; however, five major defects stand out. The failure to resolve the crisis of increased political participation and the failure to solve the Peronist problem plagued the system until the 1970s. Three others are still present today: the failure to legitimize government action, the lack of truly national parties, and the inability of political parties to become institutionalized channels for the representation and articulation of societal demands.

Failure to Resolve the Crisis of Increased Participation

Although the electorate gradually was enlarged, all of the nation's ruling elites balked at the prospect of increasing political participation in a meaningful manner. Even when forced to give in, they seldom did so gracefully; nor did they accept as final the participation of new groups. As was noted above, the conservatives, representing primarily the large landowners, ruled virtually unchallenged until near the end of the nineteenth century. When faced at that time with the demand for increased political participation, they resorted to electoral fraud or force, if needed. Various pressures, such as the revolts of 1890, 1893, and 1905, and electoral abstention by the Radicals, forced them to yield to some extent, and electoral reform came about in 1912. Increased middle-class participation was not fully accepted, however, and many leading conservatives were prominent in the revolution of 1930 that removed the Radicals from power.

After 1916, the Radicals appear to have joined the conservatives in opposing increased political participation on the part of the working class. Indeed, much of the opposition of these groups to the Peronist regime was based upon their belief that it was greatly increasing political participation. Yet what occurred between 1946 and 1955 was not real participation by the working class, but rather mobilization or controlled participation. The Peronist party was used to gain popular support for the Perón government and to ensure its security, but as Myron Weiner and Joseph La Palombara stated, "the regime was concerned with developing a subjective sense of participation, while actually preventing the populace from affecting public policy, administration, or selecting those who will."[14] However, even this controlled participation was unacceptable to the upper and middle classes, and thus one finds both conservatives and Radicals supporting the 1955 revolution.

Between 1955 and 1973, the Peronists were allowed only limited participation. Even when the party was free to enter elections, as in 1962, it was clear that it would not be allowed to gain power. In the elections of 1963, limited participation meant that Peronists were allowed to nominate candidates only for legislative offices. In 1965, when the party was given full electoral freedom, there were no executive posts at stake. It was not until eighteen years after Perón's overthrow that his party was given the opportunity to regain power at the polls, and the electoral equality granted at that time was conceded extremely grudgingly. Unfortunately, once Perón returned in 1973 he was unable to keep in check those heterogeneous groups whose demands he had encouraged while in exile. The disillusioned Left returned to guerrilla warfare, while labor and entrepreneurial and agricultural producers engaged themselves in a redistributional struggle. As the weak political institutions of the country began to collapse, the armed forces, with the backing of important socioeconomic groups, came to the conclusion that participatory democracy had failed in its last chance to work out and needed to be replaced with a new economic order based upon an autocratic regime. It took violent repression and a military defeat to convince Argentines that democracy based upon unrestricted participation was indeed the form of government that could gain the legitimacy necessary to rule the country.

Failure to Resolve the Peronist Problem

For several years, one of Argentina's major political problems, perhaps *the* major problem, was the split of the populace into two seemingly irreconcilable camps: Peronist and anti-Peronist. Not only did the nation's parties fail to solve this problem, they actually exacerbated it in the attempt to broaden their electoral base.

In their search for Peronist support at the polls in 1958, Frondizi and the UCRI posed as the one true friend of Peronism; yet after gaining power, they continued the legal ban on Peronism until 1962 while trying to "integrate" individual Peronists into their party. When in 1962 they finally allowed the Peronists to nominate their own candidates for congressional and provincial offices, *frondicistas* appealed to the anti-Peronist sector of the electorate as the only alternative to a second Peronist dictatorship. Voters were told that a vote for the People's Radicals, conservatives, or other minor parties was in reality a vote for Peronism and for the return to power of Juan Perón.

In 1963, Illia and the old Radicals also appealed for the electoral support of the Peronists by promising that should the UCRP obtain power, Peronism immediately would be granted complete legality. This appeal evidently was at least partially successful. Judging from the election returns, it appears that Illia and other UCRP candidates picked up an appreciable amount of support from Peronists who were unwilling to throw away their votes by casting blank ballots as Perón had ordered. The Illia administration did grant juridic personality to Peronism, as it had promised, but it seems to have felt that this was all that was necessary to solve the entire problem.

As the 1965 elections approached, the UCRP turned to the tactics that had failed to work for Frondizi in 1962; that is, they tried to polarize the electorate once again in terms of Peronists and anti-Peronists. They were somewhat successful in the short run, as many members of minor parties voted for the UCRP candidates as the lesser of evils. The old Radicals received more votes than at any other time in their history, and many of them must have come from non-Radicals who were afraid of a revival of Peronism. However, the Peronist vote also increased, and that movement again demonstrated that it had greater popular support than any other single party, much to the dismay of the leaders of the armed forces.

Exploitation of the conflict between Peronists and anti-Peronists was not limited to the Radicals. It was also a basic electoral tactic of many of the nation's minor parties. In the province of San Juan, for example, the Bloquistas sought and obtained the electoral support of Peronism in 1962 (largely by means of the tactics used by the UCRI four years earlier). Just one year later the Bloquistas claimed to be the only party capable of defeating the Peronists and thus preventing a return of dictatorship, and they obtained enough anti-Peronist votes to win again.

The Hour of the People and Balbín's change of strategy in 1972 marked the beginning of the solution to the Peronist problem. The reconciliation between Peronists on the one hand and Radicals and conservatives on the other continued, despite conflicts and differences, during the 1983–89 period. Neither Cafiero's 1987 victory in the Buenos Aires gubernatorial election nor Menem's triumph in 1989 constituted the traumatic events they would have in the past. The peaceful and uncontested transfer of power from a Radical to a Peronist president in 1989 testified to how much things had changed since the 1940s.

Factionalism and the Lack of Truly National Parties

One important aspect of the Argentine political party system often ignored by commentators is that the individual parties have almost always had the province, not the nation, as their fundamental reference point. This, added to the tendency toward personalistic and/or ideological factionalism at the national level, has meant that in practice national political parties have been virtually nonexistent. At the time of the 1966 coup there were three separate Radical parties, four Socialist parties, at least a dozen Peronist and neo-Peronist parties, and perhaps twenty conservative parties. Of these, and all the minor parties that existed at that time, only the People's Radicals were organized in all twenty-two provinces. Although there were nine parties and coalitions with presidential candidates in the 1973 elections, only two had a formal organization in every province.

Conservatism has always been an alliance of individual provincial parties. This was true of the Federal, Unitary, National, Autonomist, National Autonomist, and National Democrat parties, which existed prior to 1955. After that date, the conservatives gave up all pretense of being a united national party and formed the National Federation of Parties of the Center. However, not even this organization was able to affiliate all the local conservative parties. Its successor in 1973, New Force, was also unable to gain the adherence of several local parties. The decision of the CFI to turn down the Centrist Alliance in 1989 further attested to the conservative parties' inability to set aside rivalries and ideological differences in order to form a common front. Moreover, it showed UCD's inability to appeal to most provincial parties.

From the time of their formation the Radicals were split both by personal conflicts and ideological differences. At various times there have been Red Radicals and Blue Radicals, Situational Radicals and Traditional Radicals, Personalist Radicals and Anti-Personalist Radicals, and more recently Intransigent Radicals and People's Radicals. During much of its history radicalism was essentially an alliance of provincial *caudillos*. This personalism, plus factions that became virtual parties within the party (each had its own officers, program, and membership list), has long been a Radical hallmark. Party factionalism declined during the first half of the Alfonsín administration, but it returned as soon as the Radicals began to lose electoral support. In 1991, Alfonsín was unable to speak for the party, as his leadership was openly defied by Angeloz and de La Rua.

Not even Peronism was an exception to this general rule. Originally a union of the Argentine Labor party and the Radical Reorganizing Group, the Peronist party was held together almost exclusively by the personality of Juan Perón; however, even at its height, Peronism was not a unified national party with a coherent program. In the Federal Capital and its working class suburbs it was primarily a labor party, but in other areas it was essentially a Social Christian movement, an ultranationalist Catholic organization, or simply a personalistic vehicle for provincial *caudillos*. The ideological cleavage within the party was accentuated in the late 1960s and early 1970s when groups of quite radical students and clergymen joined the movement. Between 1983 and 1989, first the orthodox, then the Renovators, and later the *menemistas* controlled the party apparatus. In 1991, Menem, in spite of being the president, was unable to secure his party's support on such key legislation as labor reform. Although after the 1991 midterm elections the president's position was strengthened, many of his critics were ready behind the scene to take advantage of the next economic debacle to undermine his leadership.

The minor parties differed from this pattern only in degree, for most of them had electorates that were very narrowly circumscribed geographically. Socialists, Trotskyites, and the Left in general have traditionally received two-thirds of their votes in the city and province of Buenos Aires; the Progressive Democrats have never effectively escaped the confines of Santa Fé; and the Bloquistas, who dominated San Juan for decades, did not even exist outside that province. The Left in particular has suffered from factionalism, which frequently led to formal party splits. Besides ideological and personal differences, an additional source of internal cleavage has been the attitudinal ambivalence toward Peronism. While some argued that since Peronism was a popular force, it had an ideological affinity with Marxist-Leninist ideals and therefore alliances should be pursued; others, particularly the Trotskyites, contended that Peronism is a reactionary movement and should be kept at arm's length.

Failure to Legitimate Government Action

Speaking of political parties in general, Robert E. Scott has written:

If this informal political structure is to perform successfully the dual function of integrating the masses into the nation and legitimizing the activities of the central government for them, it must play a positive and meaningful role in the political decision-making process. Only a political party system that plugs into the central core of national political power before it sends its interpretation of government policy out and down through unofficial communications networks can speak to the general citizenry in terms that make official actions not only meaningful and acceptable but also, simultaneously, legitimate and binding.[15]

In Argentina political parties have not played a meaningful role in the decision-making process and thus have not been able to legitimate government actions. It would appear that this has been largely due to two factors: (1) a lack of independence on the part of the government party, due in turn to its reliance on the president; and (2) the lack of "loyal" opposition parties.

The entire political system in Argentina is centered around the person of the president. According to the constitution, bills can become laws only after being approved by both houses of Congress (the Chamber of Deputies and the Senate) and signed by the executive. This in theory should allow Congress to play a significant role in policymaking, like that in the United States. In practice, however, the executive office sponsors most of the bills that are approved. This affects not only the legislative and judicial branches but also the political party system and especially the government party. In such a system the political party has become primarily a means of attaining executive power and thus has been left without meaningful functions once this has been accomplished. Only rarely has a government party played an important role in the formulation of policy. Instead, congressmen and provincial legislators who were members of the party in power have been reduced to the position of enacting into law bills that originated in the executive branch.

Historically, this pattern differed little as the presidency passed from the conservatives to the Radicals and then to the Peronists. Before 1916 and again between 1930 and 1943, the conservative parties were essentially the parties of the president and the provincial governors. This was somewhat less true of the Radicals between 1916 and 1930; however, even during this period there is little doubt that major policy decisions were the prerogatives of Presidents Yrigoyen and Marcelo Alvear. Neither the Radical congressmen nor the local party leaders played an important part in this process. Presidential dominance of the government party reached its height during the first Peronist period, but it certainly did not die with the 1955 revolution.

The dependence of the UCRI upon the president can be seen throughout the Frondizi administration. For example, during his first two years in office Frondizi acted in a manner that was almost diametrically opposed to his party's platform; yet, rather than challenge this deviation from the party line, the UCRI wrote a new platform that advocated the very things the president had been doing for the past two years. A more specific example arose in 1960 when Frondizi proposed to the Congress a bill giving the chief executive power to grant private concessions for the exploitation of the nation's power resources. This was a very controversial issue, even within the president's own party. UCRP congressmen boycotted the sessions at which the bill was discussed, while some conservatives joined in the boycott, and others attended in order to vote against the bill. In order to gain passage in the lower house of Congress, Frondizi needed the support of 97 of the 111 UCRI deputies. Initially, many of the Intransigent Radicals joined the opposition boycott, but when the president threatened to have them removed from the party, most of them returned and voted for the bill.[16] Soon thereafter, the UCRI national committee removed three congressmen from the party and suspended six others for their failure to vote for this bill.

While the government parties failed to act as legitimating agents because of their subservience to the president, their opponents were even less capable of performing this function because of their unwillingness to form a "loyal opposition." To quote Robert E. Scott, Argentine "parties were monopolistic when they controlled the government and inherently disloyal oppositionists when they did not."[17] While success in a presidential election left a party virtually without meaningful functions to perform, defeat simply meant a change in tactics; the long-range goal remained the same: control of the executive branch.

Given the nature of the Argentine political system, which concentrates virtually all governmental power in the hands of the executive, electoral defeat has seldom been accepted as definitive. To accept defeat at the polls and agree to act as a loyal opposition would mean relegation to near-total impotence for a period of at least six years. Thus, the opposition parties traditionally have turned to other means of attaining power. This most often meant an attempt to provoke a military coup. If the leaders of the armed forces could be convinced to overthrow the government, the opposition parties might be able to gain power in the revolutionary government; or, failing in this, they might fare better in new elections, especially if the former government party were denied participation at the polls.

All of Argentina's "revolutionary" administrations have been supported, at least initially, by most of the major parties that had formed the opposition to the deposed government. In most instances, opposition parties were also active in prerevolutionary conspiracies. Generally speaking, only the party removed from power condemned the armed forces for breaking the constitutional order; the other parties praised the removal of an "illegitimate" government.

In 1930, the conservatives, unable to win honest elections, supported the coup of General Uriburu and soon inherited the government. Denied the presidency by means of electoral fraud, the Radicals applauded the 1943 coup; they moved into the opposition only after they realized that the revolutionary government was not going to install them in power. Both conservatives and Radicals were involved in the 1954–55 plots to remove Perón, and each party supported the revolutionary government. After the Peronist election victories in 1962, the People's Radicals might have been able to save the Frondizi administration by agreeing to serve in a coalition government. Instead, they refused and joined the chorus of those demanding that the president resign. Frondicistas reciprocated four years later, when they were influential in persuading the armed forces to remove the Illia administration. The single important exception to this rule came in 1974 and 1975 when the Radicals, and especially their leader, Ricardo Balbín, played a very responsible opposition role, thus helping to temporarily forestall the overthrow of Isabel Perón.

Throughout this century the parties out of power in Argentina concentrated much of their energies on convincing the general public, and especially the leaders of the armed forces, that the current administration lacked legitimacy and thus had no right to govern. The government parties, largely removed from the decision-making process and performing no meaningful political functions, were incapable of protecting the administration from these attacks by helping to legitimate its actions. It is little wonder, then, that political parties are not among the most prestigious of Argentine institutions.

Beginning in 1983, change appeared to be taking place. First of all, in a sharp difference from the past, both major and minor parties have refrained from plotting against the government. As a matter of fact, they were instrumental in helping Alfonsín defend the constitutional order when the latter faced military mutinies in 1987 and 1988.

Second, upon taking office, Alfonsín pledged to use Congress as a means of legitimizing governmental action by having it decide legislative proposals instead of ruling by decree. He did so in the hope that the minority in Congress would collaborate with his policy proposals. Bipartisan support was essential because the Radicals had a majority in the Chamber of Deputies but not in the Senate. In some policy areas collaboration indeed took place as a number of bills such as the National Food Plan, the Beagle Treaty with Chile, the divorce law, and the Full Stop and Due Obedience laws were ratified by Congress. Taking into account the total legislative output in the 1983–87 period, Congress approved 65 percent of the executive proposals. However, on economic matters, the Radicals faced stiff opposition by Peronists and minor parties alike. The failure to pass the Mucci Law, which would have altered the unions' legal status, convinced Alfonsín that key measures, particularly those in the economic realm like the Austral Plan and the Primavera Plan, should be put into effect by decree. The resort to rule by decree became more frequent after 1987 when the UCR lost its majority in the Chamber of Deputies. A preliminary study by Ana María Mustapic and Matteo Goretti showed that during the Alfonsín administration 89 percent of the bills presented to the floor of Congress were approved.[18] This indicates that an agreement was usually reached between majority and opposition prior to the vote, but most of the bills so approved were very specific and not highly controversial. Bipartisan agreement was much harder to find on appropriation bills or other controversial legislation. In these cases presidential legislation was usually defeated because of the lack of a Radical majority in the Senate and, after 1987, also in the Chamber. This explains why toward the end of his term Alfonsín used his decree powers more often. At any rate, while during the Alfonsín administration the behavior of majority and minority was far from perfect, it should be stressed that a noticeable attitudinal change developed; that is, the Peronists and minor parties played the loyal opposition that had been missing in the past, while the Radicals refrained from harassing or ignoring them. Within the limitations imposed by an obsolete constitution, opposition parties used Congress, more than in the past, as a forum to make their views known to the public. Congress also became an outlet for maverick politicians or party factions to assert themselves (this was particularly true of the Renovators within the PJ) and to strike occasional bargains with the UCR.

Inability to Provide Institutionalized Channels for the Articulation of Societal Demands

In Western democracies political parties provide institutions capable of representing and articulating various interests and demands coming from different groups within the society. Their task is one of simplifying such demands and translating them into policy programs. They also serve the purpose of channeling political consensus and conflict in the form of mediative institutions between society and government. In Argentina, as in most of Latin America, parties have been unable to perform such functions by their very nature. In fact, mass-based political formations like the UCR and the PJ have historically resembled *movements* rather than parties, as was noted earlier.[19] As David Rock put it, "movements confer leadership on individuals, whose ideas and personalities are believed to embody a set of general interests or goals."[20] In this sense leaders are the heirs of the *caudillo* tradition that dominated Argentine politics in the nineteenth century. Movements arise during times of crisis when political institutions lose their legitimacy.

Because of the heavy reliance upon charismatic leadership, movements' goals and composition have changed over time. Their common features have been nationalism, top-down organization, moderate reformism, and a vague political message that goes beyond the limits imposed by class cleavages and group interests and appeals to "the people," "the citizens," or the "national community" in order to create a "harmony of classes." Institution building goes counter to the premises of *movimientismo* as the former emphasizes rationality and established rules whereas the latter stresses discretionary decisions on the part of the leader and "political feelings." Thus, *movimientismo* is inclined to nondemocratic, plebiscitary forms of political participation. This pattern could be seen early in modern Argentine history. Yrigoyen himself viewed the UCR as a movement, "the union of the Argentines," which strived to correct the distortions of the previous conservative regime. With Peronism, corporatist elements were introduced in the Argentine movement-prone tradition. An outspoken admirer of Benito Mussolini, Perón saw in the state corporatism of Fascist Italy a possible solution for the corrupt restricted democratic system established by the conservatives and continued by the Radicals. Corporatism enabled the state to control the capitalist economy, to subordinate the social classes that had previously benefited from the free market economic system, and to deactivate the potentially explosive influence of the working class by making labor the backbone of the Peronist movement and incorporating it in the new ruling coalition. Emphasis on the movement rather than the party was even stronger in Peronism than in Yrigoyenism, but both had a common nature: they were responses to institutional crises. Peronism tried to solve the problem by controlling the mass mobilization process through the expansion of the breadth and scope of the state as both an employer and a regulator of socioeconomic life. The weakness of *movimientismo* rested on its loose organization and institutionalization. Interest mediation within the groups making up the movement and between the movement and other societal groups was left to the initiative of the charismatic leader, thus making the role of the movement in this regard meaningless.

The inclusion of corporatist elements in the Peronist movement's rhetoric, however, did not mean that Argentina became a corporatist state after 1946, as it had not been a true democracy until the 1930s. In a sense, old values and political institutions survived without being wiped out by the incoming ones. Elitism, liberalism, *movimientismo*, corporatism, and authoritarianism began to coexist, but in a very uneasy manner following the pattern of the "living museum" described by Charles Anderson.[21] As different values conformed to different rules of the game, elections and parties were no longer the only vehicles through which to gain power and represent interests. Military coups, co-optation and/or repression, conspiracy, and armed revolution all became parts of an uncertain political game in which the lack of consensus on basic issues became the most distinctive feature of the Argentine political system. As the country experienced authoritarian forms of government in which parties were severely limited or banned altogether, power become increasingly concentrated in the executive, the state bureaucracy, and special agencies. This accentuated the tendency of key interest groups to lobby directly the executive and the administrative branches of government, a tendency that persisted even when democratic forms of government were reinstated. The incapacity of political parties to promote stability and interest mediation led to the widespread belief that they were detrimental to the political system and that things could be accomplished without them.

Against this background of distrust and skepticism, political parties returned to the center of politics in 1983. From the start, the Radicals pitted themselves against the most powerful agricultural (SRA), industrial (UIA), commercial (Argentine Chamber of Commerce), and financial groups (Bank Association, ADEBA) as well as against the military, the trade unions, and the Catholic church, which together make up what in Argentina are recognized as the most important *corporaciones* or *factores de poder* (power holders). This approach created resentment and suspicion between the Radical administration and interest groups at a time when a social pact was solicited even by World Bank analysts. As time went by, Alfonsín resorted to ad hoc agreements that went nowhere. Toward the end of his mandate the president became so frustrated that he attributed his policy failures to what he termed terrorist activities of the most powerful *corporaciones*, namely, big business.

The Peronists fared no better once in power. When Menem decided to implement an orthodox economic program first masterminded by the Bunge & Born economists, and later by González and Cavallo, half of the CGT, the Argentine Agrarian Federation (FAA), and those industrial groups heavily dependent on government contracts and financing (*patria contratista*) attacked the president.

The UCD, on the other hand, alienated part of the industrial bourgeoisie that supposedly should have endorsed it. Large sectors of the business community that had thrived through state subsidies, state purchases, and tariff barriers found themselves at odds with the free market zeal of the UCD, which aimed at destroying the special privileges they had gained through civilian and military administrations alike. Moreover, the UCD's anticlerical message turned the Catholic Church and its upper-class followers that had supported conservative parties in the past against them.

For their part, the *corporaciones*, aware of the parties' institutional weaknesses and fearful of one another, have contributed to the gulf existing between the two. Their preferred interlocutor remains the government and its agencies, which are the source of the real power, rather than political parties. A 1988 study based on open-ended interviews came to the conclusion that businessmen and union leaders did not trust political parties as effective means of interest mediation.[22] The unstable nature of the political system has taught them that their interests are best served by ad hoc, temporary, nonbinding agreements or coalitions to achieve short-term objectives, since getting stuck with the wrong party could mean economic disaster. This short-term behavior, in turn, makes it very difficult for parties to make inroads among the *corporaciones*. Since 1983, political parties have found themselves ill equipped to reverse an old trend because of ideological stands and have been unable to present a unified leadership with whom interest groups could deal.

NOTES

1. Ricardo C. Guardo, *Horas difíciles* (Buenos Aires: A. Peña Lillo, 1963), p. 97.

2. Comisión Nacional de Difusión del Plan de Desarrollo, *La UCRI, Palanca del Desarrollo Nacional y Justicia Social* (Buenos Aires: Ediciones UCRI, 1961), pp. 28, 33.

3. Arturo Frondizi, *La Argentina. ¿Es un país subdesarrollado?* (Buenos Aires: Ediciones CEN, 1964), p. 7.

4. Ibid., pp. 8–23.

5. Manuel Mora y Araujo, "The Nature of the Alfonsín Coalition," in *Elections and Democratization in Latin America*, ed. Paul Drake and Patricio Silva (San Diego: Center for Iberian and Latin American Studies, University of California Press, 1986), pp. 175–88.

6. Torcuato Di Tella, "La situación argentina: Fin de la integración y comienzo de la coexistencia," *Cuadernos Americanos* 124, no. 5 (September–October 1962): 56–57.

7. Luis González Esteves and Ignacio Llorente, "Elecciones y preferencias políticas en la Capital Federal," in *La Argentina electoral* (Buenos Aires: Editorial Sudamericana, 1985), p. 79.

8. Ibid., p. 55.

9. Ibid., pp. 59, 65.

10. Cámara de Diputados, *Diarios de sesiones*, February 10–11, 1984, cited by Liliana de Riz, "Alfonsín's Argentina: Renewal Parties and Congress" (July 1988, Mimeographed), p. 9.

11. Quoted in "Carlos Menem defiende el indulto," *Proceso* (Buenos Aires), October 30, 1989, p. 42.

12. Ezequiel Gallo and Silvia Sigal, "La formación de los partidos políticos contemporáneos: la UCR (1890–1916)," in *Argentina, sociedad de masas*, ed. Torcuato Di Tella, Gino Germani, and Jorge Graciarena (Buenos Aires: Editorial Universitaria de Buenos Aires, 1965), p. 163. A separate study shows the same to have been true of those elected to Congress in 1916. See Darío Cantón, *El Parlamento Argentino en épocas de cambio: 1890, 1916 y 1946* (Buenos Aires: Editorial de Instituto, 1965), pp. 52–66.

13. Peter Smith, "Los radicales argentinos y la defensa de los intereses ganaderos, 1916–1930," *Desarrollo Económico* 7, no. 25 (April–June 1967): 826.

14. Myron Weiner and Joseph La Palombara, "The Impact of Parties on Political Development," in *Political Parties and Political Development*, ed. Myron Weiner and Joseph La Palombara (Princeton, NJ: Princeton University Press, 1966), p. 403.

15. Robert E. Scott, "Political Parties and Policy-Making in Latin America," in *Political Parties*, p. 335.

16. *Hispanic American Report* 13, no. 9 (September 1960): 641.

17. Scott, "Political Parties and Policy-Making," p. 338.

18. Ana María Mustapic and Matteo Goretti, "Un congreso unánime: la práctica de la cohabitación bajo el gobierno de Alfonsín," Series Documentos de Trabajo (Buenos Aires: Instituto Torcuato Di Tella, 1990).

19. Gino Germani, *Authoritarianism, Fascism, and National Populism* (New Brunswick, NJ: Transaction Books, 1978).

20. David Rock, "Political Movements in Argentina," in *From Military Rule to Liberal Democracy in Argentina*, ed. Monica Peralta Ramos and Carlos Waisman (Boulder, CO: Westview Press, 1987), p. 8.

21. Charles Anderson, *Politics and Economic Change in Latin America* (Princeton, NJ: Van Nostrand, 1967).

22. Liliana de Riz and Catalina Smulovitz, "Los actores frente al cambio institucional" (*CEDES* mimeo, 1988).

CHAPTER 3

The Armed Forces

For the first half-century after independence was attained, Argentina had nothing even resembling a national army. During this period the military establishment consisted almost exclusively of gaucho cavalrymen who were untrained and poorly equipped. Impressed soldiers were led by amateur, and often self-appointed, officers. Such were the "armies" who fought the Spaniards, the Paraguayans, the Indians, and, most often, each other.

This situation changed dramatically during the first conservative era (1862–1916), when a modern professional army was created. The process was begun by President Mitre, who nationalized the Buenos Aires War Ministry in 1862, and was continued by each of his successors. Domingo Sarmiento created the Colegio Militar in 1869 and the Escuela Naval in 1872 (these are the equivalents of the U.S. military academies at West Point and Annapolis). In 1899, Julio Roca established a war college for senior officers about to join the general staff; it was patterned on the Prussian model and staffed by German officers. By 1901, Argentina had a compulsory military training law. During the next several years the character of the officer corps was altered substantially by regulations that: (1) required graduation from a military academy prior to being commissioned; (2) established compulsory retirement ages for senior officers; and (3) created the Qualifications Commission, whose purpose was to see to it that promotions were based on merit. As a result, by 1916 the officer corps was staffed primarily by members of the middle classes who looked upon the armed forces as a professional career.

Between 1862 and 1916 there were several unsuccessful rebellions—usually organized and led by civilians, but including small sectors of the armed forces; however, each of the conservative presidents knew that he could count upon the loyalty of the military establishment as a whole. It was only after the creation of a modern, professional army, and the assumption of power by the Radicals, that serious conflicts occurred between the government and the armed forces. The process of military politicization began during the Radical administrations of 1916–30 and has continued to the present day. That the military has become a major arbiter in national political life may be seen in any of a number of simple facts: for example, since 1928 not a single civilian has served a complete term as president (Alfonsín resigned six months before his term was due to end); and, of the twenty-seven chief executives who have served during the 1928–1992 period, seventeen were active duty or former military officers, while only ten were civilians.

Today, then, the question is not whether the armed forces are actively involved in politics, but instead what part of the armed forces plays a significant political role and who is involved. What different political roles are played by the military? And, most important, why have the armed forces become so deeply involved in politics?

MILITARY RECRUITMENT

At the time of the 1930 revolution, the Argentine military establishment was composed of no more than 50,000 men; by 1943 this number had doubled, and by 1955 it had doubled again. In 1974 the army had about 85,000 men, of whom 65,000 were one-year draftees, 15,000 career noncommissioned officers (NCOs), and 5,000 officers. There were about 33,000 men in the navy and 17,000 in the air force, each of which had about 1,250 officers.[1] By 1989 the entire armed forces shrank to about 86,000 men.

Traditionally, neither draftees nor NCOs have figured in political action to any appreciable extent, nor did the officers in the professional services, such as medicine and law. Although NCOs and middle-ranking officers have come to play a significant role since 1987, as we shall see later, it is the Command Corps that traditionally has made the news, especially the 100 or fewer generals, admirals, and brigadiers. A great deal has been written about these men, their social backgrounds, and their goals and values, but very little of it has been based upon empirical evidence. A large segment of the civilian population is convinced that a definite military caste exists in Argentina, that in order to become a general it is imperative that one's father be a landowning aristocrat, preferably from one of the traditional provinces of the northwest. On the other hand, the military establishment itself insists that entrance into the officer corps is completely open, that promotions are based entirely upon merit, and that the leaders of the armed forces come from all segments of Argentine society.

In recent years it appears that potential officers, that is, those who are admitted to the military academies, have been selected primarily on the basis of universalistic criteria such as school grades and physical fitness; however, certain unwritten particularistic criteria certainly have been retained. An example of this is the extremely small number of Jewish officers, none of whom could be found in combat branches since the 1930s. While there may well exist a degree of self-exclusion here, it almost certainly due to discriminatory practices on the part of the military itself. A very knowledgeable Argentine once remarked to one of the authors, "A Jewish general? Impossible!"

The practice of admitting only "acceptable" young men to the officer corps is greatly facilitated by the oral interview that is required of all candidates for the military academies. Darío Cantón cites the example of a candidate who said that his father was dead and that he lived with his mother. When asked how his mother earned a living, he answered rather evasively, and thus the interviewer requested information on the candidate's family from the local police force. When the report came, it was not only satisfactory but too satisfactory: "The candidate's mother is a true lady; she has a very good standing in the community," and so on. This made the interviewer even more suspicious, and he ordered further investigation. He finally discovered that the candidate's mother was the mistress of the chief of police. Admission to the military academy was denied.[2]

Since it is not the entire officer corps, but rather its top echelons, that wield political power, determining what sort of person reaches the top military posts is of greatest interest here. Are such persons really members of the landowning aristocracy? Or, as the military itself claims, do they encompass the entire spectrum of Argentine society?

The works of José Luis de Imaz and Robert Potash indicate that neither of these claims is entirely accurate and that during the last half century, at least, the top leadership of the Argentine armed forces has come from the urban middle class. Between 1917 and 1961, only about 10 percent of the nation's generals were born in the traditional provinces of the northwest, while roughly 40 percent were born in the Federal Capital and its suburbs. This trend is even more pronounced in the case of admirals and brigadiers, almost two-thirds of whom were born in greater Buenos Aires, compared with about 5 percent in the northwest.[3] Also, rather than coming from "traditional" or aristocratic families, many of the generals have been second-generation Argentines; that is, their parents were born abroad, most of them in Spain and Italy. The Spanish and Italian ancestry of the generals—and of the admirals and brigadiers as well—is even more apparent if one looks back two generations.

As far as occupational background is concerned, virtually all the generals included in Imaz's study come from families that may be labeled middle class. Two-thirds of the fathers of these generals were businessmen, military officers, members of the liberal professions, or white-collar workers; less than 10 percent were in any way connected with agricultural enterprises.

It must be admitted that knowing that generals tend to come from the middle class does not tell us very much about their political attitudes. As Potash puts it:

To say that the majority of the Army officers were of middle class origin is only to say that they came from a heterogeneous sector that was itself sharply divided in outlook. Even if it were possible to know the precise segment of the middle class into which the officer was born, it would also be necessary to know the status of the family into which he married. Marriage of a second generation Army officer into a traditional family might very well lead him to take on its political coloration.[4]

What it does tell us is that the general political conservatism of the Argentine military leaders is not a result of aristocratic social origins.

Recent data on the social background of generals are not available to us. However, several senior officers recently acknowledged to us that since 1983 the low prestige into which the armed forces had fallen and the poor salaries paid junior officers have driven away from military academies many upper- and middle-class applicants who, in turn, have been replaced by lower-class cadets in increasing numbers.

TYPES OF POLITICAL ACTIVITY

The political activity of the Argentine armed forces has not been limited to the deposing of civilian presidents; rather, it is possible to discern four relatively distinct political roles played during the last half-century. The armed forces have acted as: (1) a simple pressure group with relatively limited objectives (1922–30, 1932–43, 1963–66, 1973–76, 1983–present); (2) a governmental partner, or, as the Argentines put it, cogovernment (1946–55, 1966–70); (3) a wielder of an absolute veto power (1958–62); and (4) an entity that has complete control over the machinery of government (1930–32, 1943–46, 1955–58, 1962–63, 1970–73, 1976–83). If one assumes that the mere existence of a modern military establishment gives it a political role, then a fifth category might be added, that of minimal participation in politics; this would have been the case before 1922.

When the military establishment has played the role of a simple pressure group, its actions have not placed great strain on the political system, largely because its goals have been relatively limited in scope. During most of the Yrigoyen period the military's main demand was that the government not meddle in military affairs; it was especially adamant that promotions not be based upon partisan loyalty. During the administrations of Roberto Ortiz and Ramón Castillo, military pressure was applied to see to it that Argentina remained neutral during World War II. During the Illia administration, the leaders of the armed forces tried to convince the president that Argentine troops should be sent to the Dominican Republic at the time of the 1965 uprising there and that he should react more vigorously to border clashes along the Andean frontier. Under Alfonsín, sectors of the military rebelled to force out their commanders, end civilian trials of officers, enlarge the military budget, and obtain higher salaries.

The armed forces played a more forceful role during the Perón and Onganía administrations, when they served as a partner of the government. In each case the president was a retired army officer; however, it would be a mistake to think of either as a "military regime." Under Perón, the military was forced to share power with organized labor and, to a lesser extent, with nationalist and clerical groups. During the Onganía administration, final policy decisions were made by President Onganía, not by the army's general staff.

During the Frondizi administration (1958–62), the armed forces played a third role. The military does not seem to have formulated policy, but rather to have insisted that major policy decisions made by the president be submitted to the leaders of the armed forces for their approval. In this connection, Mariano Grondona says that the revolution of 1962 was nothing more than a "motion of lack of confidence by the military parliament."[5]

The fourth role is that of deposing constitutional governments and establishing military regimes. This was done in 1930, 1943, 1955, 1962, to some extent in 1966, and again in 1976. The next question is: What leads the armed forces to take this most drastic final step?

THE CAUSES OF MILITARY COUPS

It is interesting to note that while the armed forces are frequently accused of assuming control of the government in order to retain the status quo and to prevent any meaningful reform, the reasons given by the military leaders for their revolutionary actions almost never include complaints about the major policy decisions of the deposed regimes. It is true that Juan Perón was accused of dictatorial methods, Frondizi of bargaining with the ex-dictator, and Illia of divisive electoral maneuvering; however, condemnations of major public policies adopted by these presidents were notable only by their absence.

The causes of military coups—as announced in revolutionary manifestos—are of an altogether different sort. The regimes deposed in 1930, 1943, 1955, 1962, 1966, and 1976 were accused of corruption, of immorality, and of an inability or unwillingness to maintain law and order. However, instead of being criticized for their action, these governments were criticized for their lack of action, especially for failing to take decisive action against "the spread of communism" or to alleviate pressing economic problems.

Certainly the armed forces were upset by the corruption of the Yrigoyen, Castillo, and Perón administrations and by the breakdown of law and order under Frondizi, Illia, and Isabel Perón; however, these factors do not adequately explain any of the coups—nor does the simplistic notion that the armed forces are motivated solely by a desire to maintain the status quo. Instead, it appears that the major causes of Argentina's "revolutions" have been: (1) the meddling of civilian governments in the internal affairs of the military; (2) popular dissatisfaction with civilian administrations; (3) a desire to change the very nature of the political system; and (4) from the 1950s through the 1970s, a deep-seated anti-Peronist attitude on the part of the leaders of the armed forces.

Interference in Military Affairs

One of the factors leading to military coups has been the manner in which the government has dealt with the armed forces. Particularly unacceptable is interference in what the military considers its own internal affairs. For example, under Yrigoyen, promotions were granted with little regard for military regulations; officers were rewarded for past services and promised further benefits for future support. This was pushed to an intolerable degree in 1922, when the Radicals introduced in Congress a bill to reward those military men who had rebelled in 1890, 1893, and 1905. Participation in these Radical revolts was declared to be "a service to the Nation."[6] The same pattern prevailed throughout the first Peronist era, when promotions were based more on loyalty to the regime than upon merit.

During the Frondizi administration, the major complaint of the legalist sector of the armed forces was that the president constantly played one faction of the military off against the other, often giving in to those in rebellion against authority while disciplining those dedicated to legality. This attitude was expressed by Colonel Juan Francisco Guevara on August 31, 1962:

I would remind the people that when in 1959 General Carlos Severo Toranzo Montero rebelled in order to become Commander-in-Chief of the Army, President Frondizi made a deal with the rebel, disciplined those who tried to enforce the law, and subordinated them to the insubordinate ones. Since then the civilian authorities have demonstrated an attitude which is suicidal for themselves and criminal for the country, for they have continually followed the tactic of ceding to force, crushing justice and law, and thus discouraging those who have complied with their duty. We are now living through another rebellion, initiated by another General Toranzo Montero. Once again this rebellion has been aided by the complicity of the government.[7]

The "crime" of the Illia administration was that of siding with the *colorado* faction of the military against the *azules*, who by 1963 were fully in control of the armed forces. As soon as he was inaugurated, President Illia set out to get rid of the *azul* commanders-in-chief he inherited from the Guido administration. By the end of 1963, he had managed to obtain the resignation of the commander of naval operations, and his air force secretary was working on the head of that service branch. However, by this time the army high command demanded that this sort of maneuvering cease—General Onganía was obviously the next target—and Illia then cut off all communication with the armed forces. In mid-1965 Illia further angered the legalists within the military by reinstating 64 *colorado* officers who had been forced to retire after the attempted coups of September 1962 and April 1963.

Isabel Perón was less guilty of this sort of action than most of her predecessors. However, she too angered an important sector of the army when she appointed to the cabinet an officer on active duty—without consulting his superiors. The leaders of the armed forces saw this as an attempt to portray the military as responsible, at least in part, for the actions of her administration, an implication the military totally opposed.

These sorts of actions by Yrigoyen, Frondizi, Illia, and the Peróns were probably not sufficient in themselves to lead to their overthrow; but when added to all the other factors, such actions certainly helped to tip the scales against them. It is ironical to note that this sort of government activity angered precisely the segment of the military that ordinarily would be most inclined to support constitutional government.

Popular Opposition

James Payne has written that "the root cause of military intervention in Latin America, then, is the extremity to which political opposition is carried and the moral decision this opposition thrusts upon the military. . . . A military coup will take place when (a) vigorous civilian opposition to the chief executive is extremely (unusually) high and (b) when civilian support for the chief executive is extremely (unusually) low."[8] It is assumed that when opposition reaches certain proportions, the very legitimacy of that government comes into question and that by allowing a president to remain in office in the face of such opposition, the leaders of the armed forces find themselves making a moral decision. On the other hand, it is assumed that widespread civilian support for a government will tend to inhibit a coup, for it forces the military leaders to make a political rather than an ethical decision.

When applied to the Argentine situation, this theory would appear to be somewhat oversimplified; nevertheless it does seem to explain at least part of the motivation for military coups in that nation. All of the presidents deposed by the Argentine armed forces—with the possible exception of Arturo Illia—faced extreme civilian opposition, and at the same time only Perón had any appreciable popular support.

In 1930, there was almost total dissatisfaction with the Yrigoyen administration. The president's senility and his unwillingness to delegate authority, combined with the effects of the world depression and the government's inability to do anything to counteract its effects, cost Yrigoyen the support of almost all the important sectors of society. All the opposition political parties plus important sectors of the president's own party, the university students, nationalist groups, and virtually all the nation's mass media were willing to lend their support to a revolutionary movement.

By 1943 Ramón Castillo had managed to become perhaps the most unpopular president in the country's history. The nation was under an almost continuous state of siege, thus allowing the president to limit freedom of expression and association. The government supported pro-Axis organizations, while the sentiment of a majority of the people was pro-Allies. On top of this, Castillo was preparing to impose as his successor in the presidency the one politician even more unpopular than himself.

While it is true that Perón had far more popular support at the time of his overthrow than was the case for any other president, it is also true that the opposition to his regime was more vigorous and more determined than that faced by other presidents. By 1955, he was opposed by all the non-Peronist political parties, the Church, students, and landowners, many of whom were willing to risk their lives in an attempt to overthrow the regime.

Although elected in 1958 with the support of several different political groups, by 1962 Frondizi faced the opposition of both Peronists and anti-Peronists. His intervention in the provinces won by the Peronists in the 1962 elections infuriated the Peronists while failing to placate their enemies. The People's Radicals might have been able to save the constitutional order had they been willing to serve in a coalition government, but instead they joined the growing chorus of those demanding the president's resignation.

The most vigorous opposition to Illia came not as much from the opposition parties as from business and industrial groups, nationalist organizations, organized labor, and several Catholic lay groups. In 1966, the opposition may have been somewhat less vigorous than at the time of earlier coups, but at the same time support for the regime was minimal, and it was clear that a revolutionary movement would encounter little opposition.

In 1976 there was even less public clamor for a military coup, and yet as the administration of Isabel Perón demonstrated its inability to curtail either the astronomical rate of inflation or the escalation of political violence, the general public seemed resigned to the creation of a military government. Potash even goes so far as to say that there was "clear evidence of broad public support" for this coup.[9]

In the absence of reliable polls, it is impossible to state with exactness the levels of opposition to any of the deposed governments; however, what is most important is the military's perception of this opposition. This perception is probably exaggerated by the fact that opposition leaders have not been willing to wait for the opposition to be manifested at the polls but instead have gone to their friends in the armed forces in an effort to convince them of the "necessity" of a coup. As Imaz put it:

The armed forces have been looked upon by all political groups as a potentially useful instrument for the satisfaction of their own objectives. Thus in spite of all arguments to the contrary, recourse to the armed forces as a source of legitimation has become a tacit rule of the Argentine political game, a rule which no one openly invokes, but one which has benefited all political groups at least once. Although they must all deny it publicly, Argentine politicians cannot ignore the fact that at one time or another during the past quarter-century they have gone to knock at the doors of the barracks.[10]

A New Political System

Within each of the six revolutionary movements there has been a definite faction—of varying size and strength—that has been intent upon instituting some fundamental changes in the political system. This has been most apparent in the revolutions of 1930, 1966, and 1976, but it has also been true, to a lesser extent, of those of 1943, 1955, and 1962.

In 1930, the segment of the armed forces led by General José Uriburu made it clear from the beginning that it was opposed to the form of the liberal democracy practiced in Argentina. In a letter to the daily newspaper *La Nación* published on November 30, 1930, Lieutenant Colonel Pedro P. Ramírez set forth the general goals of this group:

It is not our primary purpose to overthrow a despotic and incapable government; this single act would accomplish nothing. *That which is fundamental is to change the system* [emphasis added]. We must avoid a repetition of the present governmental chaos and dispose of political professionalism. This requires the modification of certain aspects of the country's political life. The Sáenz Peña Law [a 1912 election law that provided for compulsory and universal manhood suffrage] appears to be unsuitable to a country which is 40 percent illiterate. The present parliamentary system is not adequate for the progress and the interests of the living forces of the nation. Our Congress, subordinated to the actions of a boss without scruples, is obviously in crisis. The few voices which can be heard in protest against a suicidal majority have no purpose other than electoral propaganda. For the moment we are not seeking the cooperation of any political party. We must work without compromise in order to save the nation honestly.[11]

Almost as soon as he took power, General Uriburu dissolved Congress, declared a state of siege, and began preparations for the conversion of Argentina into something resembling a corporate state. Although he gave some indication of his political plans as early as October 1, 1930, the clearest expression of his corporatist ideas is to be found in a speech of February 20, 1932:

We cannot conceive of a country of farmers and ranchers being represented in a Chamber of Deputies by fifty-nine lawyers, thirty-six doctors, nine farmers, two workers, and an equally insignificant number of the other professions . . . as was the case prior to September 6, and as will surely occur with the present Congress. . . . We think indispensable the effective defense of the real interests of the people, the organization of professions and unions, and the modification of the present political party structure, so that the social interests may have authentic and direct representation. . . . We must say to those who believe that the last word in politics is universal suffrage . . . that corporative organization gave grandeur and splendor to the Italian communes in the twelfth and thirteenth centuries. . . . Corporative organization is not a discovery of fascism, but the modern adaptation of a system whose results during a long historical epoch justify its resurgence.[12]

The 1943 revolution was primarily the work of a secret military lodge known as the Group of United Officers or simply the GOU. Completely disillusioned with civilian government, the leaders of the GOU wanted to institute a purely military dictatorship and to reduce civilians to "the only mission for which they are fit: work and obedience."[13]

In both 1955 and 1962, the revolutionary movements contained relatively large factions that proposed military dictatorships of indefinite duration. In each case their goal was not only to eliminate Peronism as a political force but also to make fundamental changes in the political system that had allowed the rise of Peronism. In 1966, the revolutionary leaders appear to have felt almost unanimously that the political system had to be modified substantially—an opinion shared by many civilians. Throughout the Onganía administration virtually all official pronouncements included lengthy condemnations of the "old politics," which allegedly was in the process of being replaced by a "new politics"—a new politics that, to the concern of many, sounded very much like the corporatist plans of General Uriburu. Much of the criticism of the old politics was, in actuality, directed against professional politicians who were considered by many military men the basis of the nation's problems. To some, politics itself was an opprobrious term. Several officers who served as provincial or municipal intervenors following the 1962 coup were appalled by the corruption and incompetence they encountered. Some were able to institute what they considered substantial reforms, only to see them discarded when civilian politicians returned to power in late 1963. In 1976, disillusionment with civilian government was even greater. By this time, there was nearly total agreement within the armed forces that a lengthy period of military government was the only possible solution.

Anti-Peronism

The last four military coups have been, to varying extents, the result of a widespread anti-Peronist attitude on the part of much of the leadership of the armed forces. In order to understand this anti-Peronism, it is necessary to look back at the first Peronist period, which began with widespread military support for Perón.

At the time of the 1946 presidential election Perón certainly had the support of most of the armed forces, if for no other reason than that the only alternative was a return to rule by the discredited civilian politicians. Throughout the early phases of his administration Perón's emphasis upon industrialization, economic nationalism, and modernization of the military establishment allowed him to retain this support. However, by 1951 there was a segment of the military that was no longer willing to follow his leadership; it was at this time that he faced the first serious armed challenge to his regime. During the next four years, discontent within the armed forces slowly increased, and by September 1955, Perón's opponents were strong enough to drive him from power.

It is difficult to say just exactly when and why Perón encountered resistance within the military, but it seems quite likely that friction first developed concerning his wife Eva María Duarte de Perón, or simply, Evita. The leaders of the armed forces were disgusted with Perón's open affair with Evita in 1945, and there was even more opposition to their marriage. As the illegitimate daughter of a poor provincial family, and later a radio and movie actress, Evita was not considered a fit wife for a high-ranking army officer. After the marriage, military leaders were upset by her political activities and her openly antimilitary attitude. In 1951 they let it be known that they would not tolerate her as vice-president and thus a potential commander-in-chief of the military establishment. Evita's death in July 1952 might have eased the conflict somewhat had Perón not then begun a series of affairs with teenage schoolgirls that also offended the military's sense of dignity.

A second source of friction was the increased power of organized labor, which the armed forces opposed for at least two reasons: first, it was a potential counterweight to the military; and second, many of the upper-middle-class officers were never really prolabor (although not opposed to the use of the labor movement for their own ends, as in October 1945). This conflict increased in intensity after the General Confederation of Labor (CGT) began to assume an arrogant attitude toward the armed forces. The last straw came in 1955, when Perón seemed to be considering the establishment of armed workers' militias.

Another major source of friction between Perón and his military establishment was the series of anticlerical measures adopted in 1954 and 1955, legalization of divorce and prostitution, abrogation of religious instruction in the public schools, deportation of clergymen, and so on. This campaign against the Church placed Catholic officers in a position of divided loyalties. It is probably no accident that Perón was overthrown shortly after his excommunication.

After 1952, when economic problems forced Perón to abandon his nationalistic posture, he lost the support of still another sector of the armed forces. Many military leaders had sided with him because of his economic nationalism; however, his rapprochement with the United States, and especially the petroleum concessions granted to Standard Oil, cost him the support of this group, which by 1955 felt that Perón had sold out to imperialists.

On top of this, corruption in the government became so rampant that it began to cast suspicion on the honesty of the armed forces, which have always been eager to protect their reputation. The giving of Perón's name to provinces, railroad stations, football stadiums, and even army bases was also considered contrary to the severe austerity of the armed forces.

After 1955, military opposition to Peronism was probably based to some extent upon the fear that the return to power by Peronism would mean a resumption of the conflicts mentioned above; it was also feared that the return of Peronism would mean large-scale purges of the extreme anti-Peronist officers, and particularly its hard-line sectors, who since 1955 had been engaged in purging the military of those even suspected of pro-Peronist sympathies. The proscription of Peronism continued after hard-line officers (or *colorados*, see below), who advocated direct military rule, were defeated by the "legalists" (or *azules*), who favored a return of the military to the barracks in order to preserve internal unity and professionalism. The *azules'* leader, General Juan Carlos Onganía, upon claiming victory in April 1963, endorsed an "apolitical" military but kept the military veto barring the Peronists from competing in elections. By no means insignificant in the continuance of this anti-Peronism was the affiliation with Peronism of one of the nation's most active urban terrorist organizations, the Montoneros, and Perón's implicit endorsement of this group's activities in the early 1970s. However, the single most important factor explaining the anti-Peronism of the leaders of the armed forces was a continuing unwillingness to accept any regime that had the potential power to deprive the military of its role as arbiter or to eliminate it as the decisive power factor. Only Peronism, with its mass following centered around organized labor, was a potential threat to the continued hegemony of the armed forces.

By 1973, anti-Peronism within the armed forces was no longer sufficient to justify a coup d'etat. This was due in part to the failure of the Argentine Revolution and in part to the more moderate attitude shown by Perón late in his life. When Cámpora stepped down a few months after his election to allow Perón to take over, the military did not object. The 1976 coup, in turn, had more to do with the state of chaos into which the country had fallen than with the Peronist nature of the administration in office. In point of fact, quite a few Peronist union leaders and right-wing party bosses welcomed the coup as it got rid of rival left-wing elements within their own movement. The armed forces' approach toward Peronism took an even sharper turn during the Alfonsín administration. As we shall see later, many officers began to look to Peronism as an ally with whom to defy the Radical administration's policies. By early 1989, many officers were openly supporting Menem's candidacy. In their view Radicalism, not Peronism, had become the armed forces' deadly enemy.

The National Security–Economic Development Nexus

An additional factor may be either a rationale or a rationalization for military intervention. This is the doctrine of national security. From the 1950s until the late 1970s, there was nearly total agreement within the upper echelons of the armed forces that national security was not only connected to, but also *dependent upon*, economic development. The 1967 Law of National Security defined national security as "the situation in which the vital interests of the nation are sheltered from substantial interference." These vital interests were said to include the exploitation of natural resources, the development of basic industries, and the creation of an efficient infrastructure. A former secretary general of the National Security Council (CONASE) wrote, "Development has become an indispensable condition for security, for without development the nation's vital interest cannot be protected."[14]

Since the maintenance of national security was clearly the responsibility of the armed forces, and since "national security is utopian without economic development,"[15] it was only a short step to the conclusion that if civilian governments were not doing an adequate job in this realm it was the *duty* of the armed forces to assume responsibility for economic development. This was phrased only slightly differently by the retired general serving as secretary general of the National Development Council (CONADE) in 1970: "The enemy of the nation is its lack of development."[16] He did not need to add that combating the nation's enemies is a function of the armed forces.

Many military leaders went a step farther and claimed that the military was uniquely qualified to direct the development process. According to this perspective, not only did the military have the necessary hierarchical organization and discipline, but it was, unlike most civilian groups, not tied to any specific economic interest and thus able to represent the interests of the nation as a whole.

An additional twist of the National Security Doctrine was its emphasis on internal security. After the Cuban revolution and Fidel Castro's attempt to export guerrilla warfare in the rest of Latin America, U.S. and Latin American officers became preoccupied with the prevention of a communist takeover. Thus, the military became deeply involved in counterinsurgency warfare and intelligence which would later be utilized to their fullest during the dirty war.

The Revolutionary Climate

As was mentioned above, the Argentine armed forces have never even attempted to depose civilian regimes that enjoyed widespread popular support. In 1930, 1943, 1976, (to an only slightly lesser extent) 1962, and 1966, the regimes removed were badly discredited in the eyes of the general public. Only in 1955 was there appreciable support for the government overthrown—

and this was the one coup involving a great deal of bloodshed. Thus it has never been enough that the leaders of the armed forces want to depose a president; there must also exist the proper "climate" for a coup. In the words of a retired army officer:

In Argentina the breaking of legality has always involved three factors: the government, the armed forces, and a climate or atmosphere of agitation on the part of the civilian population. The government "intervenes" with its errors and its apathy which galvanize the opposition and dishearten its supporters. The political parties and the interest groups—aided by the press—create the climate that makes the filling of the vacuum acceptable; and finally, the armed forces act. What we have witnessed in Argentina during the last thirty days [July 1965] is the appearance of the first serious attempts to bring about the third factor: the atmosphere of a coup. This maneuver has not originated in the armed forces, nor obviously in the government itself. The point of the lance appears to be personified by retired officers—almost all of whom were allies of the UCRP when it was in the opposition—and in communist elements which have infiltrated the unions and universities. The legality represented by the government finds itself caught by this pincer movement. To the extent that it loses prestige by its incapacity to resolve general problems, it will precipitate the creation of the climate necessary for the failure of that legality. . . . Another characteristic of the mechanism of coups in Argentina is the fact that governmental errors do not themselves produce a coup; it is necessary to underline them repeatedly with two accusations that have profound repercussions: "communist infiltration" and "corruption." The country is now witnessing the opening of this campaign; if this action is consolidated, the armed forces will become the target of an intense psychological campaign designed to stir up their moral sentiment.[17]

This is exactly what happened during the last year of the Illia administration (the year following the publication of Colonel Garosino's article). Opponents of the government constantly described alleged Communist infiltration of the universities, radio and television, and credit cooperatives. For example, from his magazine *Leer para Creer*, Francisco Manrique charged Communist infiltration in the government-owned television channel; the major daily newspaper *La Prensa* claimed that Communists were gaining control of the credit co-ops; and all the opposition news media claimed that the government was giving the Communists a free rein in the universities.

Two of the country's three weekly news magazines, *Primera Plana* and *Confirmado*, and the monthly *Atlántida*, became major weapons in the psychological war waged against the Illia government. The campaign was two-pronged: first these periodicals accused Illia of every sin known to man; second, they attempted to convince the general public of the inevitability of the forthcoming coup. Beginning late in 1965, *Confirmado* became an almost official organ of the conspirators. In an article entitled "Predictions: What Will Happen in 1966?" (published in December 1965) was the following:

On July 1, 1966, at eight o'clock in the morning, several army vehicles full of troops stopped at strategic points in the center of town. Access to the Plaza de Mayo [the large square surrounded by executive office buildings] had already been cut, and the last inhabitant of the executive mansion had left tranquilly an hour earlier. At eleven o'clock a proclamation was issued: "Confronted by the inefficiency of a government which had led the country to its gravest economic crisis, which promoted social chaos and broke national solidarity, the armed forces have taken power in order to assure the continuance of the nation itself." Finally at two in the afternoon the public was informed that a prestigious general, who had been retired from active duty for only a few months, had been invited by the military leaders to become the chief of state.[18]

This is exactly what happened just six months later. The article missed the date of the coup by two days, and the time of Illia's departure from office by twenty minutes.

FACTIONALISM

Ever since 1930, when the armed forces became deeply involved in the nation's political life, the military has been plagued by the existence of antagonistic ideological factions. Factionalism has been a continuous problem for more than half a century; however, it is apparently most serious, and certainly most obvious, immediately following military coups. This lack of agreement within the armed forces about goals and the means of attaining them severely limits the ability of a military regime to carry out a coherent program. It also leaves at least one faction dissatisfied with the results of the revolution and thus probably stimulates future conspiratorial activity.

In 1930, there were two distinct sectors within the revolutionary movement. One group thought of the coup simply as a means of removing an inefficient, corrupt administration and of returning the government to more responsible elements, that is, the conservatives. The other group looked upon the coup as the beginning of a real revolution that would fundamentally alter the entire political system by replacing liberal democracy with a neo-fascist corporate state.

The leaders of these two factions were Generals Agustín P. Justo (of the conservative group) and José F. Uriburu (of the corporatists). These men and their backgrounds were as different as their political ideas. Justo came from a middle-class family of Entre Ríos. After graduating from the military academy, he received a degree in engineering from the University of Buenos Aires and became a mathematics professor at the Colegio Militar. During his six years as minister of war (1922–28) he was responsible for a thorough modernization of the army and greatly improved the conditions of military life. A symbol of the professional soldier, by 1928 Justo was probably the most popular officer in the Argentine army.

Uriburu was born in the northwestern province of Salta. His parents were prominent members of the landowning aristocracy who could trace their ancestry back to the early colonial era. Uriburu fought with the Radicals in the 1890 rebellion and against them in their 1905 revolt. He served as aide-de-camp to his uncle, who was president between 1895 and 1898, and in 1913 represented his native province in Congress. Sent to Germany to study military tactics, Uriburu returned a confirmed Germanophile. By 1923 he had risen to the army's top position, inspector general. He retired from active duty in 1929.

Although it was Uriburu who became president with the overthrow of Yrigoyen in September 1930, there is little doubt that Justo was more representative of the officer corps and its political ideals. As Félix Luna puts it:

The wealth of Uriburu and his wife, his membership in the most aristocratic of Argentine clubs, his kinship with those who long had governed national life, and his stay in Imperial Germany had led him to develop a mentality which was not shared by his comrades, the majority of whom were sons of immigrants who by their own effort had reached the level of the liberal and progressive middle class, and who had not known the luxuries Uriburu had enjoyed.[19]

Uriburu's corporatist plans were opposed from the beginning by conservative politicians and by Justo's faction of the armed forces. Confident, nevertheless, in his personal popularity, Uriburu allowed honest elections to be held in Buenos Aires province in April 1931. The results were disastrous; the supposedly discredited Radicals easily defeated the candidates supported by Uriburu. Almost completely lacking in public support (the major exception was a small group of Catholic nationalists), Uriburu gave in and held national elections in November 1931. Largely because of electoral fraud and the government's refusal to allow the candidacy of Marcelo Alvear, the presidency was won by General Justo. Argentina's first military regime lasted less than eighteen months.

Following the 1943 revolution, there was general agreement among the leaders of the armed forces in their distrust and disdain for civilian politicians and in their desire to build a strong military establishment; however, there was no such consensus as to the sort of political regime to be established. There emerged a split between a group of young nationalistic officers, led by Colonel Juan Perón, who looked to the working class as a group capable of legitimizing the revolutionary regime, and the more conservative and traditional sector, which was as opposed to a military-labor alliance as it had been to the Castillo administration it had just deposed.

This power struggle within the military lasted from June 1943 until October 1945, during which period three different generals occupied the presidency. Early in October 1945, the older, more conservative faction seemed to gain the upper hand; Perón was imprisoned on Martín García Island, and most of his supporters were removed from key positions in the army. However, the anti-Peronists were unable to agree upon what to do next, and on October 17, when a multitude of workers streamed into the Plaza de Mayo shouting, "We want Perón!" they capitulated. This was the end of the strictly military regime. For the next decade Argentina was governed not by the armed forces, but by Juan Domingo Perón.

Immediately after the fall of Perón in 1955, there were at least four separate groups within the armed forces: (1) a small number of Peronists, almost all of whom were soon retired from active duty; (2) a neutral group that was willing to fraternize with both Peronist and anti-Peronist officers; (3) those officers who had taken part in the 1955 revolt and, as a result, were further removed from the Peronists but still opposed to their persecution; and (4) the extreme anti-Peronists. The last-mentioned group was composed primarily of those who had taken part in the abortive revolt in 1951 and had been imprisoned for up to four years as a result. When reinstated on active duty in September 1955, these men felt that as the original anti-Peronists they had the right to govern. It was this group that was instrumental in replacing Lonardi with Aramburu in November 1955. Ironically, many of these became *legalistas* or *azules* after 1958. Extreme anti-Peronists included officers who had been fence sitters under Perón and now tried to acquire anti-Peronist credentials.

During the Aramburu administration (1955–58), when one of the major concerns of the government was the holding of elections and the return to constitutional government, the leaders of the armed forces divided into three main factions: *quedantistas*, who wanted a continuance of military government until the last vestiges of Peronism were eliminated; *continuistas*, who favored holding elections but at the same time making sure that the victors were sympathetic to the goals of the military; and a "fair play" group, which wanted to hold honest elections (although without allowing the Peronists to nominate candidates) and to respect the results at the polls.[20] The third group emerged victorious, largely as a result of the position taken by President Aramburu.

By 1962, these three groups had coalesced into two sectors: the "gorillas" or *colorados*, and the legalists or *azules*. The former were the hard-line anti-Peronists, who frequently seemed to confuse their anti-Peronism with anticommunism (indeed, some of their leaders felt that Peronism was simply the Argentine version of communism). They looked upon the 1955 coup as a fundamental revolution whose primary goal was the elimination of the conditions that allowed the growth of Peronism. Convinced that Argentina was still not ready for a return to democracy (the large Peronist vote in the elections of March 1962 was cited as proof of this), the *colorados* demanded military rule for an indefinite period—ostensibly to prepare the way for "real" democracy. In 1962 the *colorados* dominated the entire upper echelon of the navy; within the army, their strength was concentrated in the infantry and the engineers.

The *azules*, a much more moderate group, looked at the 1955 rebellion as a simple act of resistance to tyranny. The general position of this group was that the military should stay out of the political process unless the alternative was chaos or a return to dictatorship. The *azules* drew most of their support from the cavalry, which includes all mechanized forces, and especially the large Campo de Mayo garrison, which is strategically located just outside the Federal Capital.

The backgrounds and attitudes of several of the leaders of these two groups were examined by Philip Springer, who concluded that *azules* tended to come from the interior provinces, while a majority of the *colorados* were *porteños*, and that "more *azules* come from the upper class than do *colorados*."[21] The *azules* tended to be more nationalistic, more Catholic, and more pro-Franco than were the *colorados*; it also appeared that the *azules* were more interested in industrialization than were the *colorados*, who were accused of wanting to perpetuate the country's traditional pastoral economy.[22]

In March 1962, the *colorados*, who had always hated Frondizi, gained the upper hand, and the president was deposed. They had been angered by Peronist support of Frondizi in the 1958 election and by Frondizi's attempts to bring Peronists into the government party; his legalization of Peronism prior to the 1962 elections was just the last straw. The *azules* were opposed to the coup—to varying extents—but the Peronist election victories and the approaching power vacuum greatly weakened their strategic position. For several months after the overthrow of Frondizi, there was an obvious power struggle within the armed forces, which at times seemed likely to lead to civil war. The *colorados* were intent upon establishing a military dictatorship that would stamp out Peronism once and for all, while the *azules* insisted that Frondizi's constitutional successor be allowed to remain in office until elections could be held and the situation returned to normal. Finally, in an armed confrontation in September 1962, the *azules* emerged triumphant, and after April of the following year, when an attempted coup on the part of *colorado* naval officers was put down, the *azules* were in complete control.

During the next nine months, *azul* leaders were actively involved in preparations for national elections that would allow the country to return to constitutional normality. Originally they worked toward the creation of a large National and Popular Front that would unite most of the nation's major political parties; however, when the conservatives, Christian Democrats, and People's Radicals refused to participate, the *azules* became disillusioned with this maneuver. The plan was rejected completely when it became apparent that the major voice in the selection of the Front's presidential candidate would be that of Juan Perón. The *azules* soon found themselves in a position where they felt it necessary to prohibit Peronist candidates for any executive office.

With the failure of the National and Popular Front, the *azules* were forced to rely upon the effects of a new proportional representation law to attain the political unity they so fervently desired. They assumed that the use of proportional representation would mean that no candidate for the presidency could obtain a majority of the electoral votes and that no single party could obtain a working majority in Congress. This, they felt, would lead to the formation of a coalition government supported by a large majority of the populace.

Unfortunately, at least from the point of view of the *azules*, that was not the result. A plurality of the votes cast in the July 1963 election were received by the UCRP, the one Argentine political party totally opposed to any form of coalition government. Although obtaining only a fourth of the popular vote, Arturo Illia received enough electoral votes from the nation's minor parties to be elected to the presidency. He then proceeded to ignore even those parties that had supported him in the electoral college and to form a strictly partisan administration. As far as the *azules* were concerned, they had won all the battles but had lost the war.

After 1963, cleavages within the armed forces were much less severe; however, ideological conflicts continued, as did conflicts between the service branches. During the 1966–73 period, the primary conflict appeared to have been between liberals and nationalists. Throughout the administration of General Onganía (1966–70) the predominantly liberal military establishment became increasingly concerned about the influence of the president's nationalist advisers and about Onganía's own corporatist ideology. Even with the removal of Onganía in June 1970, this conflict was not resolved. Slightly more than a year later a group of highly nationalistic field grade officers attempted to overthrow the liberal administration of General Alejandro Lanusse.

In addition to those ideological conflicts that cut across service lines, there has also been appreciable conflict between the service branches, especially between the army and the navy. The navy played no role in the military coups of 1930 and 1943; however, it played a very important role in 1955, and after that it was noted for its extreme anti-Peronism. A number of scholars have attempted to explain the extremity of the navy's political position, but none of these explanations is entirely satisfactory.

In 1960 Edwin Lieuwen wrote, "Resistance to Perón had always been strongest in the navy, whose democratic traditions conflicted with Perón's increasing authoritarianism. The naval officer corps, unlike that of the army, tended to come from the rural oligarchy and the wealthier urban families, and hence was hostile to any regime bent on upsetting the nation's basic institutions."[23] Four years later he wrote, "The navy officer corps (unlike the army's, which is petit-bourgeois in class origin) tends to originate in the upper-middle class."[24]

Lieuwen's impressions are contradicted by the data collected by de Imaz, which show little or no difference in the social backgrounds of army and navy officers. De Imaz says instead, "Navy men feel personally identified with the highest social stratum, because only the values of this stratum are identifiable with the Navy value system. This identification . . . has led many senior officers and Navy ministers in recent years to assume representation of a social stratum which they did not even know."[25] Marvin Goldwert, on the other hand, attributed army-navy differences to the more cosmopolitan nature of the naval profession: "The naval career presents an opportunity for travel beyond the national soil. . . . The naval officer is thus drawn not to the xenophobic and narrow integral nationalism [of the army], but to the more cosmopolitan liberal nationalist position."[26] Unfortunately, in spite of a great deal of conjecture, much of it apparently quite reasonable, it is impossible to explain with any certainty the political differences separating these two service branches.

THE PROCESS OF NATIONAL REORGANIZATION

In 1966 the armed forces gave power to a retired general and then returned to the barracks convinced that "their" *caudillo* would perform miracles. No miracles took place under Onganía. In 1976, the military decided to rule the country as an institution.

Guillermo O'Donnell, Argentina's best-known social scientist, sees both coups as "the result of a frightened reaction to what was perceived as a grave threat to the survival of the basic capitalist parameters of society."[27] This threat was itself believed to be the result of the hypermobilization of the working class by previous populist, that is, Peronist, administrations. These two coups, then, were simply the means of inaugurating authoritarian regimes (called by O'Donnell bureaucratic-authoritarian) that were capable of deactivating, economically as well as politically, the working class. This deactivation, or exclusion, was in turn seen as the means of stabilizing the society and polity in order to create the climate necessary to attract foreign investment sufficient to "deepen" the industrialization process.

Although O'Donnell's explanation is something of an oversimplification, the actions of the administrations that succeeded these coups certainly lend some credence to his position. It must also be pointed out that neither in 1966 nor in 1976 was there any appreciable opposition to the overthrow of constitutional presidents. These coups had the approval, or at least the acquiescence, of most sectors of the Argentine public and key interest groups such as the Argentine Industrial Union and the Argentine Rural Society. In each case there appears to have been a general consensus that something had to be done. In fact, there is evidence that in 1976 the leaders of the armed forces delayed the virtually inevitable coup until the economic and political situation deteriorated to such a point that they could be sure of widespread public approval of their action.

Not only did the armed forces decide to rule as an institution in 1976, but they also resorted to an unprecedented use of repression, as described in Chapter 1. Upon taking power, the leaders of the armed forces announced the beginning of the Process of National Reorganization (or the Proceso), which would fundamentally restructure the nation's economic, social, and political systems and put an end to the need for coups. The new president, Army Commander-in-Chief General Jorge Videla, said that this coup "signifies the final closing of an historic cycle." The basic objectives announced by the 1976 military junta were no more specific than those enunciated by its predecessor a decade earlier. The sole objective of a purely economic nature was

the creation of a socioeconomic system which assures the capacity for national decision making and the complete fulfillment of the Argentine person, where the state maintains control over vital areas of both security and development and offers to private initiative, both domestic and foreign, the conditions necessary for a fluid participation in the process of rational development of our resources, while neutralizing all possibility of their interference in the political process.[28]

The Act for the Process of National Reorganization, however, forced President Videla to share power with the junta of the Commanders-in-Chief, whose approval was needed even for the appointment of cabinet members. Still burned by the Onganía experience, the junta made sure that no single man would be left in charge of the decision-making power. This was particularly true for the navy and the air force, who feared that the army could gain the upper hand in the intraservice power struggle that had long been a feature of the Argentine armed forces. The military junta, composed of the three service commanders, was named The Supreme Organ of the State. It was charged with fixing the basic objectives of the government and supervising the attainment of these objectives. It was also granted the power to choose the president and remove him at will and to approve presidential appointments of ambassadors, governors, and ministers.

What was also different from 1966 was that the armed services divided among themselves the spoils of power. The army, the navy, and the air force assumed the jurisdiction of specific geographical areas and, following specific criteria, took control of ministries, governorships, mayoralties, and state companies.[29] Such an arrangement was devised to guarantee the vested interests of each armed service and ensure some kind of collective leadership. However, this also produced an extreme decentralization of authority, often fueling intraservice conflicts and paralyzing any effective decision-making process. Such decentralization was often used by junta leaders as an argument to explain their lack of control over the "excesses" of antisubversion military units reported by the foreign press and human rights organizations during and after the Proceso. The same decentralization was also responsible for the deterioration of the internal discipline within the armed forces and the staggering corruption that involved many officers. In fact, freed from the checks and balances of the democratic process, many officers in charge of state companies and bureaucratic positions turned out to be even more in-clined to use their positions for personal advantage than the civilians they had accused before the coup.

To ensure a greater impact of the upper echelons of each high command in the regime's policies, the Legislative Advisory Commission was created. Composed of nine senior officers (three from each armed service), the Leg-islative Advisory Commission was expected to advise legislative proposals to the junta which, nonetheless, remained the highest decision-making body of the regime. In fact, it soon appeared that major legislation originated in the military junta or the presidency, with minor matters perhaps originating in the cabinet.

The relative power of the president and the junta depended to a great extent upon the personalities involved. President Videla appears to have exercised greater authority than Viola or Galtieri did, probably as a result of two factors: (1) Videla was the individual most responsible for the 1976 coup, and thus he had a degree of prestige among his military colleagues that was unavailable to his successors; and (2) while Videla was president, the com-mander-in-chief of the army, General Viola, was a fellow infantry officer and a close personal friend. President Viola, on the other hand, was faced with (and ultimately replaced by) an army commander (General Leopoldo Galtieri) who was neither a fellow infantry officer nor a close friend.

While President Videla gave Minister of the Economy José Alfredo Mar-tínez de Hoz complete control over the formulation of economic policy, much as President Onganía had earlier given such power to Adalbert Krieger Vasena, President Viola almost immediately abolished the Ministry of Eco-nomics and divided its functions among the Ministries of Public Works, Finance, Industry, and Agriculture (again in a manner quite reminiscent of President Lanusse's action after the removal of Onganía). In both 1967 and 1976, newly appointed economics ministers were given an enormous degree of policy-making authority, and in each case the failure of the policies devised by these men appears to have been blamed not only upon the ministers themselves but also on the opposition of some influential military circles. For instance, Martínez de Hoz was unable to privatize many state companies that were creating huge fiscal deficits because their military managers op-posed the idea. Similarly, while wages collapsed by one third in 1977, the junta reminded Martínez de Hoz that employment levels had to remain high to avoid possible social dislocations. Thus, plans to cut jobs in the bureau-cracy and state corporations were quickly scaled down. Last but not least, Martínez de Hoz found himself powerless when the high commands of each armed service requested ever-increasing funds for military expenditures. The minister was able to stay on the job while Videla protected him, but in return he had to make substantial concessions to his enemies within the military. Divisions within the armed forces were not confined to economic matters. Military hard-liners tried to thwart any attempt toward talks with civilian

civilian politicians over a possible relaxation of the dictatorship. In 1979, a coup attempt by one of their leaders was easily put down but testified to the deep divisions within the armed forces. The various points of contention that had been subdued thanks to Videla's skillful maneuvering exploded with a virulent force during Viola's term. With Galtieri as new army commander in 1981, the hard-line faction gained the upper hand. The unwillingness of this sector of the officer corps (which cut across services) to back up Viola's attempt to ease the repressive apparatus created in 1976 led to the president's ouster by year's end. Galtieri gave a warning to Viola only two months after the latter had taken office when he stated in an Army Day speech:

In the last 50 years other military processes, faced with the proliferation of criticism, took the wrong path and thought elections were the solution to the political problem. The history of these successive failures, the after effects of which we are still suffering, leave us with the hard but wise lesson that we must not make the same mistake.[30]

While the military hard-liners had prevailed for the moment, it was soon clear that Galtieri faced ever-increasing opposition within the armed forces. The basic issue was that despite the promises at its inception, the Proceso was a total failure. The armed forces once more showed that they could agree on what they wanted to get rid of but had no clear idea of how to build a new political order. Any time discussions arose within the military establishment on what kind of form the political regime should take, the officer corps proved to be as divided and conflictual as the politicians they so much despised.

Regardless, the Malvinas/Falklands conflict cut short the debate. The invasion plans prepared by the navy commander, Admiral Jorge Anaya, were to be carried out in May, when the Southern Hemisphere winter would have made it impossible for the British to send a task force. However, Galtieri became persuaded that the increasing civilian opposition could have gotten out of control by that time. In March the Argentines attacked. Their assumption was that the British were not going to fight back and even if they did, the United States would have stopped them. In fact, relations between the Argentine military regime and the Reagan administration had been quite cordial. The U.S. administration had appreciated Argentina's offer to send counterinsurgency specialists to Central America to fight the left-wing guerrilla movement in El Salvador and the Sandinista regime in Nicaragua. Last but not least, the United States was bound by the Rio Treaty to help Argentina in the case of a foreign aggression. Galtieri and the junta thought that the risks were quite low while the payoffs were very high. By taking the islands, they could boost the regime's waning popularity and the reputation of the armed forces. The result was just the opposite. After the initial surprise, the British fought back with the assistance of the United States.

The Malvinas/Falklands defeat not only showed the incompetence of the regime's diplomacy but, more embarrassing, made it plain that the armed forces were totally incapable of performing the very task for which they were supposedly trained. Of the three armed services, only the air force gave the British a real fight, damaging or sinking several ships. The navy, after the sinking of its battle cruiser *Belgrano* by a British submarine, only a few days into the conflict, kept the fleet safe in the ports of the mainland. The army sent to the islands for the most part ill-trained and poorly equipped conscripts. The best troops were kept at the border with Chile, around the Beagle Channel, where the two countries almost went to war in 1978. Faced with the professional soldiers of the Royal Army and Navy, the poor Argentine troops could not mount any resistance. The high commands of the three armed services, consistent with their history of rivalries and jealousies, fought three different wars without any coordination against a very determined enemy. Cut off from supply lines and left without orders from their commands and with their morale destroyed, more than 11,000 field officers and troops quickly surrendered while a thousand died. Once the fight was over, many prisoners told their British captors stories of abuses, mistreatment, and widespread corruption in which their senior officers had been engaged. Once back home, they also told their families and friends, thus giving the last blow to the credibility not only of the regime but of the military as a professional institution.

The capitulation on the field marked the end of the regime. Galtieri quit, but that could not save the day. The three armed forces became even more divided than ever. The air force pulled out of the junta altogether and solicited a return to civilian government. This left the army and the navy with the responsibility of what to do next. Former General Reinaldo Bignone was taken out of retirement to perform some last-minute miracle. He could not. The Malvinas/Falklands defeat destroyed any bargaining power that the military might have had before. Thus, unlike his counterparts in Brazil, Uruguay, and Chile, Bignone was unable to find a negotiated solution to the return of the armed forces to the barracks. What most preoccupied the military was the possibility that a new civilian administration would initiate investigations concerning violations of human rights during the Proceso. Once it was clear that neither the Radicals nor the Peronists were willing to compromise on this subject, the armed forces issued the National Pacification Law, which amounted to a self-amnesty for the crimes committed during the war against subversion. It was to no avail. The dirty war and its crimes would become the thorny issue dividing military from civilian society in the years to come.

The Military on Trial

Upon taking office in 1983, Alfonsín set for himself a goal that had no precedents in Latin American history: bringing to justice the members of the outgoing military regime. The Argentine officer corps had long believed that it constituted a separate caste in society, a group of untouchables above the rule of law. Alfonsín promised to end all that. However, aside from some general proposals announced during the speeches of the presidential campaign, Alfonsín had no clearly designed policy when his term started. The president's approach followed an incremental pattern that became more and more pragmatic as unexpected events arose in the months that followed.

To begin with, the president repealed the military self-amnesty decreed in September of 1983. Subsequently, Alfonsín took several initiatives to weaken the armed forces' political clout and subordinate them once and for all to civilian authority. To this end, the National Security Doctrine that had been used to justify the war against subversion was repealed. Moreover, the Law for the Defense of the Constitutional Order, which sanctioned heavy penalties against military and civilian people plotting against the government, was passed by Congress.

Among the first measures adopted by the administration was the reduction of the size of the armed forces. The defense budget was cut by half, two-thirds of the army generals and one-third of the navy admirals were forced into retirement, and three-quarters (about 50,000) of the conscripts were discharged because the government could no longer afford to feed and clothe them. Acquisitions of new weapons and spare parts were cut to a minimum. So were the salaries of officers and NCOs who, in defiance of military regulations, began to take second jobs to make ends meet.

The internal organization of the armed forces underwent substantial changes as well. In the past, all successful military coups had been started by or received the crucial support of the First Army Corps, whose headquarters were in the huge Campo de Mayo base just outside the Federal Capital. Alfonsín disbanded the First Army Corps and scattered its units across several bases around the country. In this way, it was hoped, the likelihood of future coup attempts would be lessened. The security forces of each armed service that had been heavily involved in the dirty war were also reorganized and placed under the authority of the Ministry of Defense, now headed by a civilian. The Ministry of Defense also took control of the large industrial conglomerate developed by the military since 1941, the General Directorate of Military Manufactures (DGFM). Most of the officers in charge of DGFM's companies were cashiered and replaced with civilian managers. Besides, the administration drew up plans to privatize many such companies that were a heavy drain on the national budget because of their heavy losses.

The National Atomic Energy Commission (CNEA) in charge of Argentina's nuclear program was also taken away from the navy, which had managed it for most of its history, and transferred to civilian authority. The military had pushed its nuclear plans hard after 1976 and just before Alfonsín took office announced that Argentina had mastered the technology for the enrichment of uranium, the first step toward the manufacturing of a nuclear bomb. For this very reason, Argentina had refused to sign the Nuclear Nonproliferation Treaty sponsored by President Jimmy Carter in 1978, charging that it was an affront to the national sovereignty of Argentina. Accordingly, the United States cut off crucial supplies for the enrichment of uranium and lobbied European countries to do the same.

While most of these measures were grudgingly accepted by the military, the issue of responsibility for the dirty war crimes ended, in the long run, in open confrontation. Even during the presidential campaign, Alfonsín stated that a line should be drawn among those who had ordered the tortures and executions, those who had gone far beyond their orders, and those who had merely carried out instructions. In his view, the first two groups were the ones to be tried.

As he started his term, the president charged the Supreme Council of the Armed Forces (SCAF) with trying the nine leaders of the three military juntas that ruled the country during the Proceso. Alfonsín wanted to have the military itself punish those who had abused their powers. In this way, the officer corps would not feel as victimized. Once the SCAF had handed down exemplary sentences to the junta leaders, the president planned to issue a sweeping amnesty discharging field officers that had carried out the war against subversion from any wrongdoing. In this way he could put the whole issue behind him and dedicate his time to other pressing problems. At the same time, to show his fairness, Alfonsín instructed the federal prosecutors to begin penal action against former members of the ERP and Montonero terrorist organizations that had survived the dirty war. Human rights organizations vehemently opposed the presidential initiative. To forestall their action, Alfonsín appointed novelist Ernesto Sábato to chair CONADEP and report to him in six months. CONADEP served the purpose of establishing the facts pertaining to the crimes during the dirty war. In a way, it also meant to pay a belated tribute to the thousands of innocent victims of the Proceso's savage repression so that human rights groups could feel in part vindicated.

Unfortunately for Alfonsín, things did not go as planned. The SCAF, after six months of hesitation, ruled that it was unable to reach a verdict, while implicitly acquitting the junta leaders whose orders to fight subversion SCAF found "unobjectionable." This was the first of a series of setbacks for Alfonsín. Hoping to have the military openly acknowledge the illegitimacy of the dirty war and make an apology had proven naive.

Immediately, the junta trials were passed on to the Federal Appeals Court of Buenos Aires. From that point on, the administration saw the initiative slowly but steadily slipping away from its hands. During the hearings many of the accused took a defiant stand. Videla denounced the whole thing and proclaimed that only history would judge him. Masera went even further when he said, "we are here because we won the armed conflict but lost the psychological war. . . . The enemy is afraid because it knows that the armed forces can return to defeat them."[31] Viola's defense council charged that the Communists were behind the trials and that the military had been true national heroes in their quest to vanquish "antinational assassins" disguised as left-wing "revolutionaries."[32] The trials were a traumatic event for Argentines. Televised daily, they showed hundreds of witnesses testifying to the horrors of the repression years. At the same time, the media multiplied its efforts to uncover hundreds of cases involving not only the former leaders of the Proceso but also junior officers and NCOs still on active duty. The end result was the creation of an enlarging gulf within society. The citizenry became outraged at discovering the atrocities of the past regime while the military felt that instead of being praised for eradicating terrorism, it was now being vilified and humiliated. After eight months of hearings, the court sentenced Videla and Masera to life terms and Viola to seventeen years; two other junta members received smaller jail terms. The leaders of the last junta were all acquitted. However, they were tried again for misconduct during the Malvinas/Falklands war by the SCAF. In mid-1986 General Galtieri received twelve years, Admiral Anaya, fourteen; and Air Force Brigadier Basilio Lami Dozo, eight.

These sentences encouraged a proliferation of lawsuits to be handled now by civilian courts against junior officers. Although the Alfonsín administration was aware of the explosive effects that these investigations could have on the armed forces, it found itself incapable of stopping the trials. Having promised to defend the rule of law, the president was unwilling to violate the independence of the judiciary.

These events deepened the split that had been developing within the armed forces, particularly in the army, where the chain of command virtually broke down. Field officers felt their generals had sold them out by allowing the civilian administration and the judiciary to prosecute them in order to save themselves. Sharpening the division between the two groups was the fact that junior officers ascribed to their superiors' incompetence the humiliating defeat in the conflict with Great Britain. While many field commanders were sent to war, their generals had rested comfortably in their offices. By early 1987, the upper echelons of the army could no longer claim to command the loyalty of many of their troops.

Alfonsín tried to ease tensions within the officer corps by having Congress pass the Full Stop Law. The law aimed at stopping further indictments against members of the armed forces by fixing at sixty days the time still available to bring new cases to court. The law was in effect a disguised amnesty. In fact, it prevented, once the stated time period had expired, further investigations, leaving many crimes unpunished. Human rights groups and individual citizens reacted angrily. With the help of sympathetic state prosecutors they hastily presented new cases to the courts. Once again, the government's attempt to end the issue was frustrated. Ironically, while the Full Stop Law freed most senior officers from pending charges, it had the unintended consequence of still leaving under indictment some 400 officers and NCOs who, in the original intention, were those who should have benefited from the new legislation.

The internal tensions that had simmered for three years finally erupted during the 1987 Easter holiday when Lieutenant Colonel Aldo Rico led a mutiny of junior officers and NCOs. Rico and his followers, quickly dubbed "painted faces" (*carapintadas*) for the camouflage paint they wore, demanded an end to the indictments, the retirement of generals who did not have their confidence, better salaries, and increased budgetary allocations for military expenditures.

The mutiny eventually ended, thanks to the massive popular support of individual citizens and opposition parties. However, despite the administration's denials, the *carapintadas* got most of what they wanted. Several generals were cashiered, and Congress passed shortly afterward the Due Obedience Law. The new law practically eliminated all pending indictments for junior officers and NCOs, leaving only twenty people still in jail. The Full Stop and Due Obedience laws were an embarrassment for Alfonsín and his credibility, as they repudiated most of his early pledges. They sanctioned the untouchable status of the military and were in open contradiction with the spirit of the constitution. Encouraged by his success, Rico led a new mutiny in January of 1988, but this time he failed and was arrested. Most officers saw in his attempt a personal feud between him and the army chief-of-staff; thus they kept out of it.

In April of that year Congress, after three years of debate, passed the new Defense Law, which aimed at specifying the role of the military in the new democratic regime. For the armed forces the law was another source of resentment. The military was limited to the defense of the country from external threats, but the law left the issue of internal security unsolved. Equally important, the new law failed to give to the armed forces specific guidelines on their new mission.

With Rico out of the picture, the cause of the rebellious *carapintadas* was taken up by Colonel Muhammed Alí Seineldín who, like Rico, had created a personal following as a trainer of commando units. In December 1988, Seineldín launched the most threatening rebellion yet. This time the *carapintadas* asked for a sweeping pardon for all military officers still in jail (including the junta leaders convicted in 1985 and Lieutenant Colonel Rico), higher salaries, and the removal of the army leadership. After lengthy negotiations, Seineldín and his men put down their arms, and once again the administration denied rumors that a deal had been made. Yet, weeks later the chief-of-staff of the army resigned and salaries were raised, but no pardon was issued.

In January 1989 a new event shocked the nation. Sixty left-wing terrorists of the then-unknown organization All for the Fatherland attacked the La

Tablada military garrison outside Buenos Aires. After three days of heavy fighting, the surviving attackers surrendered. This event gave the military another excuse to argue that the terrorist threat was still alive and that the armed forces' role in the dirty war had to be vindicated.

By the time Alfonsín stepped down, the armed forces could claim to have prevailed over the president's effort to bring military crimes to justice. However, it was a pyrrhic victory. The armed forces, and particularly the army, remained deeply divided, as the right-wing, nationalist elements that had joined the *carapintadas* movement were tearing apart the military's hierarchical structure. During the 1989 presidential campaign, the *carapintadas* openly endorsed Menem's candidacy with the expectation that if he won their leaders would be given key posts in the army's high command. Menem gladly accepted their support and after his election issued a sweeping presidential pardon. Among the 280 beneficiaries could be found 40 retired senior officers convicted for human rights violations and the Malvinas/Falklands debacle, many junior officers and NCOs jailed for the 1987–88 mutinies, and a few former terrorists. However, as time went on, the president turned his back on the *carapintadas* and sided with the upper echelons of the army, who were anxious to reestablish internal discipline. First Rico was cashiered, and later Seineldín was put under house arrest for insubordination. With their fortunes fading away, the *carapintadas* tried their last desperate gamble, and in December 1990 they staged a new revolt. This time, however, they were violently crushed by loyal troops, and their leaders were tried and convicted by military courts in the months that followed. Having defeated the most threatening element of the military, a few weeks later Menem felt strong enough to pardon all the junta members still in jail and former Montonero leader Mario Firmenich—this in spite of strong popular opposition.

Menem described his pardons as a "pacification effort," a necessary step to reconcile civil and military society in order to put the past to rest and work united to tackle the challenges ahead. The pardons, widely regarded by human rights associations, the UCR, and left-wing parties as a capitulation to the armed forces, still fell short of vindicating the role of the military during the dirty war. In spite of the controversy that ensued, Menem was capable of depriving the armed forces of one of their main grievances. He made clear to the Chiefs-of-Staff of the three armed services that the pardons were as far as he could go in that regard. For Menem there were going to be neither vanquished nor victors. The president skillfully played the divisions within the army. By helping the generals to get rid of the *carapintadas*, he forced them to accept his leadership. Having no longer to worry about keeping Rico and Seineldín in line, the army top brass had now to devote itself to promoting greater professionalism and a new sense of unity and purpose. Within this context, Menem succeeded in imposing his plans for the privatization of most of the companies making up the DGFM (that Alfonsín had been unable to carry out) with the proviso that some of the profits of those sales would be devoted to increasing salaries and purchasing needed equipment. Moreover, at the end of 1991 the president openly interfered with the promotions recommended by the army chief-of-staff. In the past such a measure could have triggered a coup, but not this time. The armed forces were also forced to accept the scrapping of the *Condor II* middle-range ballistic missile and further personnel cuts.

By early 1992, Menem seemed to have put to a rest the military issue. With Seineldín sentenced to life imprisonment for his role in the last military uprising, Rico remained the sole leader of the *carapintada* movement. This time, however, the former lieutenant colonel found a more democratic way to express his grievances by organizing his own political party, the Movement for Dignity and Independence (MODIN). In the 1991 congressional elections MODIN finished to a surprising third place in the Buenos Aires province, ahead of the much more heralded UCD. Most of Rico's support came from the poor shantytowns outside the Federal Capital, where the economic crisis had hit the hardest. Portraying himself as a Catholic, right-wing nationalist, Rico could attack the corrupt party system and Menem's unfulfilled promises of social justice most successfully to the poor, his most receptive audience.

What role the military will play in the future remains to be seen. Surely, most of the upper-class and economic groups that once looked up to the military as a means of containing populism were totally disillusioned with the Proceso's economic results. More generally, the horrors of the dirty war have made all sectors of society wary of resorting to the military as the ultimate arbiter of civilian politics. On top of that, the embarrassing performance during the Malvinas/Falklands conflict has also contributed to diminish the prestige of the armed forces. As for the officer corps, it is likely that they will remain heavily politicized. However, the debacle of the Proceso may have convinced many officers that for the time being the most important thing is to rebuild the prestige and professionalism of their institution and to restrain their lobbying effort to bread-and-butter corporate demands like salaries and equipment. This does not mean that future interventions are out of the picture. Traditionally, military coups have taken place when there was strong civilian support for them and, in most cases, such coups were associated with socioeconomic crises. If the new democratic regime proves incapable of promoting economic growth and alleviating the plight of the poor, it is not unlikely that new *carapintadas* would come to the scene and take upon themselves the task of getting rid of an ineffective and corrupt government. The recent aborted coup in Venezuela is an example that such a scenario can indeed materialize and have traumatic consequences for the consolidation of the democratic regime.

NOTES

1. James Rowe, "Argentina's Restless Military," *AUFS Reports* 11, no. 2 (May 1964): 5; and *The Military Balance, 1974–1975* (London: Institute for Strategic Studies, 1974), p. 63.

2. Darío Cantón, *Military Interventions in Argentina: 1900–1906*, Working Paper no. 39 (Buenos Aires: Centro de Investigaciones Sociales, 1967), p. 23.

3. José Luis de Imaz, *Los que mandan (Those Who Rule)* (Albany: State University of New York Press, 1970), p. 59.

4. Robert Potash, *The Army and Politics in Argentina, 1928–1945: Yrigoyen to Perón* (Stanford, CA: Stanford University Press, 1969), p. 285.

5. Mariano Grondona, "Las Cuatro Salidas," *Primera Plana* 5, no. 220 (March 14, 1967): 11.

6. Cámara de Diputados, *Diario de Sesiones* (1922), vol. 5, p. 24.

7. Oscar Alende, *Entretelones de la trampa* (Buenos Aires: Santiago Rueda Editor, 1964), pp. 116–17.

8. James Payne, *Patterns of Conflict in Colombia* (New Haven: Yale University Press, 1968), pp. 142–43.

9. Robert Potash, *The Impact of Professionalism on the Twentieth-Century Argentine Military* (Amherst: University of Massachusetts, Program in Latin American Studies, 1977), p. 16.

10. José Luis de Imaz, "Los que mandan: las fuerzas armadas en Argentina," *América Latina* 7, no. 4 (October–December 1964): 68.

11. Quoted in Carlos Fayt, "El Fenómeno Peronista," *Aportes* 1 (July 1966): 14.

12. Quoted in Juan Orona, *La Revolución del 6 de Septiembre* (Buenos Aires: N.p., 1966), pp. 227–28.

13. A secret GOU document circulated shortly before the 1943 coup, quoted in Juan Orona, *La Logia Militar que derrocó a Castillo* (Buenos Aires: N.p., 1966), pp. 110–11. Unfortunately, it is quite possible that this document is apocryphal.

14. General Guillermo Osiris Villegas, *Políticas y estratégias para el desarrollo y la seguridad nacional* (Buenos Aires: Editorial Pleamar, 1969), p. 109.

15. General N. E. Iavicoli, "La interrelación del desarrollo y la seguridad en el estado moderno," *Temas Militares* 1, no. 2 (January–February 1967): 82.

16. General Juan Enrique Guglialmelli, *120 días en el gobierno* (Buenos Aires: Edición del Autor, 1971), p. 83.

17. Lt. Col. Alberto M. Garosino, "Radiografía militar del golpe," *Confirmado* 1, no. 12 (July 23, 1965): 64. It should be noted that this article is not only a description of this phenomenon but also an example of it.

18. "Perspectivas-Pronósticos: Que Pasará en 1966?" *Confirmado* 1, no. 34 (December 24, 1965): 14–16.

19. Félix Luna, "José Félix Uriburu," in *Presidentes Argentinos* (Buenos Aires: Companía Fabril Editora, 1961), pp. 204–5.

20. Philip Springer, "Disunity and Disorder: Factional Politics in the Argentine Military," in *The Military Intervenes: Case Studies in Political Development*, ed. Henry Bienen (New York: Russell Sage Foundation, 1968), p. 150.

21. Ibid., p. 150.

22. Ibid., pp. 150–52.

23. Edwin Lieuwen, *Arms and Politics in Latin America* (New York: Praeger, 1960), p. 51.

24. Edwin Lieuwen, *Generals vs. Presidents: Neomilitarism in Latin America* (New York: Praeger, 1964), p. 15.

25. Imaz, *Los que mandan*, p. 79.

26. Marvin Goldwert, *Democracy, Militarism and Nationalism in Argentina, 1930–1966* (Austin: University of Texas Press, 1972), p. 71.

27. Guillermo O'Donnell, "Tensions in the Bureaucratic-Authoritarian State and the Question of Democracy," in ed., David Collier, *The New Authoritarianism in Latin America*, (Princeton, NJ: Princeton University Press, 1979), pp. 176–78.

28. Military Junta, "Proceso de Reorganización Nacional" (Buenos Aires: Congreso de la Nación, Oficina de Información Parliamentaria, 1976), p. 1.

29. Andrés Fontana: "Armed Forces and Neoconservative Ideology: State Shrinking in Argentina, 1976–1981," in *State Shrinking*, ed. William Glade (Austin: University of Texas Press, 1988), p. 71.

30. Quoted in *Latin America Weekly Report*, July 10, 1981, p. 3.

31. *La Razon* (Buenos Aires), October 4, 1985, p. 11.

32. *La Nación* (Buenos Aires), October 11, p. 12.

CHAPTER 4

The Labor Movement

Throughout Latin America organized labor has attained a position of some political importance. This is especially true in Argentina, where the labor movement is very large, relatively wealthy, quite well organized, and thoroughly politicized. The leader of a large union in Argentina is almost automatically a prominent national politician; the secretary general of the General Confederation of Labor (CGT) holds potential political power that is probably equal to that of the leader of a major Argentine political party.

The size of the organized labor movement has varied a good deal during the postwar period. It was probably largest during the early 1950s, when the government claimed there were 4 million union members. Today we do not have reliable statistics but because of the deep economic crisis that affected Argentina in the 1980s, it is reasonable to assume that unionized workers are around 3 million. It is not just the blue-collar workers in the factories who are organized; most white-collar employees in businesses, banks, and government offices belong to unions. In fact, of all the nation's large wage-earning groups, only the domestic servants and agricultural workers lack effective organization. Nor are all unions small. The Retail Clerks, Metallurgical Workers, Business Employees, Textile Workers, and Government Employees unions have over 200,000 members each, and several others had over 100,000.

Unions are financed largely through a check-off system. Employers are required by law to deduct union dues from employees' salaries and to deposit these funds in the bank account of the national union organization. These dues usually amount to between 1 and 2 percent of the members' wages. Most unions have also received permission from the labor ministry to retain the first month's salary increase each time a new contract is negotiated. This

money is used in a number of ways. For example, the Light and Power
Union, which has about 35,000 members in greater Buenos Aires, owns four
tourist hotels for the use of its members: one on the ocean at Mar del Plata,
two in the Córdoba hill country, and one in the mountains of Bariloche. In
and around the capital it owns six weekend recreation camps with swimming
pools and sports facilities, a 12,000 volume library, and a movie theater.
Many unions also maintain strike funds worth several millions of dollars.

Not only is the Argentine labor movement very large, extremely well
organized, and rather wealthy, it is politicized to a degree almost unintel-
ligible to many North Americans. The form and the content of this political
involvement have varied enormously over the course of the last century.
The type of political action engaged in by each generation has helped to
shape the political activities of each succeeding generation, and thus before
examining the goals and methods of the contemporary labor movement, it
is necessary to look at its historical development.

THE DEVELOPMENT OF THE TRADE
UNION MOVEMENT

Tomás R. Fillol has written that "the history of Argentine trade unions
is largely an account of internal strife, of disunity, struggle and rancor."[1]
Prior to the mid-1940s, this internal struggle was among anarchists, syndicalists, socialists, and communists. Each of these groups had radically different ideas about the ultimate goals of the labor movement and the best
means of attaining these goals. In the decade between 1945 and 1955, organized labor was relatively well united under Peronist control, but with the
fall of Perón the movement split once again. With only the exception of the
1973–74 interlude, labor has been plagued by internecine rivalries to this
day.

The first union established in Argentina was probably the Printing Trades
Workers Union, which was founded in 1858. However, the union movement
did not really get going until the turn of the century. The nation's first labor
federation was the Argentine Regional Labor Federation (FORA), which
was founded in 1890 by socialists but was soon captured by anarchosyndi-
calists who proclaimed its goal to be the establishment of anarchist communism. By 1927, there were three important labor federations: the anarchist
FORA, a socialist-dominated Argentine Labor Confederation (COA), and a
syndicalist Argentine Syndical Union (USA). In 1930, just a few weeks after
the military coup, most of the components of these organizations united to
form the General Confederation of Labor (CGT), which has dominated the
labor movement ever since, although it split into rival factions shortly after
its founding in 1935, and again in 1943, 1968, 1982, and 1989.

Before 1910, the dominant ideological faction within the union movement
was that of the anarchists, who looked upon political authority of any form

as both unnecessary and undesirable. Their ultimate goal seems to have been the creation of a society resembling the guild system of medieval Europe. Preferring solidarity strikes, general walkouts, and sabotage to negotiation, the anarchists resorted frequently to violence.

Largely because of government repression, the anarchists lost control of the labor movement by 1910, and for the next quarter-century, dominance passed into the hands of syndicalists. Argentine syndicalism was at least theoretically apolitical; it accepted the Marxist analysis of class struggle but denounced political action on the part of the proletariat. The syndicalists were intent upon using the general strike as a means of creating what they called a "just society," which was evidently to involve some form of cooperativism.

About 1935, control of the labor movement passed into the hands of socialists, who differed greatly from the anarchists and syndicalists in that they were willing to work within the existing political system. Argentine socialists—social democrats might be a more accurate label—insisted upon improving the conditions of the working class by means of legislative action.

Communists have never held a dominant position in the Argentine labor movement. They got their start in the 1930s, when the new industrial workers, ignored to a large extent by the socialists, became organized. During the late 1930s and early 1940s the socialist-communist struggle within the labor movement was essentially between the haves and the have-nots. "The socialists controlled the older, more highly skilled, and more conservative transportation unions, as well as the commercial employees and the municipal workers. Many of these unions had obtained property in the form of union buildings, vacation colonies, and hospitals. Some had social security and pension systems, and others were seeking them.... The communists, on the other hand, represented the newer industrial unions. They had few buildings, vacation colonies, hospitals or pension funds to protect. They had little or nothing to conserve, and their leaders came from a younger, more aggressive generation of workers."[2]

The development of an effective trade union movement was opposed not only by employers but also by the government. Before 1916, both looked upon unions as inherently subversive. The government did all it could to destroy the union movement. One of the most potent measures in this direction was the Residency Law passed in 1902. It empowered the government to deport any alien who it felt was a menace to the security of the state. Hundreds and perhaps thousands of foreign workers were deported during the nearly sixty years that this law remained on the statute books. Native Argentines were jailed or deported to a kind of concentration camp in the Patagonia region of the far south.[3] Similarly, the 1910 Law of Social Defense was used to destroy the anarchist movement. "It prohibited anarchists from entering the country, propagating their ideas, or holding public meetings."[4]

The government's attitude toward organized labor shifted appreciably after 1916. President Yrigoyen protected both the right to organize and the right to strike, and there was a great deal of union activity during his first administration. However, the UCR had no specific labor program, and both Yrigoyen and his successor, Alvear, dealt with labor in a completely ad hoc manner. Very little labor legislation was enacted during the Radical era, and neither the Residency Law nor the Law of Social Defense was repealed.

The administrations of the second conservative era (1930–43) were somewhat less hostile toward labor than their predecessors of 1862 to 1916 had been—perhaps because by this time the labor movement was under the control of the Socialists, who obviously were willing to abide by the rules of the political game. During this period some relatively modern labor legislation was enacted, primarily through the initiative of Socialist congressmen, but the conservative governments were quite willing to look the other way while many, perhaps most, employers ignored such legislation almost completely.

LABOR AND PERONISM

Between about 1920 and 1940, there was a drastic change in the composition of the urban working class. During this period, migration to the cities came primarily from the countryside, not from Europe as had previously been the case. In 1914, about half the people living in greater Buenos Aires had been born abroad (and among the working class the percentage was much greater), while only one out of ten had moved there from the interior. By the time of the 1947 census, greater Buenos Aires contained more migrants from the countryside than from abroad (29 percent compared with 26 percent). Seventy-five percent of the unskilled workers, 60 percent of the semiskilled, and 50 percent of the skilled workers of greater Buenos Aires were migrants. Most of these migrants were recent arrivals. The new workers from the interior were not nearly as interested as the preceding generation in such European ideas as socialism, syndicalism, or communism; indeed, many had probably never heard of these terms. Instead of a foreign ideology, they were more likely to look for a new *patrón*, and shortly after the 1943 military coup they found one in the person of Colonel Juan Domingo Perón.

Although many of the original leaders of the military government of 1943 seem to have been intent upon following the pattern set by General Uriburu thirteen years earlier, there were some field grade officers, including Perón, who realized that, in order to endure, the military regime had to find a substantial base of popular support. Perón soon decided that the logical source of this support was the formerly suppressed or ignored labor movement.

Within three months of the revolution, Perón managed to gain appointment as head of the National Labor Department (a bureau arbitrating strikes and collecting labor statistics), which was soon given cabinet status as the Ministry of Labor and Welfare. It was from this position that Perón gained personal control of the organized labor movement and, soon after that, of Argentina.

Soon after its creation, the labor ministry became the sole collective bargaining agency. Although Argentina's first collective bargaining contract was signed in 1901, prior to 1943 such agreements were used in very few industries. The normal practice was for an employer to deal with each worker individually. Only under Perón's aegis did collective bargaining become the norm. Initially, Perón saw to it that the unions using his office were rewarded by gaining what they sought—a fact that was given widespread publicity. Soon unions were being encouraged to strike with the assurance that Perón would see to it that their demands were met. It did not take long for the workers to realize that Perón was much more important in their contract demands than either their union leaders or management. In October 1945, an executive decree announced that if a union desired to sign a valid collective bargaining contract, it must be done through the labor ministry—and only unions officially recognized by the ministry were allowed to use its facilities.

At the same time that Perón was gaining the personal support of the workers, he was moving to gain control of the CGT. He saw to the formation of a number of new unions where organization formerly had been impossible (notable examples were the Packinghouse Workers of Buenos Aires and the Sugar Workers in Tucumán), and he encouraged the growth of older industrial unions that were loyal to him personally. For instance, the Textile Workers and Metallurgical Workers unions each had about 2,000 members in 1943; by 1946 they had 85,000 and 100,000 respectively.[5] Many important labor leaders were lured away from their former positions and into Peronist unions with very high pay or exceptionally good posts. Perón's efforts to obtain the support of labor paid handsome dividends in October 1945, when a spontaneous labor demonstration saved Perón's career, and again four months later, when the votes of the workers elected him to the presidency.

By mid-1945 an appreciable segment of the armed forces wanted to turn power over to an elected civilian government and return to the barracks; this group was especially opposed to the political maneuvering of Perón. On October 9, Perón was forced by this group to resign from all his official posts (by this time he was minister of war and vice-president, as well as minister of labor); three days later he was arrested and imprisoned on Martín García Island. The workers responded almost immediately. Pro-Peron union leaders like Luis Gay of the Telephone Workers and Cipriano Reyes of the Packinghouse Workers were instrumental in staging mass labor demonstrations on October 17. A day later, the central committee of the CGT, which had dragged its feet until then, called for a general strike. More important, on October 17 hundreds of thousands of workers filled the Plaza de Mayo, in front of the Government House, to demand the return of Perón. The anti-Perón military leaders, confused, disunited, and unwilling to resort to massive repression, acceded to the demands of the workers and released Perón. This was one of the most significant political events in Argentine history. As Baily put it:

October 17 was significant for many reasons. Perhaps most important was the fact that it intensified the workers' growing feelings of national identification by making them aware of their own political power. By their presence in the Plaza de Mayo they had forced what they considered to be the conservative anti-labor opposition to restore Perón—the symbol of the egalitarian nation they envisioned—to power. Now, after years of frustrated attempts to establish their influence within Argentine society, they had succeeded, and they were determined to enjoy and protect their new status.[6]

Shortly after Perón's return from Martín García Island, an Argentine Labor party was created by several of the leaders of the CGT. At its first national convention, the Labor party nominated Juan Perón as its presidential candidate and wrote a platform advocating constitutional government, industrialization, agrarian reform, nationalization of public services, and restrictions on the political prerogatives of the Church and the armed forces.

After he assumed the presidency, Perón continued the prounion policies he had inaugurated in 1943, while at the same time restricting labor autonomy. Wages were increased dramatically, and even though prices also went up, by 1948 real wages for unskilled workers were 37 percent higher than they had been in 1943; the real wages of skilled workers went up by 24 percent during the same period.[7] As a consequence, the share of salaries in terms of national income rose from 38.7 percent in 1946 to 45.7 in 1949.[8]

Perón also was careful to provide the workers with psychological as well as material benefits. He constantly referred to his administration as a government of the masses, and labor leaders were named to head the ministries of interior, foreign affairs, and labor.

Dissolution of the Labor party, government intervention in individual unions, and the imposition of personal friends in the top positions of the CGT gave Perón complete control over the labor movement. The constitution of the CGT was amended to state that the fundamental purpose of the organization was to support Perón and to carry out his policies.[9] Between 1946 and 1951, the number of union meetings held per year in greater Buenos Aires declined from 760,000 to 168,000, "reflecting the growing uselessness of such expressions of union democracy."[10] The number of working days lost to strikes declined by 99 percent.[11]

During Perón's second term (1951–55), his support from labor declined somewhat. By this time he had used up the financial reserves accumulated during the war, inflation had set in, and the agricultural sector of the economy had deteriorated. While the wages of urban workers continued to increase during this period, they did not do so nearly as rapidly as did the cost of living. Between 1948 and 1955 the real wages of unskilled workers declined 24 percent, and those of skilled workers 30 percent.[12] Nevertheless, the administration retained its image as a labor government; and even at the time he was overthrown by the military, Perón was more popular among Argentine workers than any other president before or since.

POST–1955 FACTIONALISM

Soon after the overthrow of Perón, the military government intervened in the CGT and many of the nation's unions, replacing Peronist leaders with military men. However, when the union elections were held a few months later, a majority of the unions reverted to Peronist leadership. The individual union leaders, however, were new. The "revolutionary" government banned from union office all those who had held office between 1946 and 1955, and thus an entirely new generation of union leaders emerged. A few unions were captured by the communists, while others reverted to the radical, socialist, or anarchist leadership of the pre-Perón period. These political sectors soon came to be referred to by the number of unions they controlled in 1957. The "62 organizations" referred to the Peronist-dominated group, the "19" was the communist group, and the "32" was the noncommunist, anti-Peronist group, which was also referred to as the "democratic unions." By 1958 there was also an "independent" sector, which included unions leaving the "62" or the "32."

During the Frondizi administration, a combination of honest union elections and government intervention cost the communists most of their former power; when reduced to a half-dozen small unions, this sector reorganized as the Movement of Syndicalist Unity and Coordination (MUCS). The "democrats" managed to gain control of several unions, largely as a result of fraudulent elections, but the "32" virtually disappeared, as most of its component unions passed into the Independent sector. Most of the honest union elections held at this time resulted in victories for the Peronists. The majority of the unions of white-collar workers, such as the commercial employees and government workers, belonged to the Independent sector, while those of blue-collar workers—the Metallurgical and Textile Workers, for example—were most often affiliated with the Peronist "62."

In January 1963, the CGT held its second national convention since the fall of Perón. The Independents and the "62" agreed in advance to divide equally the seats on the General Secretariat; however, real control of the CGT passed into the hands of the Peronists, as one of the "62" leaders, José Alonso, was chosen to be secretary general. Neither the "32" nor MUCS received any representation on the national governing body; by this time neither controlled any appreciable number of unions.

At about the same time that Peronism regained effective control of the national apparatus of the CGT, the "62" began to have serious internal problems. A so-called orthodox faction, led by Alonso, was opposed by a more moderate group under the leadership of Augusto Vandor, the powerful leader of the Metallurgical Workers Union. The *alonsistas* were in violent opposition to the administrations of Frondizi, Guido, and Illia; on the other hand, the *vandoristas*, while claiming to be loyal to Perón, were more prone to negotiation than to open confrontation with the government. The latter attempted, at almost all costs, to avoid renewed government intervention in the CGT. The possibility of intervention did not seem to bother the *alonsistas*, nor Perón himself; in fact, at times they seemed intent upon provoking it.

During the Illia administration, conflicts within the CGT were intensified, not just within the "62" but between that sector and the Independents. The latter conflict reached a peak in 1964, when the Peronist-controlled General Secretariat decided to embark upon the Plan de Lucha, which involved general strikes and the occupation of factories. The Independents, who had consistently opposed such a covert political action, responded by withdrawing from the CGT, leaving the two factions of the "62" to fight for control of the organization.

The struggle between Vandor and Alonso was resolved in favor of Vandor in February 1966, when the executive council of the CGT removed Alonso from his post as secretary general. Three months later a provisional council was established with Francisco Prado of the Light and Power Union as secretary general. The "orthodox" Peronists then took their unions out of the CGT, leaving in that body only the *vandorista* unions and the three or four unions then controlled by the communists. With Vandor in complete control of the "62," as well as the formal apparatus of the CGT, Alonso created a new sector called the "62 unions which stand up for Perón," usually referred to simply as the "62 *de pie.*" The "62 *de pie*" and the Independents soon rejoined the CGT, but the former refused to accept any formal leadership positions in the organization.

At the time of the 1966 revolution roughly 70 percent of the organized labor force belonged to Peronist-dominated unions. About 15 percent of the Peronist group was "nonaligned," while the rest were divided almost evenly between Vandor's "62" and Alonso's "62 *de pie.*" Communists controlled three or four small unions, which had perhaps 2 percent of the CGT membership. The remaining workers belonged to unions that were, at least nominally, Independent. About all the Independents had in common was opposition to Peronism and to the claim of that group that the CGT was simply the labor branch of the Peronist movement.

Not long after the 1966 revolution, the CGT split once again. This time the dispute involved the sort of position to take vis-à-vis the Onganía government. Those unions in favor of at least a degree of cooperation with the government, led by Vandor, formed what was generally referred to as the "participationist" CGT. The unions intent upon total opposition to Onganía and his administration united in an "oppositionist" CGT, also called the CGT of the Argentines, led by Raimundo Ongaro. Only the "participation-ist" CGT was officially recognized by the government, which intervened in several "oppositionist" unions and arrested many of their leaders. The po-sition of the "oppositionists" was summarized by Ongaro in the following manner:

The working class has as its historic mission the destruction of the capitalist system. The government of General Onganía is the expression of this system. Dictatorial in form, "gorilla" in tradition, "sellout" in content, it is beyond all redemption.... There will be no pact between the working class and General Onganía... nor will there be workers behind a new military coup.... The CGT of the Argentines does not propose the holding of elections, nor does it support any candidates—civilian or military—because it does not believe that this is the honest road to the solution of the country's problems. We reject the entire system and all the alternatives it offers. ...We are not disposed to negotiate our truth, our rights, or our dignity. Besides, we are convinced that the process of history leads inevitably toward the triumph of the people.[13]

In June 1969, Augusto Vandor was assassinated. A Peronist whose primary loyalty was to the workers rather than to Perón, Vandor had been the most powerful figure in the labor movement for more than a decade. Although at one time or another he opposed all post-Perón administrations, he always stopped short of an all-out confrontation; in the end, he could be counted upon to negotiate. His death left the "participationist" CGT virtually lead-erless and gave the far more radical Ongaro a greater opportunity to expand his power base, thus ending the possibility of a reunification of the labor movement in a manner acceptable to the government.

Within two weeks of Vandor's assassination, Onganía intervened in the CGT—a move he had refused to make during the first two years of his administration. The intervenor (who was not given that title, but instead was referred to as "the government's delegate for normalization of the CGT") was given all the power normally held by the CGT's elected leadership. The labor movement remained badly split until Perón ordered its reunifi-cation preparatory to the 1973 presidential election.

By the time he was elected for his third term in office, Perón could count on the loyalty of most of the labor movement. Its support had been necessary for the creation of the social pact that the CGT and the General Economic Confederation had agreed upon a year before. In the Perón administration's own words, the pact was signed

with the intention to do away with the injustices suffered by the workers for almost two decades as well as the economic imbalance and lack of control brought to us by the strategies of colonialism, for which this act requires and demands the unconditional observation of all. This Act of Commitment is not a circumstantial price and salary agreement. It is the definition of an irreversible political action to increase worker participation in the national income within a framework of a new concept of worker compensation and relations among the social sectors—a starting point for the process of national reconstruction and liberation.[14]

Back in power, Perón proceeded to purge the left-wing sector of Peronism that had become prominent during the brief tenure of the Cámpora administration. This purge did not just include the Montoneros and the left-wing of the Justicialist party but also those radical unionists that had emerged after the Cordobazos. In fact, in the late 1960s and early 1970s many rank and file had begun to openly attack the leadership of the union bosses loyal to Perón (many of whom had compromised with the Onganía regime) and were pushing for free elections for the selection of union delegates. Therefore, the old leader modified the old Law of Professional Associations in order to protect union bosses from workers' demands and possible attempts to oust them. Severe restrictions were also established to control initiatives by rank and file that could jeopardize the social pact calling for wage restraints. Factory lockouts were also outlawed. In return, wage hikes were decreed, and compulsory arbitration and job security were reintroduced. Moreover, labor leaders were appointed to a number of crucial posts within the administration, and their economic clout strengthened to induce workers' compliance. However, the consolidation of the power of the old union bureaucracy triggered a new wave of violence. Montonero and ERP terrorists began to kill right-wing labor leaders who were accused of "selling" the workers to the "capitalists" and thus preventing the proletariat revolution. Soon after Perón's election, José Rucci, the CGT general secretary, was assassinated. In response, union bosses organized their personal bodyguards to fight back and allegedly became involved with the criminal activities of the right-wing death squads of the AAA.

The internal situation within unionism became extremely tense after Perón's death in mid-1974. A power struggle soon developed pitting José López Rega, the reactionary minister of social welfare who wanted to impose a tough stabilization plan at the expense of labor, and the most powerful union bosses, headed by Lorenzo Miguel, who had replaced Vandor as the new leader of the UOM and the "62." In June and July 1975, the CGT called general strikes against the government decision to repudiate previously signed collective bargaining agreements. The strikes were the first ones ever launched against a Peronist administration. In the end, the CGT prevailed and López Rega was forced to quit, but in the process the administration of President Isabel Perón lost whatever credibility it had left. With the country quickly falling into chaos, divisions among union leaders deepened. Some, like Miguel, insisted that it was in the best interest of the labor movement to support an administration that the unions now virtually controlled. Others thought that the best way out of the crisis was to endorse the military coup in the making.

It was this split that in part explains the different treatment that the military meted out to some unions. The leaders most compromised with the Isabel Perón administration, above all Miguel, were arrested. The CGT, the "62," and many of the largest unions (telephone, metallurgical, textile, machinists, oil, and bank employees unions) were purged of their leaders and taken over by military intervenors. Equally important, the bank accounts and assets of the intervened unions were frozen. To prevent any meaningful opposition to the Proceso's policies, strikes and work stoppages were declared illegal. Labor intimidation went a step farther than during past authoritarian regimes as the security forces proceeded to kidnap and murder many rank-and-file factory leaders. Of all social groups, the working class was the one that suffered the greatest number of casualties during the dirty war, according to the 1984 CONADEP report. Nonetheless, the Videla administration spared those unions, many of them small, willing to compromise with the regime. For the union bureaucracy, what was important was to survive the purge that the military was enforcing and find a working relationship with the new authorities. In many ways, the execution and kidnapping of left-wing union leaders and rank and file played into the hands of the conservative old guard of the labor movement. The latter had always considered Marxism and the democratization of the internal organization of the union structure deadly to its interests. In 1977, labor leaders of both intervened and non-intervened unions created the "Commission of 25," an organization whose role was to represent a united front for labor demands before the military regime. However, labor's attempt to gain concessions from the Proceso proved extremely difficult. It could hardly have been otherwise as the objective of the military regime was to destroy those institutional mechanisms that had enabled the labor movement to exercise the socioeconomic clout it had achieved since Perón's first term. The strategy of the armed forces was to emasculate union power by dividing and conquering its leadership, reducing its economic resources, and subordinating unions to strict governmental control through the introduction of new regulatory schemes.

Divergence of opinions on how to react to the Proceso's unwillingness to make significant political and wage concessions led to a split within the Commission of 25. A moderate group of unionists inclined to cooperate with the military left the Commission of 25 and in 1978 formed the Labor Action Committee which, after further reshufflings and splinters, became the National Labor Commission (CNT). Those unions that remained with the Commission of 25 stiffened their opposition to the Proceso's policies. Their intent was to replace the old "62" as the hub for Peronist unionism. In April 1979, the Commission of 25 tried to launch a general strike but met with a violent government repression effort that frustrated its intended goals.

Only with the unraveling of the military regime and the relaxing of the repressive apparatus in 1981 was the labor movement capable of mounting an effective opposition. By that time, the Commission of 25 had renamed itself the CGT-Brasil, whereas the National Labor Commission had become the CGT-Azopardo (both names were taken from the streets where their headquarters were located in Buenos Aires). The two rival CGTs once again were divided on how to deal with the crumbling authoritarian regime. The moderate CGT-Azopardo still argued that more concessions could be gained from the military by negotiating than by going on strike. The CGT-Brasil, on the other hand, thought that only by adopting a combative stand could labor push the armed forces out of power. Accordingly, it called a first general strike in July of that year. Internal dissent was momentarily put aside after the Malvinas/Falklands fiasco. After December 1982, the two organizations sponsored three general strikes in an effort to speed the return to democratic process and to gain economic concessions. Finally, as the 1983 presidential elections came to a close, the two CGTs worked together in support of the Peronist candidate, and in 1984 they finally reunited in one CGT under the provisional leadership of four general secretaries. This arrangement was devised to appease different union factions in preparation for the CGT national congress that would normalize the status of the labor umbrella organization under the new civilian regime.

The labor movement continued to be plagued by internal squabbles for most of the Alfonsín administration. The composition of the factions varied over time, depending on the specific economic juncture of the moment. Splits originated over: (1) ideological issues, (2) political strategies in dealing with the Radical administration and the Justicialist party, and (3) personal rivalries among union leaders. One of these factions was the resurrected "62," once more under the leadership of Lorenzo Miguel. Between 1983 and 1985, Miguel was able to impose his control over the Justicialist party through the establishment of several alliances with other union leaders and party politicians. The Peronist electoral debacles in the first three years of the new democratic regime forced Miguel to relinquish his post of Justicialist party chairman, but he continued to remain a key political broker both within the PJ and the labor movement. The second faction was made up of the "Group of 25," a somewhat center-left grouping tied to the Justicialist party leadership. The *ubaldinistas* were the followers of Saúl Ubaldini, leader of the small Beer Workers Union, who had gained a reputation for organizing the strikes during the last period of the military regime. His combativeness earned him quite a personal following and one of the four general secretary posts of the CGT in 1984. The last faction was made up by the "Group of 15." It brought together many of the moderate unions that had participated in the CNT first, and the CGT-Azopardo later, and had in Jorge Triaca of the Plastic Workers Union and Carlos Alderete of the Light and Power Union two of its most prominent spokesmen. According to James McGuire, each of these factions adopted a different stance toward involvement in the Partido Justicialista. The "62" and "25" involved themselves actively (on opposite sides) in the struggle between the party's orthodox and renewal sectors. Both factions fought for key positions in party leadership organs and for choice slots on the party's candidate lists for national deputy seats, expending energy and resources to develop party-mediated forms of political influence. In contrast, the *ubaldinistas* and the "15" by-passed party and legislative channels, preferring to advance their interests by pressuring or bargaining with the national executive. The *ubaldinistas* staged general strikes and mass demonstrations to pressure the executive from the outside, whereas the "15" tried to influence the executive from within by bargaining with Alfonsín's advisors and cabinet ministers (for six months in 1987) by occupying posts in the labor ministry.[15]

Internal squabbles were momentarily set aside when in early 1984 the Alfonsín administration sent to Congress a bill designed by Labor Minister Antonio Mucci, a Radical union leader who had long opposed the Peronist domination of organized labor. The explicit goal of the Mucci Bill was to bring to an end the power of the Peronist union bosses. It called for minority representation in the executive committees of each union and government supervision of internal elections. In the past, labor bosses had used fraud and intimidation to prevent internal opposition, thus perpetuating their leadership. Freed from checks and balances, some of these leaders often acted in gangster-like fashion, ignoring the pleas of their rank and file and plundering union funds for their personal aggrandizement. The defeat of the bill by only one vote in the Senate compromised the whole Radical strategy to neutralize labor power.

From that point on the government alternated carrot and stick tactics with the labor movement. Unable to pass any reform through Congress, the Radical administration resorted to ad hoc negotiations with those leaders willing to cooperate. Conversely, union leaders were divided on how to respond to such tactics. Some leaders like Miguel and Triaca, while suspicious of each other, were often inclined to strike temporary deals with the Alfonsín administration. Previously labeled as "union thugs" by the president, these two bosses turned out on occasion to be his tactical allies in isolating or under-cutting the most radical elements of the labor movement. On the other hand, the union hard-liners found in CGT General Secretary Ubaldini their spokes-man. Ubaldini adamantly favored a tough stance that made use of continuous threats, rank-and-file mobilization, and general strikes to bring the Radical government to its knees.

In early 1987, Triaca and other pragmatic leaders grouped in the heter-ogeneous "15" unions came to the conclusion that Ubaldini's radicalism was becoming a liability. Thus, they decided to support the government eco-nomic plan in return for their involvement in the decision-making process. Alfonsín appointed Alderete to the powerful post of labor minister and granted higher than average wage hikes to those unions making up the "15." The accord, however, did not last long. Although strike activity diminished for a while, Alderete continuously undermined Alfonsín's economic team policies and after the September Peronist victory over the UCR in the congressional and gubernatorial elections, he resigned, thus ending the uneasy relationship.

As strikes and union militancy in general kept disrupting the administration economic policy, Alfonsín was forced to make major concessions in 1988 that the economic team had strongly opposed before. The most important one was the reintroduction of free collective bargaining, which allowed employers and unions to agree directly on wage hikes even if they exceeded governmental guidelines. In addition, Congress passed the same year a new Professional Associations Law that represented a clear victory for the labor leadership. In fact, the authority of the government to intervene in the way unions elected their leaders and dealt with internal matters was greatly restricted, which was tantamount to strengthening the union bosses' power.

Competition for labor leadership remained fierce throughout the 1984–89 period. In 1986, Ubaldini succeeded in his bid to become the sole general secretary of the CGT. Yet he could not count on the continuous backing of the other three factions. The volatility of the labor situation was in part due to the nearly equal strength across factions. Moreover, tactical alliances were made and unmade to keep any given faction from prevailing. In this context, Miguel gradually acquired the role of the "balancer," siding with either Triaca or Ubaldini when one or the other's position appeared to weaken.

The Peronist primary elections of 1988 saw the different factions still divided. The "25" threw their support to Cafiero, and Ubaldini decided not to take sides. On the other hand, Triaca and the "15," still burned by the association with the Alfonsín administration, found in Menem the chance to redeem themselves. They were later joined by Miguel and the "62." All factions eventually decided to support Menem once the La Rioja governor won the Peronist nomination, but it was the "15" that became crucial in the 1989 presidential campaign by providing money and organizational networks.

The labor movement believed that Menem's election would allow the labor movement to have the same socioeconomic clout that it had experienced during the heyday of Peronism. Menem's campaign promises of a "productive revolution" (creation of more jobs) and massive wage increases (*salariazo*) fueled such expectations.

However, Menem's honeymoon with labor was short-lived. His decision to embrace free-market economics took the unions completely off-guard. Menem realized that the main obstacle to the structural reforms advocated by his advisers was the labor movement. Therefore, he proceeded by slowly but steadily emasculating union power. In less than three years Menem accomplished more in diminishing the labor union influence in Argentine politics than did Radical and authoritarian administrations after 1955. Ironically, it took a Peronist president elected with strong union support to undo many of Perón's prolabor policies.

Menem's decision to attack the labor movement's vested interests rested not only on economic grounds. The unions had always claimed to be the backbone of the Peronist movement, and as long as they remained a powerful political actor, they represented a liability to his personal plans. In other words, if Menem wanted to transform the Peronist movement into a personal vehicle supporting his neoconservative political agenda, the union bosses had to be subdued. This is what Menem has tried to do between 1989 and 1992. His strategy did not differ from that of previous administrations. It consisted of dividing and ruling the union bosses. However, Menem could count on a crucial advantage over his predecessors. He was first and foremost a Peronist, and rallying support among the rank and file for strikes against him could prove difficult. In fact, the first few months of the Menem administration were relatively strike free. By counting on the surprise factor, Menem quickly moved toward rewarding those unionists willing to comply with his plans. Triaca was appointed as minister of labor, and other leaders of the "15" were given important governmental posts. From their official positions, the leaders of the "15" could dispense money and favors to their friends while keeping at bay their rivals within the union movement. However, the CGT general secretary refused to go along with Menem and soon became the focal point of labor opposition to the president's policies. Consequently, the labor movement split again in yet another power alignment, this time pitting *menemista* against *ubaldinista* factions. In October 1989, a special two-day congress of the CGT was convened. The *menemista* delegates gained control of the meeting's agenda and voted to replace Ubaldini with one of their own, Guerino Andreoni of the Shop Workers Union. Ubaldini, in retaliation, claimed that the meeting had been "packed" with *menemistas* and walked away from the congress along with those union delegates loyal to him. After that, the labor movement divided into two rival umbrella organization: the pro-Menem CGT-San Martín and the *ubaldinista* CGT-Azopardo. In this situation, Miguel and his "62" took an ambivalent position, refraining from attacking the government while avoiding the endorsement of the president's policies. However, this did not pay off, as the old union boss was incapable of securing fat wage increases for his union as he had in the past.

Once the split materialized, Menem switched to yet another strategy, acting as a mediator between the two rival CGTs while supporting behind the scene *menemista* unions in wage negotiations. In the meantime, the president began to push legislation that would make it increasingly difficult for the labor movement to mount any meaningful opposition to his plans. Menem first had Congress approve legislation that allowed the government to privatize most state enterprises. He also sent to Congress a bill restricting the right to strike. Once it became clear that legislators were dragging their feet, the president acted decisively and enforced the proposed law through a decree which bypassed congressional approval. In 1991, Congress approved an executive bill rewriting the labor code in a way that favored business over labor by increasing employers' latitude in hiring and firing.

All this legislation strengthened the government. The first round of privatizations allowed the administration to get rid of more than 60,000 employees. An additional 100,000 were shed from the state bureaucracy. On top of these measures, the administration kept salaries of government workers well behind the inflation rate, in part as a means to force early retirements.

The labor response was slow in coming. The unions most affected by the administration policies, that is, those representing government and state corporation employees, joined Ubaldini's CGT-Azopardo and stepped up confrontation by staging a number of strikes, but to no avail. A general strike in March 1990 was aborted as many unions withdrew their support. At the same time, the government effectively used the new legislation to break strikes by telephone and railway workers. Although Ubaldini kept attacking the government, he found himself increasingly isolated, as many union bosses preferred to negotiate one-on-one agreements with the administration and business rather than resorting to conflictual behavior that was not paying off. A final blow to Ubaldini's credibility came in September 1991, when he unsuccessfully ran for the governorship of Buenos Aires. He was humiliated on receiving only two percent of the vote.

In early 1992, the administration proposed new legislation attacking the last bastion of union power: its control over welfare funds and obligatory union membership. The deregulation attempted by the administration in these two fields was meant to reduce the unions' finances and their membership strength.

POLITICAL METHODS

In his analysis of the Peruvian labor movement, James Payne explains that there are three principal types of labor relations systems. The first, collective bargaining, is a system based upon economic coercion in which the strike is an effective withdrawal of labor; decisions, agreed upon by labor and management, are made at the firm or industry level, and are relatively independent of government action. Requiring a scarcity of labor and a neutral government, this system cannot be relied upon exclusively by Argentine unions. The second system, legal enactment, involves lobbying for laws to settle disputes; activity is centered upon influencing political parties or upon the formation of a labor party. This requires a stable electoral system and relatively efficient national bureaucracy, neither of which is prominent in Argentina. The third system, labeled political bargaining by Payne, involves coercion of the executive by means of violence or the threat of violence, which if not pacified may lead to the removal of the president by the armed forces. According to Payne, where political bargaining is used, "the concessions made to any group of workers will tend to be proportionate to the degree to which that group threatens the security of the executive."[16]

The methods employed by the Argentine labor movement have varied a great deal. Those used at any given time have depended upon two factors: the political group in control of the labor movement and the type of government in power. During the period of anarchist or syndicalist domination, when the national government considered the very idea of labor organization subversive, there was an attempt to destroy the state completely, as labor relied on general strikes, widespread violence, and even assassination. During the period of socialist control, when the national administrations were somewhat less hostile to labor, reliance was placed on legislative enactment—which failed almost as completely as had the violence of the earlier period. Between 1943 and 1955, when the government was openly sympathetic to the aspirations of labor, reliance was almost exclusively upon the goodwill of the president. Since 1955, labor has been badly split ideologically; it has confronted various types of governments and has used a number of different tactics.

Following the 1943 revolution, labor began to flex its muscles at the polls. In the presidential elections of 1946, 1951, 1973, 1983, and 1989 the bulk of the Peronist votes came from the urban working class. Labor votes also provided much of the margin of victory in 1958 and 1963. In 1958 the workers voted en masse for Frondizi—in accordance with the wishes of Perón, then in exile in Caracas—and in 1963 a large number of workers voted for Illia in an attempt to defeat General Aramburu. In the gubernatorial elections of 1962, it was the votes of workers in the suburbs of the federal capital that elected the Peronist labor leader Andrés Framnini to the governorship of Buenos Aires province.

Between 1955 and 1973, the electoral strength of labor lost much of its significance, as the armed forces refused to allow Peronism any opportunity to regain executive power. Thus, while the votes of labor certainly were influential in 1958 and 1963, the workers constantly were forced to choose between the lesser of evils, because Peronist candidates were prohibited. In 1962, when the Peronists were given full electoral freedom, their victories were quite ephemeral since they led to a military coup and the annulling of the election results. It was the potential strength of the Peronists—due to their labor support—in the elections scheduled for March 1967 that precipitated the 1966 revolution. With its electoral strength virtually nullified, the labor movement was forced to turn to other means of political expression.

Labor tried to intimidate President Frondizi by means of sporadic violence and a number of politically motivated strikes; however, it is the 1964 Plan de Lucha and the 1967 Plan de Acción that provide the best examples of political bargaining. Shortly after his inauguration, Illia was faced with labor demonstrations, inflammatory public speeches, and a general strike. Then in

May 1964, the executive committee of the CGT decided to adopt a plan of systematic seizure of industrial plants. The country was divided into eight zones, each of which was subjected to a twenty-four-hour demonstration of labor's ability to seize control of the sources of industrial production. Between May 21 and June 24, more than 11,000 plants were occupied by almost 3.2 million workers.

The ostensible purpose of the Plan de Lucha was to show labor's disapproval of the economic policies of the Illia administration. In actuality, its basic goal was to show the government's intrinsic weakness and to invite a military coup. The nation's labor leaders hoped that the government would react either by applying massive repression, thus making martyrs of the workers, or by doing nothing. President Illia chose the latter course, refusing to call out the army to dislodge the workers from the factories they were occupying. Under different circumstances this might well have been the proper response; however, in the Argentina of 1964 it satisfied no one. It failed to placate labor, it angered the business and industrial community, and it infuriated the leaders of the armed forces.

Soon after General Onganía assumed the presidency, he set out to eliminate inefficiency and featherbedding among the railway and dock workers. This soon led to the firing of many railway workers and the jailing of the leaders of the longshoremen's union. The response of labor was a general strike on December 14, 1966. The strike was quite successful, stopping 70 to 80 percent of the nation's transportation, industry, and commerce. Onganía almost immediately announced a delay in putting into effect the new railway work rules, and soon after that fired his ministers of interior and economics, both of whom were intensely disliked by labor. This action seems to have given labor a false sense of power, for on February 3, 1967, the central committee of the CGT decided to embark upon a Plan de Acción, quite similar to the 1964 Plan de Lucha.

This Plan was scheduled to begin with "agitation" between February 8 and 17, and then partial strikes between February 20 and 24; a twenty-four-hour general strike on March 1 was to be followed by forty-eight- and seventy-two-hour general strikes shortly thereafter. The leaders of the CGT appear to have felt that the Onganía government, having lost a good deal of popular support, could be forced into a more conciliatory stance. Onganía was expected to react much as Illia had in 1964 or to lose face by resorting to armed force.

Instead, the government responded in an altogether different manner. The day after the March 1 general strike the labor secretariat issued a decree depriving six large unions of their juridic personality, and the Central Bank announced the freezing of their bank accounts. The loss of legal status deprived these unions of their ability to represent their members at contract time and relieved employers of their obligation to retain union dues from salary checks; the latter cost the metallurgical and textile workers unions an estimated $200,000 a month. The blocking of union funds left these unions unable to meet their mortgage payments or to pay their officials. In the face of such vigorous, yet nonviolent, government action, the CGT central committee called off the subsequent states of the Plan. It obviously was beaten.

Union opposition to the Proceso was largely ineffective throughout the Videla administration (1976–81). General strikes were called by the "25" as late as April 1979 and again in July 1981 in attempts to force the military dictatorship to change its economic policies and make wage concessions. Reportedly, 30 to 40 percent of the work force adhered to the strikes, but their effectiveness was impaired by the tough repression employed by the military and the refusal of the CNT to join in. It was only after the economic situation began to unravel in mid-1981, and more so in the months following the Falklands/Malvinas debacle, that labor was able to gain the upper hand. Successful general strikes and mass street demonstrations were carried out between July 1981 and March 1983, adding to economic demands the demand that the military withdraw from power.

In asserting its political autonomy and defending its economic privileges, however, labor militancy has not been confined to weak Radical administrations or authoritarian governments. When in June 1975 President Isabel Perón, upon the recommendation of Interior Minister López Rega, decided to disallow a 100 percent wage increase that labor and capital had already negotiated, the CGT had no hesitation on what to do. For the first time ever, the CGT called a two-day general strike against a Peronist government. Without a base of support of her own, Isabel Perón was forced to capitulate. An even greater wage increase was decreed, and López Rega and his close associate, Economy Minister Celestino Rodrigo, had to resign. Labor came out from of this impressive display of strength as strong as ever and thus enabled to exercise its hegemony over the Peronist movement until the military coup a few months later.

During the Alfonsín administration, labor successfully resisted the president's attempt to pass the Mucci Law, which aimed at breaking Peronist dominance over the union movement. Furthermore, government-labor relations were exacerbated by the government's unwillingness to involve labor in the drafting of economic policy on the one hand, and on the other, by the high rates of inflation, which under the Radical administration eroded real wages by 56 percent. Further troubling the waters was the behavior of Ubaldini, who used strikes rather than negotiations. Between January 1984 and June 1989, Alfonsín had to endure thirteen general strikes called by the CGT leader. Nonetheless, rather than changing the government's course of action, they ended up by disrupting economic activity even further. Interestingly, strike activity diminished after 1987, as Menem argued that his candidacy could be hurt by a wave of strikes

During the Menem administration the use of the right to strike was severely curtailed and with it the major weapon that unions had in order to force a bargain. By 1992, the Argentine labor movement was experiencing one of the most difficult moments of its history. Under attack by an administration it had helped to elect, union leaders found themselves completely unprepared to cope with a challenge they could have never envisioned. Deeply divided among themselves, union bosses found it difficult to mount a counteroffensive against an administration that in its third year in office had gained appreciable popularity by bringing some economic stability to Argentina. The labor movement seemed in disarray and isolated.

Several factors help explain this new trend. First, large segments of the public opinion approved Menem's effort to restrict union power. Conversely, the union bureaucracy enjoyed much lower prestige than in the past, as many union bosses were perceived as furthering their personal interests rather than those of the people they represented. Second, unemployment and underemployment had grown steadily in the late 1980s. The result was a decrease in unionized jobs and a surge of workers employed in the underground economy, where unionization was minimal. Consequently the influence of the large unions, particularly in manufacturing, suffered a severe blow. Third, and closely related to the previous point, many unionized workers were afraid to go on strike for fear of losing their jobs in an economy still struggling to come out of a depression.

For the first time in decades, labor bosses look powerless. Their future, and, to a large degree, their survival will depend very much on how successful Menem is in completing his economic reform program. If the Argentine economy turns around, the labor movement will have to reconsider its political role and establish a new relationship with both government and business based upon greater responsibility, less demagoguery, and more responsiveness to the rank and file.

NOTES

1. Tomás Roberto Fillol, *Social Factors in Economic Development: The Argentine Case* (Cambridge, MA: MIT Press, 1961), p. 76.

2. Samuel L. Baily, *Labor, Nationalism and Politics in Argentina* (New Brunswick, NJ: Rutgers University Press, 1967), p. 64.

3. Robert J. Alexander, *Organized Labor in Latin America* (New York: Free Press, 1965), p. 37.

4. Baily, *Labor, Nationalism and Politics*, p. 26.

5. Robert Alexander, *The Perón Era* (New York: Columbia University Press, 1951), p. 31.

6. Baily, *Labor, Nationalism and Politics*, p. 89.

7. Bertram Silverman, "Labor Ideology and Economic Development in the Peronist Epoch," *Studies in Comparative International Development* 4, no. 11 (1968–69): 245.

8. United Nations, Economic Commission for Latin America, *Economic Devel-*

opment and Income Distribution in Argentina (New York: United Nations, 1969), p. 170, Table 39.

9. Alexander, *Organized Labor*, p. 46.

10. Baily, *Labor, Nationalism and Politics*, p. 116.

11. David Rock, *Argentina, 1516–1987: From Spanish Colonization to Alfonsín* (Berkeley: University of California Press, 1987), pp. 257, 313.

12. Silverman, "Labor Ideology," p. 245.

13. "Habla Ongaro," *Cristianismo y Revolución* 13 (April 1969): 20.

14. República Argentina, Poder Ejecutivo Nacional, *Plan Trienal para la reconstrucción nacional, 1974–1977*, cited by Juan Carlos D'Abate, "Trade Unions and Peronism," in *Juan Perón and the Reshaping of Argentina* ed. Federick Turner and José Enrique Miguens (Pittsburgh, PA: University of Pittsburgh Press, 1983), p. 64.

15. James McGuire, "Union Political Tactics and Democratic Consolidation in Alfonsín's Argentina, 1983–1989," *Latin American Research Review*, 27, no. 1 (1992): 37–38.

16. James L. Payne, *Labor and Politics in Peru: The System of Political Bargaining* (New Haven, CT: Yale University Press, 1965), p. 19.

CHAPTER 5

The Church and Catholic Lay Groups

Throughout much of Latin America, nineteenth-century politics was dominated by a bitter struggle over the proper relationship between Church and state, as the original cleavage between Conservative and Liberal parties was in large part a conflict between Catholic and anticlerical. The Catholic Church, which began playing a major political role, was gradually removed from the political arena, and in most of Latin America ecclesiastical issues have not been prominent in twentieth-century politics. To a certain extent, this pattern has been reversed in the case of Argentina. There, most ecclesiastical issues were settled fairly amicably during the nineteenth century, only to return following the military coups of 1930, 1943, 1955, and 1966. Like the other institutions so far examined, the Argentine Catholic Church has been highly politicized and plagued by deep divisions. The Church has usually pursued a policy of close ties with the government of the day in order to gain economic and political privileges and influence over specific policies, particularly on educational matters. The Church seems to have been at its strongest, at least in this century, during periods of authoritarian government. The reason behind this is reasonably simple. Authoritarian governments need to rely on the cooperation of the Church, if not to legitimize, at least to maintain social control over the population. In this way, when parties, labor unions, and other interest groups have been banned, the Church has acted as a mediator between civil society and the government. Conversely, in times of democratic government, the Church's influence has been limited and its relationship with the elected authorities more constrained; this is true in part because it has had to compete with other groups and in part because it has had to abide with more institutionalized rules to exercise its influence rather than the informal channels employed under authoritarianism.

The Church's influence has been declining in the last decade, but it still remains one of the most powerful institutions in the country. It makes its voice heard not just through the pulpit but also through a well-organized and financed media empire made up by a news agency (Agencia de Informaciones Católica), eight publishing houses, three newspapers, and several magazines. In addition, the Church receives free access to the state-run television and radio networks. Last but not least, in 1984 the Catholic Church controlled the majority of private educational institutions in the country; 1,348 primary schools, 964 secondary schools, and 10 universities.[1] In this chapter, attention is focused first upon the development of the Church-state relationship—emphasizing the major issues in the politicoecclesiastical conflict—and then upon those Catholic groups that have played an important role in contemporary Argentine politics: the Christian Democrats, the Catholic Nationalists, and the more recently formed Catholic Left. In its concluding section, the chapter analyzes the Catholic Church's role during the Proceso and the subsequent period of transition to democracy.

CHURCH AND STATE

After the attainment of independence, Argentine political leaders were by no means eager to alter fundamentally the relationship between Church and state that had existed for almost three centuries. The nation's first constitution, written in 1819, said in its very first article, "The Roman Catholic Apostolic Religion is the religion of the state. The government owes it the most effective and powerful protection, and all the inhabitants of the territory will respect it, regardless of their personal opinions." This document also guaranteed the Church permanent representation in the upper house of Congress in the person of a bishop and three lesser ecclesiastics and empowered the president to name bishops and archbishops from a list of three names submitted to him by the Senate. The 1826 constitution repeated these provisions almost verbatim and also gave the president the power to prohibit the circulation of papal messages.

The one major dispute between Church and state that arose with the attainment of independence was over the question of patronage. The government insisted that it had inherited from the Spanish king the right to appoint members of the upper clergy, while the Vatican claimed that the right of patronage was not transferable and that it must renegotiated by means of a concordat. In 1834, the Argentine government appointed a committee of thirty-nine theologians and jurists to study the question; of these, thirty-seven signed a report saying that: (1) ecclesiastical patronage is inherent in sovereignty; (2) the government has the right to prohibit papal documents and communications; and (3) the government can alter at will the boundaries of ecclesiastical units.[2] This report formed the basis of the government's position from 1834 until 1967. There were no concordats during this period; but as far as patronage was concerned, a tacit agreement was reached by the middle of the nineteenth century. When a vacancy occurred, the Senate sent three names to the president, who in turn forwarded one of them to the Vatican; the pope virtually always appointed this person, while at the same time insisting that he did not recognize the government's right of patronage.

The Church has often been criticized for its support of the dictatorship of Juan Manuel de Rosas (1835–52); but while the Church did freely ally itself with Rosas at the start, it was soon hopelessly subjected by him. Rosas originally gained the support of the Church by protecting it from its anticlerical enemies, but he soon came to use it to further his absolutism. By 1850, the clergy had been ordered to counsel obedience to Rosas's Federalist party and to condemn the Unitarians. Red, the Federalist color, had to be used in altar decorations, and Rosas's picture was ordered placed on all altars. With the fall of Rosas in 1852, the Church was certainly happy to be relieved of his subjugation; however, it must have been somewhat worried about the possible anticlericalism of his successors.

The constitution written the year after the overthrow of Rosas—which except for the period between 1949 and 1955 has been in effect ever since—declares in its second article that "the Federal Government supports the Roman Catholic Apostolic Faith." It also requires that the nation's chief executive belong to the Catholic Church; however, it gives him the right of ecclesiastical appointment and the power to "approve or withhold application of the decrees of the councils, bulls, briefs and rescripts of the Supreme Pontiff of Rome."

Under the liberal constitution of 1853, the relations between Church and state were serene for three decades. However, in 1884, during the administration of Julio Roca, religious instruction in the public schools was abolished, and four years later President Miguel Juárez Celman pushed through the Congress a law requiring a civil wedding ceremony. Both of these laws were bitterly resented by the Church and, indeed, by an appreciable segment of the country's more devout Catholics. It was the law abolishing religious education in the public schools that led to the First Assembly of Argentine Catholics, which met to discuss politicoreligious questions and ended up laying the groundwork for the establishment of Argentina's first Catholic political party, the Unión Católica. This party succeeded in electing a few congressmen, but it soon disbanded, as most of its members left to join the Civic Union in 1890. During the next four decades several other Catholic political parties were formed, but all were short-lived, and none was able effectively to escape the confines of the Federal Capital and a very few cities of the interior—most notably Rosario and Córdoba.

After the resignation of President Juárez Celman in 1890, the conflict between the Church and the Conservative party diminished appreciably. For the next forty years, the Church remained relatively neutral in the struggle between the Conservatives and their middle-class opponents in the Radical Civic Union. Relations between the Church and the UCR administrations of 1916–30 were also serene. Late in 1922, when the Chamber of Deputies was considering a bill to legalize divorce, President Yrigoyen made clear his opposition to the measure; he claimed that it was too fundamental a change to be accomplished by the normal legislative process and that to be valid it would require a constitutional amendment. Nevertheless, the Church was obviously pleased with the 1930 revolution, which replaced the second Yrigoyen administration with a military government headed by General José Uriburu.

Between 1930 and 1943, the major political goals of the Church were the continuance of the ban on divorce and the legalization of religious instruction in the public schools. With regard to the latter, the position of the Church was stated very succinctly in a pastoral letter of November 15, 1945, "On the Duty of Catholics at the Present Time."

The Church received the right to teach from God himself. It can then demand it in the name of God. But it can also demand it in the name of the interests of the child, who demands that he be given an integral education, making him aware of his divine origin, his immortal destiny, and the sacred rights of his person. It can also be demanded in the name of the Constitution and the Argentine tradition.[3]

General Uriburu, who was evidently quite sympathetic to the goals of the Church, did not remain in power long enough to be of any real use to that institution. While the conservative administrations of 1932–43 were certainly not hostile to the Church, neither were they interested in altering the existing Church-state relationship. Throughout most of this period the Church's major opponent was the Socialist party; neither the Radicals nor the conservatives seem to have considered ecclesiastical issues of any real importance (although there was a rapprochement between the Church and the conservatives following the 1934 Eucharistic Congress).

Following the 1943 revolution, religious issues became prominent in Argentine politics for the first time in almost sixty years as the revolutionary government set out to gain the political support of the Church. This was accomplished in a number of ways, the most important of which was an executive decree of December 31, 1943, which reestablished religious instruction in the public schools. The decree said, in part, "The teaching of the Catholic religion will be imparted as ordinary material in the plan of study."[4] The Church obviously was very happy with this decree. Pope Pius XII sent a personal message saying, "We are pleased with this recognition of the rights of the Church in the field of Christian education."[5] It is important to note that although religious instruction was something fervently desired by the Argentine Church for over half a century, the adoption of this measure was not a result of clerical pressure, but rather an attempt to enlist the future support from the Church.

This and other similar measures did indeed gain the support of the Church, not only for the revolutionary government but also for its candidate—Colonel Juan Domingo Perón—in the 1946 presidential election. For example, in 1944 Acción Católica announced that any of its members who criticized the government or its policies would be expelled from the organization,[6] and, more importantly, a pastoral letter issued shortly before the 1946 elections said: "No Catholic can join political parties nor vote for candidates who include in their programs: (a) separation of church and state; (b) revoking the legal stipulations which recognize the rights of religion; (c) secular education, or (d) legalization of divorce."[7] Since Perón's opposition was united in a Democratic Union that included these items in its platform, this pastoral letter was in effect saying to the nation's Catholics that they should vote for Perón or stay at home on election day. In what turned out to be a rather close election, it is entirely possible that the Church swung enough votes to put Perón in office.

While Perón had the near-total support of the Church in 1946, by about 1951 its position had changed to one of hesitant neutrality, and by 1955 to virtually complete opposition. The Church appears to have begun to worry about its relationship to the regime when Perón required religious instruction in the schools to include the idea that Peronism is "the one true faith of all Argentines." Then in September 1954, Perón began signing a series of anticlerical decrees, as a result of which "the drift of Roman Catholic priests, especially the younger ones, away from Perón became more like an ebb."[8] During 1954 and 1955, divorce and prostitution were legalized, a number of clergymen were jailed, and the ambassador to the Vatican was recalled. The biggest blow to the Church came in April 1955, when an executive decree discontinued religious instruction in the schools. The reason given by the government was that it "could not tolerate any interference or competition with its indoctrination of future citizens with pure Peronism and Justicialism."[9] By December 1954, the Church was beginning to protest energetically against these anticlerical measures, principally by means of pastoral letters and public demonstrations. Finally on June 15, 1955, Pope Pius XII excommunicated "all those who have trampled on the rights of the Church."

For a decade following the overthrow of Perón, the Catholic Church remained relatively aloof from partisan politics; however, this neutrality appears to have been abandoned, at least temporarily, in 1966 when the Onganía administration assumed heavy clerical overtones. Many of President Onganía's original appointments went to persons known only for their militant Catholicism; Jesuit advisers were prominent in most ministries; and the president seldom appeared publicly without the Cardinal Primate at his side. When, in the first public opinion poll taken after the coup, the people of greater Buenos Aires were asked to characterize the general orientation of the government, 15 percent responded with the label "clericalist"; the only label given with greater frequency (16 percent) was "nationalist," a term that itself has clerical overtones in Argentina.[10] This image of the Onganía administration was fortified in October 1966 when a concordat was signed with the Church—the first in the nation's history. In apparent violation of the constitution, this concordat gave the Vatican complete control over the selection of bishops and archbishops.

By early 1967, the government's image began to change somewhat. The Church hierarchy began to disassociate itself from the government, while at the same time being careful not to criticize Onganía or his administration. In January 1967, a reshuffling of the cabinet resulted in the replacement of most of the extreme right-wing Catholics with more moderate Catholic nationalists. By this time the number of *porteños* describing the government as clericalist had dropped to 4 percent, a level at which it remained for the remainder of the Onganía administration.[11]

By mid-1969, the Church had begun to shift from an essentially neutral position to one of moderate opposition. The official statement issued by the nation's seventy bishops after the 1969 plenary meeting, while not directly attacking the government, could easily be interpreted as critical of its policies. It called for liberalization "in all sectors where there exists oppression, the political, the economic, and the social." The statement also condemned economic liberalism, which it referred to as "the morally erroneous concept of global economics and business which makes profit its only or principal raison d'être and the subordination of the social to the economic imposed by the action of outside forces and internal pressure groups which is manifested in regional disequilibria, internal migration and rationalizations which bring about unemployment and insecurity."[12] For the first time in Argentine history, an openly clerical stance on the part of the government was not enough to retain the support of the Church.

THE CHRISTIAN DEMOCRATS

The Catholic inspiration of the original Argentine Christian Democrat party (PDC) was pointed out by one of the party's founders, who wrote: "Its ideological roots are nurtured essentially in the contents of the Gospel, the doctrine of the Fathers of the Church—expounded principally through the encyclicals *Rerum Novarum* of Leo XXII, *Quadragesimo Anno* of Pius XI, *Mater et Magistra* and *Pacem in Terris* of John XXIII, and the allocutions of Pius XII and Paul VI—and by the elaboration of Catholic thinkers."[13]

At the time of its formation the PDC contained two major factions. The first was a neoliberal group centered in Buenos Aires. Its members were almost all upper-middle-class professional men, primarily lawyers. They were quite anti-Peronist; interested mainly in the welfare of the middle classes, they were bitterly opposed to the social changes of the 1946–55 period. The second group came largely from the earlier Social Republican Movement.

Its members were somewhat younger than those of the first group and tended to come from the lower-middle class; most had belonged to Acción Católica or to the Liga de Estudiantes Humanistas. They were orthodox Maritainites, very much influenced by the Chilean Christian Democrats. Interested, at least to some extent, in improving the conditions of the working class, this group appears to have been more opposed to the political than the social policies of Perón.

Some indication of the original appeal of Christian Democracy may be obtained from the results of the 1957 election of delegates to a constitutional convention (which served as a sort of testing ground for the presidential, congressional, and provincial elections of the following year). Entering candidates in the Federal Capital and all twenty-two provinces, the Christian Democrats received 420,000 votes, or just under 5 percent of the total—a percentage that remained relatively constant through 1965. Women contributed 65 percent of the PDC vote.[14] In the Federal Capital, where the party received 5.7 percent of the total vote, it received 13.4 percent of the vote in upper-class districts, 8.7 percent in upper-middle-class and 4.4 percent in lower-middle-class areas, and 2.8 percent in lower-class neighborhoods.[15]

This general pattern of electoral support was repeated in the elections of 1958 and 1960, thus convincing many PDC leaders that their only hope for the future lay in increased working-class support. At the 1961 national convention, the younger, more social-minded wing gained control of the party from the more rigidly clerical faction. After that time the Christian Democrats made a concerted effort to gain the support of those Peronists of an essentially Social Christian persuasion, while insisting that "Democratic Christian doctrines must be paramount in any Peronist-inclusive alliance."[16] While this position appealed to those PDC members who wanted very badly to increase the party's electoral strength and who remembered the Catholic basis of much of the original Peronist movement, it completely alienated the right wing of the party, which thought of Peronism only in terms of the anticlericalism of 1954–55. This opening toward Peronism, usually referred to as the Línea de Apertura, had as its avowed purpose "the bringing together of all the popular sectors in a great national movement of Christian inspiration, one capable of realizing the spiritual, moral, cultural, economic, social and political revolution that the country demands."[17] This Línea de Apertura was first attempted in the 1962 elections in the provinces of Formosa, La Rioja, Catamarca, Jujuy, Chaco, Tucumán, Santa Fé, and Santa Cruz. In La Rioja the PDC included several Peronists in its list of legislative candidates. In Formosa the PDC nominated one of its leaders for governor and a Peronist for vice-governor; in that provincial capital a combined slate resulted in the election of a Peronist mayor and a PDC majority on the city council. In Jujuy, the Peronist movement simply supported all Christian Democrat candidates.

Before the 1963 elections, the Christian Democrats were among the first

to give their support to the creation of a broad-based National and Popular
Front, but they were also among the first to pull out, claiming that they
could not possibly support the "reactionary" economic program of the Intransigent Radicals. After their withdrawal from the front, the PDC began
to compete with that organization for the support of the Peronist movement.
Horacio Sueldo, the father of the Línea de Apertura and the Christian Democratic presidential nominee, praised the Peronists for "having achieved full
identity with Christian Democracy."[18] Late in the campaign, Sueldo resigned
his candidacy in favor of Raúl Matera, a well-known neurosurgeon who was
also a prominent Peronist leader (although without strong ties to the 1946–
55 regime). Matera's candidacy was very short-lived. The government almost
immediately announced that all votes cast for him would be considered void,
and Perón expelled him from the movement for having accepted the PDC
nomination. Thus at the very last moment Sueldo resumed the number one
position on the Christian Democrat ticket. He came in a distant fifth, with
about 435,000 votes (out of a total of 9 million cast).

The Christian Democrats did elect their first congressmen in this 1963
election; however, the seven PDC deputies owed their election almost exclusively to the change in electoral law that replaced the two-thirds incom-
plete list with proportional representation. Between 1963 and 1966, these
Christian Democrat deputies consistently opposed the Illia administration,
voting most often with their Peronist colleagues.

The Christian Democrats supported the Onganía administration during
its early days, as a number of PDC members accepted economic positions
in both the national and provincial governments. The most prominent of
these was Felipe Tami, who became president of the Central Bank, but
Christian Democrats were also appointed as economy ministers in the provinces of Entre Ríos, Córdoba, San Luis, and Chaco. However, within six
weeks of his inauguration, Onganía began to lose his Christian Democrat
support. By October 1966, his minister of economics had provoked the
resignation of Tami and his PDC staff; six months later the party's leaders
decided to make the break complete. Shortly after that the PDC virtually
disintegrated. A few of its members, primarily those belonging to its right
wing, continued to support the Onganía administration; some joined various
Social Christian groups identified with the Catholic Left, while most appeared to abandon politics altogether.

When political parties were allowed to reorganize in 1973, the former
Christian Democrats formed two separate parties. One, called the Christian
Popular party (PPC), joined the Peronists, MID, and other small parties in
the Justicialist Liberation Front (FJL, Frejuli). The other, the Christian
Revolutionary Party (PRC), joined the Intransigent Party (the former UCRI)
to form the Revolutionary Popular Alliance (APR); its leader, Horacio Sueldo,
was the vice-presidential nominee of this coalition, which received only 7
percent of the popular vote. In the congressional elections both the PPC

and the PRC won three seats in the Chamber of Deputies; the PPC also won a Senate seat.

The PDC returned to active political life by joining the Multipartidaria in 1982. As was noted in Chapter 2, since 1983 the Christian Democrats have remained a small, center-left party whose support has come predominantly from the middle and lower-middle classes of Metropolitan Buenos Aires. In the early 1980s, it once again allied itself with the Peronists for two basic reasons. First, through such an alliance the PDC could compensate for its chronic electoral weakness and manage to send one or two representatives to Congress. Second, the PDC, like its Chilean and Venezuelan counterparts, has fostered a political platform that cuts across social and economic cleavages. It is neither capitalist nor socialist, but it is guided by principles of "Christian humanism" and "social justice." Therefore, they have identified in the Peronists a natural partner who shares many of their ideals and whose political behavior they have tried to influence from within a coalition front. The Christian Democrats' point of view has been synthesized by one of their leaders as follows:

Christian Democracy proposes to replace the present model of [capital] accumulation with another one more compatible with the exercise of popular sovereignty. In its judgment, the dependent, speculative, concentrated capitalism is the principal obstacle to democracy. The latter is based upon popular mobilization and political party pluralism and comes systematically into contradiction with the demands of a diversified and transnational bourgeoisie which resists the class compromise.[19]

The PDC has also advocated the return to a strong and independent interventionist state which is to be the main vehicle of economic development. This should be accomplished by increasing state investments and welfare state benefits, imposing strict control over private domestic and foreign capital, and granting more delegation of authority from the federal government to the provinces. The PDC has also emphasized the greater role that parties should play to strengthen the democratic system.

In order to solve the country's problems, the Christian Democrats have advocated a social pact (*pacto de transformación*) aimed at involving not only government and peak business and labor organization, as advocated by the Peronists, but also the new social movements that have emerged during the last years of the military dictatorship. In so doing, they have argued, it is possible to "socialize power" and make institutions more responsive to the popular will. The problem with this approach is that it contradicts the emphasis on parties as agents of interest aggregation and by increasing the number of players entering the negotiation process, it makes it very difficult if not impossible to have any real chance of success. In the end, the true dilemma of the Christian Democrats, like the Socialists and the Communists, is the fact that Peronism long ago stole from them their core constituency.

The end result has been that the PDC remains today a party of intellectuals with little popular following.

THE CATHOLIC NATIONALISTS

Ever since the first presidency of Julio Roca (1880–86), many militant Catholics in Argentina have tended to equate liberalism with laicism and anticlericalism. In the political sphere, Catholic opposition to liberalism was almost completely impotent for half a century; however, during this period "there emerged a growing psychological resentment which longed for the opportunity to express itself in the institutional order. This brought with it the search for a radical change in the political realm, one which would return the situation to that which existed prior to 1880."[20]

During the late 1920s, the more militant Catholics became attracted to the extreme nationalist movements being formed. This attraction was due largely to the traditionalist and antiliberal stand taken by these new organizations. Many Catholics, especially those in Buenos Aires and Córdoba, saw in nationalism a means of turning back the clock to the pre-1880 period. They thought of liberalism in such terms as the following:

An objective foundation for the moral and legal order; rejection of all norms; uncertainty; a state which does nothing... life divorced from tradition... praising of the rights of man, the French Revolution, socialism and communism... dominance of intelligence... wordiness... the prototype is the petit bourgeois: mediocre, prudent, lacking in sacrificial spirit, wanting a tranquil life without complications, sentimental and insipid, if not cowardly.[21]

On the other hand, nationalism, at least as they saw it, was the antithesis of these values; it was:

a religious foundation for the moral and legal order; strict norms... certainty of revealed truth; a state which protects and exacts respect... life regulated by custom, history, tradition and legend... subordination of intelligence to the precepts of the Church and to the greatness of the fatherland... instead of words, concrete deeds realized with ardent enthusiasm... the prototype is the cavalier of the crusades: daring, sacrificing, wanting to dominate and to impose his will for the greater glory, honor and power of the Church and the fatherland.[22]

Catholic nationalists were pleased with the 1930 revolution that removed President Yrigoyen. They became overjoyed when they discovered that the provisional administration of General Uriburu was intent upon dismantling Argentine liberal democracy and replacing it with a form of corporatism patterned upon that of José Antonio Primo de Rivera in Spain. With the failure of the Uriburu experiment, and the return to liberalism under Presidents Justo, Ortiz, and Castillo, the Catholic nationalists devoted most of

their energies during the next decade to the formation of short-lived organizations, the editing of periodicals of scant circulation, and the rewriting of
Argentine history. Then came another military coup in 1943, and, as Marysa
Gerassi put it, "Although the nationalists did not participate in the coup,
though they did not even know its leaders' political position, and though
like the rest of the population they were taken by surprise, they viewed the
coup as their own revolution."[23] The Catholic nationalists became even more
convinced that this was the revolution they had been advocating when the
provisional government of General Pedro Ramírez dissolved Congress, reestablished religious instruction in the public schools, and appointed a number of prominent nationalists to government positions.

During the next two years, Catholic nationalism was near the pinnacle of
success. It appeared that all its old dreams were being realized: exaltation
of the Argentine nation, elimination of the political forces of liberalism, and
the return of the Church to a powerful position in the political system.
However, at the same time that a portion of the military was following a
course not dissimilar to that of Uriburu, another sector—led by Colonel Juan
Perón—was intent upon building a popular following and thus avoiding the
errors of 1931. By October 1945, the period of dominance by the Catholic
nationalists was at an end. When, with the support of the laboring masses,
Perón assumed control of the government, Catholic nationalism was replaced
with a form of popular nationalism that stressed social justice. Many of the
Catholic nationalists, especially the more aristocratic ones, began moving
into the opposition at this time; a few remained loyal to the Peronist regime
until 1954, when the government assumed a violently anticlerical posture.

Again following the 1955 coup, Catholic nationalists appeared on the
scene. Indeed, during the brief administration of General Lonardi (September–November 1955) theirs was the dominant voice in the government.
Prominent nationalists were named to head the ministries of foreign affairs,
labor, and war; another, who happened to be Lonardi's brother-in-law, became presidential secretary. At this time the nationalists appear to have
attempted to establish a sort of Peronism without Perón. According to Tulio
Halperín Donghi:

For the nationalists the solution was to be found in a pilgrimage to the sources of
Peronism: in a return to a clerical-military regime which would concede a place in
its structure to the forces of labor. . . . They hoped to obtain the aid of the working
masses who would prefer this to a complete dismantling of the structures built during
the Peronist decade.[24]

Unlike the case in 1930 and 1943, in 1955 the Catholic nationalists had
relatively little support in the armed forces, which were dominated by liberal
anti-Peronists. On November 13, when Lonardi tried to replace his liberal
minister of the interior with an extreme nationalist, he was overthrown in a

bloodless palace coup, and with him went the Catholic nationalists—several of whom were briefly imprisoned.

Beginning in 1956, the Catholic nationalists began to form a number of political parties—something they had been loath to do earlier, claiming that parties were appendices of the liberal state that they wanted to abolish. The most important of these nationalist parties was the Unión Federal Demócrata Cristiana (UFDC), which according to its founders was established for two reasons: "In the first place, the necessity to express a political philosophy which, true to the Catholic tradition of the country, is rooted in the historical exigencies of Argentina and in the social and economic necessities of its people; in the second place, the need to represent politically those Argentines who do not feel represented by the traditional political parties."[25]

With the failure of the UFDC in the 1957 elections (it received about 2 percent of the total vote), most of its leaders decided to support Arturo Frondizi in the presidential elections of the following year. Many of them were rewarded with posts in the 1958–62 Frondizi administration.

THE CATHOLIC LEFT

If the Catholic nationalists, who maintained a prominent position within Catholic lay groups into the 1970s, were to the far right, new groups emerged on the left partly as a result of the two Vatican councils held in Rome in the early 1960s. The term *Catholic Left* appears to have been coined by a faction of the Christian Democrat Party in 1961 when Sueldo's policy of an "opening to the left" was adopted. It has been used in reference to a large number of Catholic groups both clerical and laic. The one thing that these groups have in common is adherence to what is usually referred to as the theology of liberation. According to a North American scholar,

the theology of liberation has been developed at least in part as an attack on older dualist theology which attempted to maintain a rigid separation of the religious and profane spheres. Among its most basic premises has been the notion that dualist theology merely served to bolster the status quo by effectively removing the Church, a potentially influential social critic, from public involvement in sensitive social and political issues. . . . The theology of liberation affirms that the Christian eschatology, God's plan for mankind, entails not only a salvation after death, but, more fully, a liberation from the structural sin that plagues man's temporal existence.[26]

This view encourages Catholics to attempt to identify this structural sin, and also to eliminate it. In the late 1960s and early 1970s, there was general agreement within the Catholic Left that the basic "sin" was capitalism; however, there was some disagreement as to the means to be used to eliminate it. One group, under the intellectual guidance of Juan García Elorrio, was convinced of the necessity of the violent overthrow of the existing system by means of guerrilla action. Their hero-martyr was Camilo Torres, the Colombian guerrilla-priest. One of the major villains, from their point of view, was the top level of the Church hierarchy. Other groups were more moderate in the means espoused to bring about widespread change. This is particularly true of most clergymen in the Catholic Left.

THIRD WORLD PRIESTS

In August 1967, fifteen bishops from Third World nations issued a statement calling for the implementation of Pope Paul's social encyclical *Populorum Progressio*. This statement was almost immediately countersigned by 270 Argentine priests who soon thereafter formed an organization called the Movement of Third World Priests. That this was a Catholic Left group was made clear in its initial statement of principle, which said, "We are obliged to join in the revolutionary process for urgent, rapid change of existing structures and formally to reject the capitalist system. . . . We shall go forward in search of a Latin American brand of socialism which will hasten the coming of the New Man."[27]

Many of the Third World Priests had gained their early experience among working-class groups who were solidly Peronist. It is not surprising, then, that this movement immediately endorsed Peronism. This attachment seems to have been based on a rather naive view of both Perón and his movement. Like many who came to Peronism in the late 1960s and early 1970s, they tended to see in Peronism only what they wanted to see—for example:

Peronism gave force, identity and victory to the Proletarian Movement. It is obvious that Perón did not create the proletariat, but it was he who unified it, gave it objectives, and led it. . . . [Now] it is necessary to move on to the revolutionary organization of the people around their historical representative—Peronism—and to the formulation of an aggressive revolutionary policy. . . . Peronism is the inexorable road to Socialism.[28]

Such an open endorsement of a political party by a group of priests was justified on the grounds that Peronism is not really a political party, but instead is a "movement," a "social force," and "the highest level of consciousness attained by the Argentine working class."[29]

The political program originally adopted by the Third World Priests called only for raising the consciousness of the poor and publicly denouncing the injustices of capitalism and imperialism. However, as the priests discovered that the oppressed groups they wanted to assist had neither organization nor leadership, they decided that they had to assume these responsibilities as well, at least temporarily. They soon began to organize peasants and shantytown dwellers and to lead labor demonstrations; they were accused of also aiding, if not taking an active part in, terrorist organizations. According to Paul Lewis, they operated a network of clandestine clubs throughout the country, which they used for consciousness raising [*conscientización*] among students and workers. Their ties to the Church did not prevent them from cooperating with Marxist groups, either, and although they insisted that they were nonviolent, some of them were closely involved with the Montoneros, providing safe houses to hide guerrillas, arms, and underground presses. One, Father Alberto Carbone, was indicted as an accomplice in the kidnapping and murder of ex-president Aramburu. During the *cordobazo*, third world priests were conspicuous organizers of barricades and pickets.[30]

The first public protest of this group took place at Christmastime in 1968. Several members of the movement took part in hunger strikes, refused to celebrate the Mass on Christmas Eve, and held a series of press conferences where they denounced social, economic, and political injustice in Argentina and criticized President Onganía for his failure to do anything to alleviate them. Some also picketed the presidential office building.

These radical priests exercised considerable influence among young university students and members of Catholic Action. Among them could be found Mario Firmenich who later would become a Montonero leader; Juan García Elorrio, a former seminarian and editor of *Cristianismo y Revolución*; Emilio Maza, a student leader at the Catholic University of Córdoba; and Rodolfo Galimberti, who would eventually take the leadership of the Peronist Youth. Third World Priests not only were apologists of Peronism, but they also spent a great deal of effort in attempting to facilitate the return to power of Juan Perón—which many of them seemed to see almost as a panacea. One of the leaders of the movement wrote that their goal was "not the peaceful return of a venerable old man, but the combative return of a Leader and all the movement he represents. . . . His return implies the return to power of the people and the resumption of the National, Democratic and Proletarian Revolution."[31]

That this was little more than wishful thinking became clear very soon after Perón returned to power. In fact, his return marked the beginning of the end of the Movement of Third World Priests. It had been relatively easy to obtain agreement within the movement that Perón must resume the presidency; it was much more difficult, indeed impossible, to find agreement on the role the movement should play either within or outside a Peronist government. Some members wanted to give virtually unqualified support to Peronism, but to remain aloof from its internal conflicts; others would struggle within Peronism for a more revolutionary policy; and still others quickly became disillusioned with a Peronism that they decided was the voice of a labor elite unconcerned with the plight of the marginal elements of society. This split, plus the assassination in May 1974 of the movement's best-known leader, Carlos Múgica, virtually ended the group's political activities.

THE CHURCH AND THE PROCESO

The Catholic church as an institution, and particularly its ruling body, the Argentine Episcopal Conference (*Conferencia Episcopal Argentina*, CEA) which is made up of about eighty cardinals, bishops, and archbishops, bears heavy responsibilities for a role that has often been that of complicity with, and justification for, the military regime's brutal repression that took place during the late 1970s.

On the eve of the 1976 coup, General Videla and Admiral Massera met privately with archbishop Adolfo Tortolo, the chairman of the CEA and vicar general of the armed forces.[32] Although the content of the meeting was never made public, and probably never will be, it is reasonable to speculate that the military commanders wanted to secure the support of the Church upon embarking in the Proceso. Such support was indeed crucial in view of the fact that similar military takeovers in Brazil (1964) and Chile (1973) had found in the Catholic Church their most outspoken critic, around which civilian opposition could organize. Because of its following across social classes and the protection exercised by the Vatican, military governments in those two countries found it extremely difficult to silence the Church's charges of human rights violations, which increasingly constituted an embarrassment both domestically and internationally for the legitimation of their authoritarian regime. In the end, it appears that a deal was made. The junta leaders assured Tortolo and the CEA that it was going to act to defend the values of the "Western and Christian civilization" cherished by the Church against the threat posed by the atheist Marxist guerrilla movement. They also promised to strengthen the Church's privileged access to state protection and financing. In addition, the military reminded the CEA that

the "terrorists" of the 1960s and 1970s had exercised their early militancy as members of university action groups like Catholic Action and had received the formal blessing of priests linked to the Third World Movement. . . . members of the Bishops' Conference were even shown videos of interrogation sessions, during which prisoners confessed their links to certain priests.[33]

The arguments and goals espoused by the military found sympathy within the CEA. The armed forces' view of the Church as an instrument of social control and a pillar of the authoritarian state did coincide with the ideals of Catholic nationalism that were shared by many bishops.[34] By the way they behaved, it seems that the Catholic Church hierarchy had more in common with the principles of national security than with those of the Second Vatican Council. The pastoral letter of May 1976, the first since the coup, set the tone for the CEA's ambiguous behavior toward the regime. In the first part it condemned the abductions, torture, and summary executions without specifically naming the armed forces, but then it added that the military intervention had been carried out for the "common good." The document also emphasized that "we should remember that it would be a mistake to believe that the security forces can act with the purity of action of peacetime when there is already blood on the streets. It is necessary to accept some constraints on our liberties as demanded by the circumstances."[35]

Four other pastoral letters were issued between 1976 and 1981, all of which repeated the CEA's "concern" for the violation of human rights regarded as "sins." However, they always fell short of an open attack against the Proceso. In practice, the executive commission of the CEA gave justification and legitimation to the regime's policies and publicly denied knowledge of violation of human rights. While they refused to intercede for the families of those who disappeared, they seldom missed an opportunity to be seen amicably mingling with the military authorities during the celebration of national holidays or at public events. Jimmy Burns insists that such public display made it quite plain that the hierarchy of the Church was an integral part of the new political order.[36] It came no surprise when, in 1977, Tortolo declared, "The Church thinks that the government of the armed forces is a necessity at this time. . . . Therefore, we believe that the armed forces, by accepting the heavy and serious responsibility of the hour, will comply with their duty."[37]

Besides the CEA, within the clergy three main groups could be identified: (1) a sizable group of collaborators made up primarily of military chaplains; (2) those who preferred to ignore what was happening or disagreed with it but were afraid to speak up, which constituted the bulk of the Church; and (3) a minority that denounced the armed forces' repression and actively collaborated with human rights groups.

The military chaplains, including bishops, were instrumental in actively supporting the repression effort. Bishop José Miguel Medina, who replaced Tortolo as vicar general of the armed forces in 1981, reportedly said, "Sometimes physical repression is necessary, is mandatory, and as such, is legitimate."[38] A survivor of the armed forces' extermination campaign interviewed by CONADEP reported that during torture, Medina had tried to persuade him to collaborate with the authorities and told him that the military officers were acting for the good of the country. Medina never denied the allegations. An even more outspoken supporter of the military was the vicar of the army, Bishop Victorio Bonamín, who was calling for a coup as early as 1975. Bonamín went as far as to say that "the fight against subversion is a fight for the Argentine Republic, for its integrity, but also for its altars. . . . This fight is a fight for the defense of morality, human dignity, and in the end is a fight for God. . . . For this I ask the divine protection for this 'dirty war' in which we are engaged."[39] Military chaplains with individual units, often present during torture sessions, tried to gain information from detainees and gave moral encouragement to those military officers who, at times, had doubts about their actions.[40] A security officer testified that after having executed a prisoner, Father Christian Von Wernich, a military chaplain, told him that "what we had done was necessary; it was a patriotic act and God knew it was for the good of the country."[41] A former prisoner declared that upon his telling chaplain Pelanda López that he could no longer endure torture, the father replied, "You have no right to complain about torture."[42]

The second group, probably the largest within the clergy, may have worried about the military repression, but its members refrained from openly condemning it as such an act would have meant, as Mignone points out, "breaking" with the establishment.[43] In other words, political compromise and close ties with the government seemed to be the paramount preoccupation for both the top hierarchy and their subordinates. For some, this conciliatory behavior was more conducive to influencing the authorities than was open confrontation. For others, taking a tough stance could be interpreted as siding with the terrorists, an unacceptable act.

The third group, comprised of those few who, in the face of constant intimidation, denounced the abductions, stayed close to the families of the disappeared, and collaborated with human rights organizations. They were led by a handful of bishops, Enrique Angelelli of La Rioja, Carlos Ponce de Leon of San Nicolás, Jaime de Nevares of Neuquén, Miguel Hesayne of Viedma, and Jorge Novak of Quilmes. The first two paid with their lives for their defiance of the military authorities. They died in car accidents under mysterious circumstances that had all the characteristics of an ambush set up by the security forces. Other priests, nuns, and seminarians who had been suspected of left-wing leanings or, more simply, had voiced their dissent were arrested, and the most fortunate were told to leave the country. The others were either executed or simply disappeared. When physical repression was not sufficient, the CEA intervened by using its censorship powers to discipline recalcitrant clergy.[44] The CEA's desire to avoid any quarrel with the regime was equally clear when it downplayed the awarding of the 1980 Nobel Peace Price to Adolfo Pérez Esquivel, a well-known Catholic and human rights activist.[45]

Catholic lay groups mirrored the splits existing within the clergy. Many members of Catholic Action and other groups that had been active in helping shantytown dwellers became prime targets of the security forces. The same is true of those laypeople who at the risk of their lives organized associations in defense of human rights. Catholic schools, which comprised the majority of private educational institutions in the nation, underwent strong repressive measures as the military believed that they were a breeding ground for terrorists because some Montoneros had graduated from them. To this end, the government issued a decree that enabled it to dismiss teachers in Catholic schools regarded as "subversive." The measure, which in different times would have created an uproar, was tacitly accepted by the CEA.

Catholic nationalist groups, on the other hand, actively supported the authoritarian regime as in the past. During the Proceso, conservative Catholics were appointed to the Supreme Court while others headed the education and justice departments and the National University of Buenos Aires.

In foreign policy the Church displayed ambivalent behaviors. In 1981, it played an important role in averting a war with Chile over a territorial dispute regarding the Beagle Channel in the South Atlantic. This strong stance was also facilitated by the Vatican's intention to prevent a war between two Catholic countries. As a matter of fact, it was through Vatican mediation that in 1984 Argentina and Chile signed a treaty ending the long-standing conflict.

However, when the armed forces decided to occupy the Falklands/Malvinas, the Church was carried away by the nationalistic fervor that swept the country; the upper clergy gave unconditional support to the military's initiative. It is worth noting, though, that the CEA, like the labor movement, sensing the increasing weakness of the regime after General Videla had transferred power to General Viola, became increasingly critical of the military government. In 1981, the CEA for the first time publicly broke with the Proceso and endorsed in a pastoral letter the call for the return to democracy. Criticism of the war against Great Britain came only from the pro–human rights groups within the Church, namely Pérez Esquivel, Bishops de Nevares, Novak, Federico Pagura, and their followers, but their plea was ignored by the CEA.[46] On the other hand, bishops, military chaplains, and religious-related media justified the military gamble on theological grounds, as if it were a new crusade of Catholicism against barbaric Protestantism. As Bishop Manuel Menéndez wrote, "We Catholics fight for peace, but we also know that the Fourth Commandment tells us to love our country, and, if necessary, give up our lives for it. In the present circumstances, the commandment is quite clear: if they attack us, we have to defend ourselves." Bishop Menéndez failed to mention the fact that it was the Argentine Army that attacked first.[47]

After the defeat in the South Atlantic, the Church joined labor and political parties in convincing the caretaker administration of retired General Bignone to accelerate the timetable for the new presidential elections. During this phase, bishop Justo Laguna of Morón played an important role as a mediator between the outgoing military government and the civilian political forces in order to smooth the transition process. At the same time, the CEA kept a low profile during the election campaign of 1983, avoiding partisanship. That did not mean that all members of the Church followed suit; quite the contrary. Antonio Plaza, the ultraconservative archbishop of La Plata and one of the strongest supporters of the Proceso, is a case in point. Plaza had been, throughout his career, a politically active member of the CEA. Invariably, he sided with authoritarian governments from which he obtained considerable influence over educational and financial matters in the Buenos Aires province. In 1983, he was one of only two bishops that approved the self-amnesty decree that the armed forces issued before withdrawing to the barracks. During the same year, he publicly supported the candidacy of Herminio Iglesias, the right-wing Peronist candidate for the governorship of Buenos Aires. Other conservative clergy, while less outspoken about their political preferences, privately sympathized with the Peronists. In fact, the old guard of the Peronist movement, represented by Luder and Iglesias, had traditionally been tied to the Church. The Radicals, on the other hand, had a long-standing reputation for being "anticlerical" and close to Jewish, Masonic, liberal, and progressive Catholic circles. Moreover, Alfonsín's clear stance on the human rights issue created uneasiness among many bishops and priests who had been associated with the Proceso. At any rate, religious issues (abortion, divorce, Catholic education) remained conspicuously absent from the campaign as Luder and Alfonsín, as well as the CEA, wanted to prevent any such polemics.

THE CHURCH AND THE RETURN
TO DEMOCRACY

From the end of 1984 on, relations between the Church and the Alfonsín administration became progressively more difficult. The conservative nature of the Argentine Catholic Church was seen once again when the government lifted censorship provisions implemented by the Proceso. Clergy and lay groups alike openly attacked the government for allowing the spread of prostitution, homosexuality, and pornography. In their view, Marxist and liberal elements were infiltrating and corrupting the country's schools and cultural life as part of a government plot to destroy Christian and Western values and, in the end, the Church as an institution. Arguments depicting democracy as evil and prone to moral corruption or just as a disguised means to promote a Marxist takeover had been heard many times before. What was troublesome for the new democracy was the fact that eight years of harsh dictatorship had apparently had little impact on those people's minds. Alfonsín responded with moderation but could not avoid an open confrontation when in 1985 he sent to Congress a bill regulating family relations. The Family Law gave equal legal rights to both legitimate and illegitimate children. It also eliminated the archaic *patria potestad* legislation, which gave only to men the right to make decisions over their children's upbringing and finances, even when the father had walked away from his family.[48] The bill was eventually passed, but not without a considerable lobbying effort on the part of the Church hierarchy, which was joined by Peronists, provincial parties, and even some UCR representatives.

The other major battle occurred over the proposed divorce bill in 1986. Unlike many Latin American countries that had legalized divorce long before, in Argentina the whole issue remained taboo leading to many anachronistic situations. For instance, it had become common for wealthy Argentines to leave their spouses and then marry someone else in Uruguay,

Chile, or Brazil and return back home, where they "legally" could start a new family. Those who could not afford such an expedient just ignored the whole issue and moved in with their new companions. In any case, the end result was always the same, an increasing number of children born outside wedlock, a number estimated to be around half a million at the time.[49] If the Catholic Church was not willing to adjust to the changed times, Alfonsín was, but it took him some time. The Church fiercely opposed the bill and mobilized once again the support of conservative members of Congress, labor, and the military. The bill's approval was portrayed by a Catholic weekly as the beginning of the end because "after divorce we can expect . . . the legalization of abortion, drugs, euthanasia, and homosexuality."[50]

All things considered, both laws were a clear victory for Alfonsín. By the same token, their passage demonstrated the Church's inability to steer events according to its own wishes once decisions were open to discussion in a democratic environment. Furthermore, it showed the Church's incapacity to come to grips with its own past and make the necessary changes to adapt itself to the challenges posed by a young democracy and a society in transition. The CEA has adamantly refused to promote self-criticism for its complicity during the Proceso, as requested by Bishops de Nevares and Novak. Even less outspoken bishops like Laguna, while rebuffing any churchly responsibility, admitted that "today I cannot say that my soul is at peace, because if it is true that we [the Church] spoke clearly, not always was our denunciation accompanied with gestures and concrete action."[51] The CEA's silence on those matters has created a profound chasm between the clergy and many laymen. This has important implications for the Church's pastoral future because, as Pérez Esquivel commented, "A Church that refuses to recognize its own martyrs is a Church that has lost its soul."[52] However, if the CEA and the Catholic Right have not apologized, neither has the Third World Priests movement, whose links with the Montoneros were used by the security forces to justify their barbaric repression.

During the Menem administration some members of the Church's top echelon continued to show their conservatism. In 1991, Buenos Aires Archbishop Cardinal Antonio Quarracino attacked the Health Ministry's decision to distribute free condoms as a safety measure against AIDS by saying, "it seems like an invitation or a call for young people to participate in homosexual relationships." The cardinal also vehemently attacked the spread of pornography, prostitution, and drugs that in his view made the campaign against AIDS useless.[53] On the other hand, the progressive wing of the bishops began to switch their focus from human rights to general social issues. At the annual Episcopal Synod convened in San Miguel de Tucumán in November of 1991, some bishops expressed their criticism for what they perceived as "the lack of concern for the suffering of the poor in various sectors of society, and even within the government." The most outspoken critic of the Peronist administration economic policy was Monsignor Geraldo Sueldo,

Bishop of Salta. Sueldo attacked an earlier statement by the president, who had declared that only those who do not want to work cannot find jobs in Argentina. Bishop Sueldo reportedly stated that "many people do not work because they cannot, not because they do not want to."[54] Concerns were also voiced by some bishops about the staggering corruption and "frivolity" involving administration officials. Menem reacted bitterly to the remarks, which were given wide coverage in the press. Cardinal Quarrancino toned done the polemic at the end of the Synod, but nonetheless the charges constituted an embarrassment for the administration, particularly in view of the fact that those criticizing were moderate bishops who flatly exposed the absence of a well-defined social policy in Menem's reform program.

What role is the Church going to play in the process of democratic consolidation? So far the signs have been mixed. As noted, the CEA and important sectors of the laity have remained as conservative as ever. The Catholic Church has adamantly defended its vested interests and has allied itself with traditional partners like Peronist labor and the military to oppose governmental initiatives not of its liking. On several occasions the CGT's general secretary, Ubaldini, rallied Church support in his attacks on the government economic policies. Metalworkers union leader Lorenzo Miguel, on the other hand, joined the Church in opposing the Divorce Law (Ubaldini remained neutral on the matter). In regard to the military issue, the Church advocated a presidential pardon in the name of "national reconciliation" long before Menem granted it. Aside from the rhetoric, the truth is that the pardon, while helping the armed forces, would automatically forgive the Church's responsibilities during the Proceso. Moreover, many clergy hardly disguised their sympathy for fundamentalist Catholics like Muhamed Ali Seineldín and Aldo Rico, the *carapintada* leaders who seem to personify the ideals of Catholic nationalism. In all likelihood, the Church will remain politically involved in the years to come and will position itself along with the country's conservative institutions (i.e., the military and orthodox Peronism). Although its influence has been weakened, partly as a result of its unwillingness to change and its authoritarian legacy, the Catholic Church will remain a crucial player. Until there are attitudinal changes within the upper clergy about the Church's mission and its relationship with political power, the commitment of Argentine Catholicism to democracy will remain an open question.

NOTES

1. Jimmy Burns, *The Land That Lost its Heroes* (London: Bloomsbury, 1987), p. 22.

2. J. Lloyd Mecham, *Church and State in Latin America*, rev. ed. (Chapel Hill: University of North Carolina Press, 1966), p. 231.

3. *Criterio*, 18, no. 923 (November 22, 1945), p. 497.

4. Decree 18,411, quoted in John J. Kennedy, *Catholicism, Nationalism and De-*

mocracy in Argentina (Notre Dame: University of Notre Dame Press, 1958), p. 196. This religious instruction was not compulsory; if parents so desired, their children were given "moral instruction" instead.

5. Quoted in Virgilio Filippo, *El Plan Quinquenal, Perón y los Comunistas* (Buenos Aires: El Ateneo, 1948), pp. 465–66.

6. Peter Masten Dunne, S.J., "Church and State in Argentina," *Review of Politics* 7, no. 4 (October 1945): 414.

7. *Criterio*, 18, no. 923 (November 22, 1945), p. 497.

8. Frank Owen, *Perón: His Rise and Fall* (London: Cresset, 1957), p. 211.

9. Paul Hutchinson, "Argentina's Church Struggle Grows More Severe," *Christian Century* 72, no. 21 (May 25, 1955): 613.

10. "Tres años despues," *Correo de la Tarde* 11, no. 1931 (July 1, 1969), p. 12.

11. Ibid.

12. *Latin America* 20, no. 20 (May 16, 1969), p. 157.

13. Ricardo Parera, *Democracia Cristiana en la Argentina* (Buenos Aires: Editorial Nahuel, 1967), p. 82.

14. Eduardo Zalduendo, *Geografía electoral de la Argentina* (Buenos Aires: Ediciones Ancora, 1958), pp. 57–58.

15. Peter G. Snow, "The Class Basis of Argentine Political Parties," *American Political Science Review* 63, no. 1 (March 1969): 163–67.

16. Peter Ranis, "Parties, Politics and Peronism" (Ph.D. diss., New York University, 1965), p. 207.

17. Parera, *Democracia Cristiana*, p. 235.

18. *Buenos Aires Herald*, February 26, 1963, p. 6.

19. Ariel Colombo, "El Partido Demócrata Cristiano: una interpretación de su proyecto político," *Plural*, no. 10/11, 1988, p. 99.

20. Joaquin Aduríz, "Religión," in *Argentina: 1930–1960* (Buenos Aires: Editorial Sur, 1961), p. 424.

21. Luis Adolfo Estevez, *¿Liberalismo o nacionalismo?* (Buenos Aires: Editorial Difusión, 1941), as quoted in Oscar A. Troncoso, *Los nacionalistas argentinas* (Buenos Aires: Ediciones S.A.G.A., 1957), pp. 65–66.

22. Ibid., p. 66.

23. Marysa Gerassi, "Argentine Nationalism of the Right," *Studies in Comparative International Development* 1, no. 12 (1965): 189.

24. Tulio Halperín Donghi, "Crónico del período," in *Argentina: 1930–1960* (Buenos Aires: Editorial Sur, 1961), p. 67.

25. *Mayoría*, 1, no. 7 (May 20, 1957), p. 4.

26. Michael Dodson, "Priests and Peronism: Radical Clergy in Argentine Politics," *Latin American Perspectives* 1, no. 3 (Fall 1974): 59–60.

27. *Sacerdotes para el Tercer Mundo: crónica, documentos, reflexión* (Buenos Aires: Publicaciones del Movimiento, 1970), pp. 69–70.

28. Rolando Concatti, *Nuestra opción por el Peronismo* (Mendoza: Publicaciones del Movimiento Sacerdotes para el Tercer Mundo, 1972), pp. 21, 58, 141–42.

29. Ibid., p. 11.

30. Paul Lewis, *The Crisis of Argentine Capitalism* (Chapel Hill: University of North Carolina Press, 1990), pp. 377–78.

31. Concatti, *Nuestra opción*, p. 69.

32. Emilio Mignone, *Iglesia y Dictadura* (Buenos Aires: EPN, 1987), p. 17.

33. Burns, *The Land*, p. 22.
34. Mignone, *Iglesia*, p. 170.
35. Ibid., p. 21.
36. Burns, *The Land*, pp. 22–23.
37. Mignone, *Iglesia*, p. 20.
38. Ibid., p. 30.
39. Ibid., p. 24.
40. Argentine National Commission on the Disappeared (CONADEP), *Nunca Más* (New York: Farrar Straus Giroux, 1986), p. 248.
41. Ibid., p. 249.
42. Ibid., p. 251.
43. Mignone, *Iglesia*, p. 55.
44. Ibid., p. 211.
45. Ibid., p. 221.
46. Burns, *The Land*, p. 71.
47. Ibid., p. 70.
48. Daniel Poneman, *Argentina: Democracy on Trial* (New York: Paragon, 1987), p. 112.
49. Burns, *The Land*, p. 188.
50. Ibid., p. 189.
51. Mignone, *Iglesia*, p. 57.
52. Poneman, *Argentina*, p. 111.
53. *Buenos Aires Herald*, 28 July, 1991, p. 4.
54. *Buenos Aires Herald*, 10 November, 1991, p. 3.

CHAPTER 6

Students and Politics

Student political activity in Argentina is a phenomenon very much misunderstood in the United States. At least part of this misunderstanding stems from a lack of knowledge of the university system within which the student operates. Thus, before examining student politics, it is important to look briefly at some of the characteristics of the Argentine university.

The Argentine university is divided into individual schools or faculties (*facultades*), which correspond roughly to the colleges or schools within a North American university. The number of faculties and their names differ somewhat from one university to another. The National University of Buenos Aires (UNBA) has the largest number, with thirteen faculties: agriculture, agronomy, architecture, dentistry, economics, engineering, exact sciences, law, medicine, pharmacy, philosophy and letters, psychology, social sciences, and veterinary science.

At most universities these faculties are quite isolated, both geographically and intellectually. To begin with, there is no central campus; the faculties are spread throughout a city (as with the National Universities of Buenos Aires and La Plata) or cities (the National University of the Litoral has faculties in Santa Fé, Rosario, Paraná, and Corrientes). In addition, students rarely take courses in more than one faculty; instead, they begin their professional training (in law, medicine, engineering, and so on) immediately after graduation from high school. There is virtually no such thing as a liberal arts major.

Instruction traditionally has been given by poorly paid, part-time professors. A very large percentage of the professorial staff is composed of doctors, lawyers, or members of other professions who teach a few classes a week at a local university. Classes tend to be very large with a minimal amount of student-professor contact. Exceptionally low salaries discourage the formation of a full-time professorial staff, while at the same time the prestige associated with a university professorship encourages members of the liberal professions to compete for the part-time posts. Between 1974 and 1985, real salaries for university personnel dropped by 47 percent. In metropolitan areas, those people committed to teaching are often forced to work at different universities to put together a meager salary. In 1992, a full-time professor at the peak of his/her career made less than $1,000 a month, while an associate received $600. The meager pay induces professors to look for part-time contracts. Untenured faculty are paid by the number of courses they teach in a given academic year. The situation of assistant professors and instructors is even worse. Most of them, particularly in private universities, hardly receive any meaningful compensation (at best, $300 monthly). However, they keep giving one or two classes a week because of their devotion to the profession or because they believe that in so doing, they can get their name established. Most research in the social and hard sciences is carried out in private institutes funded by foreign foundations or governmental grants.

Between 1918 and 1946, from 1955 to 1966, and again after 1983, the administration of most Argentine public universities has been based upon the principle of tripartite government; that is, all administrative bodies are composed of professors, students, and alumni. Within individual faculties the principal administrative body is the directive council, composed of eight professors, four students, and four alumni, all of whom are chosen by the groups they represent. These councils elect the deans and select the new members of the professorial staff. At a higher level is the university assembly—composed of all the members of the various directive councils—which chooses the university's rector and its superior council. The latter is the university's highest policy-making organ; it is composed of five professors, five students, and five alumni, with all deans ex officio members.

Since each faculty renews its student councils and faculty representatives every year, Argentine public universities are in a virtually permanent state of electoral campaigning. Because the most important student organizations are closely tied to political parties, university elections are often regarded as a barometer of national politics; they receive exposure in the national news that would be unthinkable in North America and in many European countries. While such elections are a showcase of current trends, the importance of university politics rests in the role that students have played in affecting the content and means of politics in Argentina's modern history.

THE UNIVERSITY STUDENT

During this century both the number of universities and the number of students enrolled in them has increased dramatically. At the time of the

University Reform Movement in 1918, fewer than 15,000 students were attending Argentina's three national universities. By 1985, Argentina could count on twenty-seven public universities, with a total enrollment of 588,000 (88 percent of total university matriculation). The remaining twenty-two private universities, many of which are Catholic, had a total enrollment of 76,000. University enrollment has increased at a annual rate of 6 percent since 1961. Private universities are a relatively new phenomenon in Argentina. In 1967 there were only thirteen of them. Their rapid growth began in the early 1970s and continued well into the 1980s, primarily as a consequence of the state of disarray into which public education had fallen.

Argentine universities have been highly politicized, plagued by erratic instruction, and disrupted by frequent teachers' and students' strikes that have often prevented the regular completion of course work and the holding of regular exams. Within this context, private universities offer affluent families prestige, steady teaching, and an apolitical environment. Although it is highly disputable that private universities are, academically speaking, better than public ones, they have been very effective in creating for themselves a superior reputation. They are primarily teaching institutions staffed with faculty who also teach in state universities and research centers.

To this day, the nation's most prestigious school is the National University of Buenos Aires (UNBA). Enrollment there increased from slightly less than 100,000 in 1973 to almost 240,000 in 1975; it reached 270,000 students in 1986.[1] In 1992 the School of Architecture alone had an enrollment of more than 13,000 students. The overcrowding affecting many state universities like UNBA is the direct result of an open admission policy and the absence of tuition. Unfortunately, this enrollment increase has not been matched by an equal increase in the teaching staff and an improvement of research facilities. Actually, the severe economic crisis that developed in the 1980s has made existing problems all the more difficult, as funds available for higher education have become more and more scarce.

A 1979 report on UNBA pointed out that most students could not pass more than two out of six courses in any given year.[2] This problem rests on the fact that although tuition is free, a large number of people lack the financial resources to be full-time students and are therefore forced to find a job; about two-thirds are believed to hold part-time jobs.[3] Consequently, few students receive degrees. According to the 1980 national census, only 37 percent of those people between 25 and 29 years of age completed their university education, but the graduation rate rose to 56 percent when people between 30 and 34 were considered.[4] However, since then things have deteriorated further. In 1985, it was estimated that only one in ten students enrolling in public institutions actually was able to graduate,[5] and in 1989 that figure had shrunk to one in 19.[6]

The social background of Argentine university students, despite efforts to diversify its composition, has remained very much skewed toward the middle and upper-middle classes. A World Bank study recently concluded that "the upper 20 percent in income receive as much as 40 percent of direct public expenditure on higher education; the lowest 20 percent receive less than 10 percent of the public resources devoted to higher education."[7]

STUDENT ORGANIZATIONS

The primary unit of student organization is the facultywide center, which is governed by a general assembly (composed of all its members) and a smaller directive council (whose members are elected annually by the assembly). Within each university, the various centers are united in a university federation—such as the Federación Universitaria de Buenos Aires (FUBA)—which is also governed by a large assembly and a smaller council. At the apex of this hierarchy is the Argentine University Federation (FUA), which (theoretically, at least) represents all the nation's university students. FUA is run by a junta composed of two delegates from each university federation.

Primarily because of the isolation of the various faculties within each university, it is the center that claims the allegiance of most students. These centers provide such things as libraries, discussion groups, movies, cheap meals, and textbooks at discount prices. Judging from the number of votes cast in student elections, it would appear that a vast majority of the students belong to a center, although—much to the chagrin of many student politicians—they are under no compulsion to do so.

Between 1918 and 1950, all levels of the student movement were dominated by a group calling itself Reformists and claiming to be the heir of the University Reform Movement. Here it is probably best to digress a moment to look at the origins of the University Reform Movement before attempting to analyze the political position of the Reformists.

As earlier noted, beginning late in the nineteenth century, Argentina entered a period of rapid economic development, and in the political sphere a reform-minded nonaristocratic administration was elected for the first time in 1916. Yet the nation's universities remained as traditional and conservative as ever. The University of Córdoba, even more than the other two national universities (Buenos Aires and La Plata), was an excellent example of a colonial, Catholic, and conservative institution whose primary function was the preparation of aristocrats for professional careers (primarily in law and medicine) and the preservation of the status quo.

By 1918 the University of Córdoba included a number of young, liberal, middle-class students who were intent upon changing the very nature of Argentine higher education. As Richard Walter puts it, "The Reformists of 1918 were seeking to modernize the Argentine university, to update the Republic's institutions of higher learning in correspondence with the larger national developments which had occurred in the past few decades. The

Reformists hoped to make the university an agent of, rather than an obstacle to, change."[8]

The educational goals of the original Reformists were: (1) free university education; (2) university extension courses; (3) optional classroom attendance; (4) administration of the university by professors, students, and alumni; (5) open competition for professorial positions; (6) academic freedom; and (7) periodic review of professorships.[9] These reforms were meant to open the universities to the poor, to improve the quality of instruction, and in general to help the entire university system.

Between March and October 1918, a series of student strikes, classroom boycotts, demonstrations, and counterdemonstrations led to an executive decree promulgated by President Yrigoyen that acceded to virtually all the demands of the students. These Reform principles were soon extended to the other Argentine universities, and fairly quickly spread throughout Latin America.

Concern with university reform was soon enlarged to include concern for political reform and even reform of the society as a whole. The general political position of the Reformists during the last half-century can be summarized in terms of nationalism and anti-imperialism, populism and anticonservatism, anticlericalism, and antimilitarism.

Reformist nationalism was primarily political in nature; emphasis was placed on defense of national sovereignty against "foreign designs." However, it was closely related to the anti-imperialist posture of the group. This anti-imperialism has long been essentially anti–United States. Russian intervention in Hungary and Czechoslovakia tended to be ignored, while American intervention in Cuba, the Dominican Republic, Nicaragua, and Panama was bitterly denounced. Reformists were critical of everything from U.S. military intervention in Central America and the Caribbean to "cultural imperialism"—which was the label given anything from technical assistance and Point Four to scholarships to attend American universities and research grants to Latin American scholars. Typical of this position was a message sent by the Argentine University Federation to Secretary of State Cordell Hull in April 1936, which said in part, "FUA protests energetically against your country's armed invasion of Puerto Rico. In Hispanic American territory every soldier of yours is an invader."[10]

While not identified with any of the nation's political parties, the Reformists were extremely anticonservative. The various conservative parties, and conservatism in general, were equated with retention of the status quo and with paternalism—both of which ranked high on the Reformist list of enemies. Their alternative to the paternalism of the conservatives was a rather vague concept of populism that reflected their preoccupation with the living conditions of the lower sectors of society. For half a century the Reformists attempted, unsuccessfully, to effect an alliance with organized labor; yet they were totally opposed to the country's one labor government, that of Juan Perón (which, incidentally, might be labeled populist).

The anticlericalism of the Reformists appears to have originated as a result of the political conservatism of the Church, which in 1918 was tied to elements of the conservative parties and also vigorously opposed to educational reform. Anticlericalism manifested itself primarily in opposition to the establishment of Catholic universities, although it must be admitted that the Reformists were opposed, in principle at least, to the establishment of any type of private universities.

In spite of the fact that they opposed only two of the six military coups of the twentieth century, the Reformists were quite antimilitarist. Reformist leaders were enthusiastic supporters of the military coups of 1930 and 1955, which they considered as enforcement of the popular will, and they were not opposed to the coups of 1943 and 1962; however, these same Reformists were bitter opponents of the military regimes that followed all these coups. The proper role of the military establishment, as far as the Reformists were concerned, was that of "the arm of the people," which can be called upon to depose unpopular regimes, but which should never itself assume control of the government—a more than slightly unrealistic position, at least in Argentina.

It was not until 1950 that the Reformists faced any serious challenge to their hegemony within the student movement. Their first major competition came from the Humanists, who were basically the Catholic alternative to Reformism. Somewhat liberal Catholics whose political thought was similar to that of Latin American Christian Democracy, the Humanists agreed with many of the goals of the Reformists but differed appreciably as to means. To begin with, many Humanist leaders preferred to restrict student political activity to the university level and to leave national political issues to the politicians. Also, the Humanists were much less anti-American than the Reformists and, as Christian Democrats, were naturally not opposed to the establishment of private (that is, Catholic) universities. During the 1960s, the split between Humanists and Reformists widened appreciably because of the increased Communist influence in many Reformist centers. Humanists gained their greatest strength at the National University of Buenos Aires, where their candidates were elected as rectors in 1962 and 1965.

Reformism appealed primarily to students of lower-class and lower-middle-class backgrounds, and the independent, largely conservative movements to students from the upper and upper-middle classes; the appeal of Humanism, on the other hand, seemed to transcend class lines. At least that appears to be the case at UNBA. There, in the 1964 student elections in eight faculties (there were no elections in the faculties of dentistry or philosophy and letters), the correlation between the percentage of the vote received by Reformist candidates and the percentage of the students of lower-class origin was $+.86$; in other words, 74 percent of the variance in the Reformist vote from one faculty to another could be explained by variance in the lower-class composition of these faculties. There was also a very strong relationship between the presence of upper-class and upper-middle-class students and the vote received by independent (that is, non-Reformist, non-Humanist) candidates. On the other hand, the Humanist vote did not appear to be related to the class composition of the various faculties, thus leading one to the conclusion that the appeal of Humanism was spread rather evenly across class lines.

In the 1960s, the university student movement was subject to extreme factionalism, as literally dozens of student parties were formed. Most of these groups claimed some ties either to Reformism or to Humanism (more often the former), but more than ever before their primary ties appeared to be to national political parties.

POLITICIZATION

In the 1950s and early 1960s, it was assumed that Argentine university students were much more thoroughly politicized than nonstudent youth of a comparable age and that the university was the agent of this politicization. Research on the subject eventually confirmed the first assumption, but not the second.

In 1963, to determine "the role played by the university in developing an interest in politics," David Nasatir interviewed 630 students at the University of Buenos Aires and 489 nonuniversity young people living in greater Buenos Aires.[11] As was hypothesized, students manifested appreciably greater interest in politics than did nonstudents. For example, 38 percent of the students, compared with 26 percent of the nonstudents, said that they "frequently get as excited about something that happens in politics as about something that happens in personal life"; on the other hand, 14 percent of the students and 32 percent of the nonstudents responded that they "never" got excited about politics.[12] In addition to this difference in subjective orientation, there was also a difference in the behavior of the two groups, for 45 percent of the students, compared with 26 percent of the nonstudents, claimed to discuss politics "frequently" with friends; at the same time, 22 percent of the nonstudents, but only 4 percent of the students, denied they ever did so.[13]

While Nasatir was able to show that university students were more politicized than were nonstudent youths of comparable age, he was unable to demonstrate that the university was the agent of this politicization. If that were the case, one would expect increased contact with the university to lead to a greater degree of political interest and participation; yet neither age nor year in school was related significantly to interest in politics. In fact, the percentage of students replying that they "never get as excited over something that happens in politics as about something that happens in personal life" was highest among the fifth- and sixth-year students and those 26 years of age and older.

Variables that did account for much of the difference in degree of politicization were the father's occupation and his educational level. While interest in politics on the part of students was unrelated to their fathers' educational attainments, that was decidedly not the case with nonstudents, whose political interest increased dramatically with increased educational levels on the part of their fathers. In fact, among youths whose fathers were university educated, nonstudents were just as interested in politics as were students. This led Nasatir to conclude that

a considerable part of the differences observable between the population of students and that of nonstudents, with respect to political interest at least, is due to factors antecedent to the university experience. The differences in political interest are associated with the level of education and the type of occupation engaged in by the youth's father.[14]

Likewise, an Argentine scholar concluded from the same data that "the impact of university life upon political interest tends to be minimal."[15]

It is much easier to demonstrate that Argentine university students have a fairly high degree of interest in politics than to define the form taken by this interest. One generalization may be offered, however: for several years there was a trend toward extremist attitudes on the part of the student body. In 1957, a poll in the faculty of philosophy and letters showed over half of the students basically centrist in their political beliefs, with 7 percent communist and 8 percent rightist. A similar poll taken six years later showed 37 percent leftists, 36 percent rightists, and only 15 percent centrists.[16] And this pattern of extremist attitudes was general throughout the University of Buenos Aires—at least if such a pattern is measured by voting patterns in student elections. There, the leftist votes tended to be cast by advanced students whose fathers were poorly educated. Rightist votes (and those cast for parties which cannot readily be placed on a left-to-right continuum) appear to have come primarily from beginning students whose fathers were relatively well educated.

POLITICAL EFFICACY

The apogee of student political influence was reached in 1918 with the attainment of university reform. As Richard Walter puts it:

The accomplishments of Argentina's university youth in the year 1918 were significant and lasting. Through effective organizational techniques and direct action, they succeeded in forcing the national government to accept their demands for profound change. . . . Moreover, student organizations had entered into national affairs. Students had met with the President of the Republic, had occupied much of the time and concern of executive and legislative officials, had attracted large numbers of people to their cause. . . . Student political activity, with its corresponding educational and social interests, had become a permanent and important part of Argentine life.[17]

However, as university students moved from educational questions to broader social, economic, and political issues, their effectiveness waned appreciably.

By mid-1930, university students had begun an intensive campaign to get rid of President Yrigoyen. They advocated a military coup and at first supported the revolutionary regime of General Uriburu. They moved into the opposition only when it became apparent that Uriburu was not immediately going to return the government to civilian hands. The student movement opposed the conservative administrations of 1932–43, but rather ineffectively. It was even more opposed to the first Perón regime; this opposition was directed against Perón himself, his administration in general, and his university policies in particular. From the 1940s on, the autonomy of Argentine universities was routinely violated and faculty and students purged by military and populist governments. After the 1943 coup, General Pedro Ramírez dismissed many professors, including future Nobel laureate Bernardo Houssay, who had protested the military's attempt to create a fascist regime.

Shortly after Perón's inauguration in 1946, the government intervened in all the national universities; this was followed by wholesale purges of the professorial staff. Somewhere between half and two-thirds of the university professors were fired, and many of them had to leave the country. Their places were taken by Peronists, most of whom were of inferior intellectual ability and scholarly achievement. In October 1947, a new university law destroyed both university autonomy and tripartite government. This law gave the president power to appoint all university rectors, who in turn chose the deans of their faculties. Student participation in university government was limited to one representative—without a vote—on directive councils.

In spite of the use of intimidation and violence by the government, the student movement was never brought under Peronist control. The Peronist student federation, the Confederación General Universitaria (CGU), founded in 1950, was remarkably ineffective. As late as 1954, in the engineering faculty at the National University of Buenos Aires the Reformist centers had 4,000 members and the CGU centers only 200; in the faculty of architecture there were four times as many students affiliated with Reformist centers as with those belonging to the CGU.[18] Throughout the 1946–55 period, student demonstrations and strikes were important in showing the failure of Peronism to enlist the support of this prestigious element of society. Unfortunately, by the time the Peronist regime collapsed, the academic standards that had made Argentina a model of higher education in Latin America had been irremediably compromised.

After 1955, the student movement failed to make any significant contribution to national politics. According to Walter, "having been in a position of opposition to national governments for almost twenty-five years (1930–55), the student federations seemed to have great difficulty in moving away from this stance and in adopting positive rather than negative solutions to national issues."[19]

The opposition of the student movement to the establishment of private universities is a good example of this negative stance and also of the failure of the movement's political demands. The argument began in August 1958, when President Frondizi announced that he was in favor of allowing the establishment of private universities. The rectors of the national universities, all of them Reformists at this time, sent a petition asking the chief executive to reverse his stand, and Reformist students paraded outside the halls of Congress carrying signs saying "State Yes—Private No," "Secular Yes—Free No," and "Priest No—Books Yes."[20] The rector of the National University of Buenos Aires—and brother of the president—led a delegation of students to the Congress building, where he made a long speech asking Congress not to legalize private universities. After President Frondizi made a radio speech justifying his position, general strikes of university students were proclaimed. Police and students clashed in front of the Congress building, and many university faculties were the scenes of riots as Reformists and Humanists tried to occupy the buildings. On September 19, about 300,000 persons attended a FUA-sponsored rally to hear speeches by student leaders, alumni, politicians, and labor leaders, all of whom attacked the bill to legalize private universities.

Late in September the Reformists appeared to have won when the lower house of Congress rejected the administration bill 109 to 52; however, a few days later an amended version was passed by the upper house, and its opponents in the Chamber of Deputies could not muster the two-thirds vote needed to defeat it. This amended version, sponsored by the UCRI, allowed the establishment of private universities whose plans of study were to be regulated by the Ministry of Education.

The nation's university students lost completely on an issue of major importance to them. They had mustered the adherence of an impressive segment of public opinion, a number of important politicians and labor leaders, and the vast majority of the student body. Nevertheless, they were powerless in the face of a national administration that was paying a political debt and at the same time enacting legislation felt to be in the best interests of the entire nation—including the university community.

In most cases, the students were even less successful in their opposition of military governments. In June 1966, the universities were almost the only major source of opposition to the overthrow of President Illia. This opposition was largely a result of fear of future government policy toward the university. Most expected Onganía to abolish the system of tripartite government and perhaps to dissolve student political organizations; what they were not prepared for was the complete destruction of university autonomy.

Just a month after his inauguration, Onganía announced a provisional university statute that contained three main provisions: (1) complete control over national universities was transferred to the education secretariat, with rectors and deans relegated to positions as provisional administrators of government policy; (2) university officials were given forty-eight hours to communicate to the government their acceptance of this provision, with a lack of communication signifying their resignation; and (3) student organizations were denied the right to take part in any form of political activity under the penalty legal dissolution.

The day this statute was announced, federal police occupied the National University of Buenos Aires. They entered the various faculties and told all occupants to leave—an order that was obeyed in eight of the ten faculties. In the faculties of exact sciences and architecture, however, violence ensued. There students and professors refused to leave the buildings, whereupon the police forced their way in, beat up a number of students and professors, and then arrested them.

The first protest against these actions came from professors, who resigned en masse. The total number of resignations has been estimated as high as 3,000. At UNBA the faculty of philosophy and letters lost 41 percent of its staff, and the exact sciences faculty 51 percent. The protests of students took the form of mass demonstrations, hunger strikes, the occupation of university buildings, and violent confrontations with the police. Quite predictably, this all came to naught.

The new university law, enacted in 1967, attempted to remove the university completely from the political realm. It contained provisions such as: "The university authorities will abstain from the formulation of political declarations or the assumption of positions which compromise academic prestige" (Art. 9); "all forms of political militancy, agitation, propaganda, and indoctrination are prohibited on university grounds" (Art. 10); "within the university students who take part in any type of political activity, reunions, demonstrations, assemblies, or any other type of activity which contradicts the provisions of article 10 may be punished by the dean" (Art. 98); and "student centers which violate the previous article will be deprived of their juridic personality" (Art. 99).

These actions by the Onganía administration were largely the result of the extremity to which student political activity had been pushed—the minister of interior was exaggerating only slightly when he announced that intervention was a response to the clamor of public opinion—and by a sincere desire on the part of the government to modernize the universities (albeit without any clear ideas as to what modernization entailed). It is also likely that Onganía was under pressure from the military, and from his more conservative advisers, to "clean out the communists."

The students, totally removed form the decision-making process, resorted to violence in ever increasing degrees. Why did this happen? In the previous sections we saw how in the early 1960s students had become increasingly alienated from the political system as a whole. The repression of the Onganía regime made the situation much worse. By the late 1960s, university students saw no real short-term prospect of changing the country's state of affairs. While many of them advocated a profound socioeconomic overhaul according to a nebulous idea of an "Argentine way to socialism," the Onganía regime represented in their eyes a conservative restoration which was going to perpetuate the dominance of "transnational capitalist exploitation." These repressed tensions overlapped with the rapid sequence of international events. The Second Vatican Council, the Second General Assembly of the Latin American Bishops' Conference and its impact on the development of liberation theology, the exportation of the Cuban revolution to other nations of Latin America, the 1968 French student revolution, and the building up of the pacifist movement opposing the Vietnam War in the United States all deeply affected Argentine student leaders. While the old Reformist-Humanist debate became obsolete, many student groups tried to elaborate the ideals that ensued from these events and adapt them to the Argentine reality. In this way we can partly explain the variety of splinter groups that arose at this particular juncture and the often contrasting ideologies and methods adopted accordingly. As Onganía had abolished all the institutional channels allowing students to express their demands for reform, a large number of young people came to believe that the only way to promote change was through violence. The spark that turned all these tensions into open rebellion came in early 1969, just at the time when many commentators thought that Onganía was consolidating his power. In March of that year the police fired upon students in the city of Corrientes, who were protesting a price hike in cafeteria meals, leaving one person dead. Student strikes eventually spread to Rosario and later to Córdoba, where youth were joined by auto workers. In that city protest quickly turned into a riot and to an unprecedented escalation of violence that became known as the *cordobazo*. Why was Córdoba rather than Buenos Aires the center of the students' uprising, and why were they joined by workers? According to David Rock:

The automobile workers' participation in the *cordobazo* resulted in part from the fact that many day students worked night shifts at the factories, and many young car workers were night students; these two groups served as a conduit between affairs in the university and those in the factories. Beyond this . . . [autoworkers' unions] had no tradition of Peronist regimentation from the CGT. In this new working-class city, which had doubled in size during the past twenty years, the unions were smaller, plant-based, more democratic, and independent. Thus these union members were able to act even as the labor movement at large was paralyzed.[21]

The rebellion was eventually put down by the army, but by the time peace was restored, the authority of the government had been irremediably compromised. While there is to this day a heated polemic on whether or not foreign agitators were behind the *cordobazo*, the fact remains that the event constituted the political coffin of the Onganía regime. Furthermore, it was in the aftermath of the *cordobazo* that guerrilla groups, whose membership came predominantly from university students, began to carry out their first operations. In the words of William Smith:

The *cordobazo* . . . fueled the emergence of important revolutionary movements dedicated to guerrilla warfare that were without parallel in Latin America in terms of their characteristic combination of theoretical sophistication, mass appeal, and impact on the course of politics. However, in their drive to become the "armed vanguard of the proletariat," the revolutionary organizations born in the late 1960s made a deeply ambiguous contribution to Argentine politics. While they helped to block the consolidation of the authoritarian regime, revolutionary violence provided a justification for state terrorism and left a legacy of militarization of politics, ideological polarization, pervasive cynicism, and retreat into civic privatism.[22]

Militancy across the nation's universities built up in the last few years of the Argentine Revolution. During this time four main student organizations emerged as the strongest: the Maoists and Guevarists of the FAUDI (linked to the small Revolutionary Communist party); Franja Morada (literally purple fringe, tied to the Radicals); the Peronist University Youth (JUP); and the Reformist National Movement.[23] In 1970 Franja Morada and the Reformists took control of the FUA and dominated university politics until 1973. It was during this period that Radical and Peronist student organizations, unlike their counterparts from the Left, began to participate actively in the internal debates of their respective parties. In 1972, Franja Morada supported Alfonsín's challenge for the party leadership against Balbín. The JUP, on the other hand, was very active in paving the way for Perón's return and in supporting the left wing of Peronism in its struggle with the right wing of the movement.

The trend toward extremism continued after the return to constitutional government in 1973, but by this time the extremists were almost uniformly of the Left. In the 1973 university elections, leftist candidates received almost two-thirds of the total vote. The Communists received 23 percent, the "ultra-left" (such as Maoists and Trotskyites) 12 percent, and the Peronists 31 percent. (Although the national Peronist party was certainly not uniformly to the far left, its youth sector was.)

The Peronist victory in the 1973 presidential elections coincided with a shifting of the balance of power in the universities as the JUP displaced Franja Morada as the hegemonic force within the student movement. This was helped by the Cámpora administration, which during its brief tenure handed over the university administration to left-wingers. In the name of "popular" education entry examination requirements (for example, the holding of a secondary school diploma) were abolished, and university enrollment skyrocketed from 300,000 to 450,000 in only one year. Many professors that did not conform to the criteria of the new administration were forced to leave. Those instructors holding degrees from foreign universities were particularly targeted because they were considered agents of "foreign imperialism." According to James H. Street, in the Faculty of Economics of the UNBA, "thirteen tenured professors were dismissed while three hundred new teachers were hired, few with academic credentials, to staff the crowded classrooms."[24] However, a few months later, after Perón began his third term, the pendulum swung back in the opposite direction. In 1974, the government decided to intervene in the universities by appointing vice-chancellors of its liking and curtailing the universities' independence. And in the process academic standards fell one step further.

This initiative prompted the JUP to attack the Isabel Perón administration (and the right wing of Peronism which supported her) and to form an alliance with Montoneros. In the aftermath of the 1976 military coup, the universities became a prime target of the military's repression effort, as the bulk of the guerrilla movement and its supporters came from student organizations. The new minister of education fired 3,000 professors, staff members, and researchers. Later on, in events similar to what Onganía had done in 1966, "ninety-five career fields [were eliminated] from the universities, including most social sciences and such newer scientific fields (in the Argentine system) as ecological studies and oceanography."[25] These purges took place amid a climate of kidnappings, murders, and arbitrary arrests. Of the total number of disappeared people verified by CONADEP, 21 percent were students (the second largest number after workers), and 5.7 percent were teachers. During the Proceso the military made a point of "depoliticizing" the university system; student associations were made illegal. The depoliticization process was facilitated by the fact that many professor and student activists who had not fallen into the hands of the security forces had gone into exile. Consequently, between 1976 and 1981, university political activity for all intents and purposes ceased to exist.

STUDENT POLITICS AFTER 1983

It was only after the Malvinas/Falklands war that student politics was resumed. The sudden debacle of the military regime created great enthusiasm across Argentine universities. Many groups were created spontaneously, and often independent of national political parties. For seven years university organizations had been banned, and thus the new student generation that grew up during the repression years had no experience in politics or organizational matters. Between 1982 and 1983, many contending groups began to scramble to position themselves within the university debate and to redefine the characteristics of representative institutions. Some traditional institutions like the student assembly were eliminated while the councils were reinstated. The first FUBA congress was finally held in 1983; it elected as its leader Andrés Delich of Franja Morada.

With the beginning of the new democratic regime, the universities regained their autonomous status and instituted an open admissions policy. The UNBA created a one-year pilot program (*ciclo básico*) for freshmen, dividing it into two fields: social sciences and exact sciences. Unfortunately, the program was poorly organized and was quite ineffective.

In the 1986 academic year, the University of Buenos Aires alone had over 270,000 students, including 78,000 in the basic program—classroom facilities have been makeshift, student-teacher ratios high, and faculty salaries woefully low. An example is the "Introduction to Modern Civilization" course that was offered to students enrolled in the basic program. Thirteen thousand students registered for this course; the lectures were given by videotape on a round-the-clock basis; and the professor in charge of preparing the course, a distinguished sociologist, received a stipend of $300 a month. The army of teaching assistants who actually met with the students received considerably less.[26]

Alfonsín devoted much more money for education than did the military regime and allocated some funds to revamp research through the National Council of Scientific and Technical Research (CONICET) that had been heavily purged during the Proceso. However, as the economic situation progressively deteriorated, the Radical administration was forced to cut funds for higher education. The result was grossly underpaid teachers who were often on strike, thus preventing students from attending courses regularly enough to graduate. Under the Menem administration the Ministry of Education proposed to solve the state of bankruptcy of the university system by introducing a bill in Congress which, while increasing university autonomy, introduced a highly controversial tuition fee. In May 1991, the FUBA rejected the bill outright arguing that education was a "social investment not a macroeconomic variable." It also added that tuition fees would be the prelude for an elitist education that would exclude the lower classes. Such criticisms were echoed by the National Interuniversity Council of Deans. Not only did the deans attack tuition fees; they also denounced the Ministry of Education's attempt, in its reform bill, to divert funds to those schools judged to be more "efficient." In the deans' view, this was a gimmick by the government to reward universities that were willing to follow the administration's educational programs while punishing those that refused to follow suit. Even more bitter criticism came by the end of 1991, when the government announced its intention to transfer education to the jurisdiction of the provinces.

What made student activity different in the mid-1980s was the emphasis on pragmatic issues and the weakening of leftist ideology. The radicalism with which the earlier generation of university students had identified was rejected and held responsible for having provided a justification for the abuses of the Proceso. The new student leadership, regardless of its political affiliation, showed a great concern for themes linked to the consolidation of the nation's democratic institutions, among them, tolerance, respect for the rule of law, and the rejection of violence as a means of conflict resolution. Students also brought to the attention of political parties the importance of tying their platforms to the new issues raised by human rights groups and grass-roots movements. Another substantial departure from the past was the emergence of strong center-right groups that were instrumental in reshaping the political debate at the university level. The four main university student organizations of the period between 1983 and 1990—Franja Morada, the Union for University Opening (UPAU), JUP, and the Intransigent University Youth (JUI)—merit individual attention.

Franja Morada

Throughout the 1983 to 1990 period, this Radical-dominated organization regained its hegemonic role in student politics. Its leaders actively campaigned for Alfonsín in 1983 and took as their own many of the president's reform plans. Besides the emphasis on the strengthening of democratic values, Franja Morada strongly endorsed university reform, advocating academic freedom, university self-government, autonomy from government intervention, revision of academic curricula, new representative institutions, and the selection of new faculty through a system of examinations.[27] At the same time, its leaders became heavily involved in the internal politics of the UCR, siding consistently with the left wing of the party. They became disillusioned with Alfonsín when the president failed to promote those socioeconomic changes he had promised early in his term.

Franja Morada's ideological stand remained moderately to the left, and this enabled the group to capture swing voters who might otherwise have voted for the JUP, the JUI, and other left-wing formations. On the other hand, the group has been unequivocally clear in articulating students' demands on bread-and-butter issues much like its toughest competitor, UPAU.

UPAU

UPAU is the new element in Argentine student politics. A small group in 1983, it became the second largest university organization in the UNBA by the mid-1980s. UPAU's political discourse was quite different from that used by other groups. According to Edward Gibson,

Capitalizing on widespread student discontent with an overburdened state university system, UPAU leaders shifted the terms of the debate which had traditionally governed university politics. Critics of UPAU (as well as conservative admirers) have labeled its electoral strategy as one of depoliticization due to its deemphasis of broad political issues and its focus on such prosaic issues as university curricula, student cafeterias, and other issues related to the practical and administrative aspects of university life. To conservative admirers, such as the daily *La Nación*, the UPAU "depoliticization" was a welcome relief from the "used and abused" sweeping radical discourse of university politics in the past. To critics on the left, UPAU's "depoliticization" was continuous with the depoliticization ethic of the previous liberal military regime.[28]

UPAU has put its opposition on the defensive and has forced Franja Morada, JUP, JUI, and other minor left-wing groups to compete on its home turf. To sum up:

the UPAU stress on practical themes sought: (1) to bring issues formerly considered as "non-political" back into life and (2) to shift the terms of the political debate to new terrain as part of a strategy of political mobilization and power creation. Here lay the deeply political purpose of UPAU's young militants: to establish a beachhead for Argentine conservatism in the public university system and use it as a resource in the national electoral arena.[29]

Contrary to conservative student groups of the 1970s, UPAU's activists made plain their commitment to constitutional democracy and repudiated the "old Right" tradition of inviting a military coup to oust its enemies. As Oscar Jiménez Peña, one of UPAU's founders, stated, "Regardless how difficult the situation is, there is no justification for a coup. We cannot tolerate any more coups. After every coup the situation got worse."[30] Many of UPAU's leaders quickly turned to party politics and joined the ranks of the up-and-coming conservative UCD, to which they brought a great deal of enthusiasm, organizational skills, and new strategies and ideas. Indeed, it was on issues dealing with the party platform that the young UPAU's activists came into conflict with UCD's president and founder, Alvaro Alsogaray. In their opinion, Alsogaray's exclusive emphasis on economic issues severely limited the UCD's electoral appeal. The UPAU's leaders proposed to enlarge the party's political discourse to other themes such as education, ecology, human rights, foreign policy, and problems related to local government. In the view of these young activists, politics had to transcend the abstract principles of economics and come down to the solution of problems encountered every day by the average citizen.

JPI

The Intransigent Party Youth (JPI) is a minor organization whose strength has been primarily concentrated in metropolitan Buenos Aires and whose fortunes have been intimately tied to that of the Intransigent party. About a third of the JPI's activists have also been part of the PI's leadership. The JPI's greatest moment came between 1984 and 1985, when it was able to attract a lot of left-wing voters at the UNBA. However, thereafter things unraveled, in part because of the heterogeneous nature of its membership. Some of its activists were originally Radical and Peronist émigrés, others were socialists, and the rest were just young people who identified with a vague notion of "modern Left," which the JPI claimed to represent. The JPI's main plan of action has mirrored that of the Intransigent party, that is, the creation of a left-wing, nationalist student organization based upon "popular and revolutionary" principles. In spite of its rhetoric, the JPI has not been able to spell out a clear ideology of its own, nor has it been capable of distinguishing itself from the Peronist University Youth. In practice, the JPI's insistence in forging electoral alliances with the JUP has worked to its disadvantage, as many former Peronists and Radicals returned to their respective student organizations because of their disenchantment with the JPI's lack of a clear identity.

JUP

The Peronist University Youth has been associated with the Renovation faction of the Peronist party since the electoral debacle of 1983 when the Renovators took control of the PJ, and the JUP gained some influence within the party structure. Although not nearly as radical as in the 1970s, the JUP has positioned itself toward the center-left of the political spectrum in university politics and has made alliances with Intransigents and Christian Democrats. Nonetheless, the JUP has failed to capture a large following among students, a fact that is not at all surprising given that Peronism has seldom fared very well at the university level.

STUDENT ELECTIONS, 1983–1990

Between 1983 and 1990, university politics reached its climax, when student elections come to a close. Because most of the schools making up Argentine state universities renew their ruling bodies every year, electoral campaigns are a never-ending process. On the other hand, private universities have not experienced such a trend because they have made a point of remaining apolitical—at least officially. Of all elections, the most important are those held at the UNBA. Table 6.1 portrays electoral trends in five of the UNBA's thirteen schools. As it can be seen, Franja Morada has remained the dominant force in student politics. This has also been true at the national level, as at the 1987 FUA national convention Franja Morada had 36 percent of the delegates, by far the single most important group. Its hegemony in the UNBA came into jeopardy when the up-and-coming UPAU was able to capture the schools of architecture (1987), law (1988, 1989), and engineering

Table 6.1
Student Elections in Selected Schools, 1986–1990 (in Percentage)

	1986		1987		1988		1989		1990	
Architecture	Franja	43.1	Franja	34.8	Franja	42.0	Franja	45.2	Franja	54.4
	UPAU	20.1	UPAU	37.6	UPAU	30.0	UPAU	29.2	UPAU	23.6
	JUI	15.3								
Law	Franja	39.3	Franja	36.9	Franja	36.6	Franja	34.2	Franja	33.4
	UPAU	30.4	UPAU	37.6	UPAU	39.6	UPAU	35.4	UPAU	24.6
	JUP	11.2	JUP	13.4						
Economics	Franja	36.6	Franja	38.4			Franja	45.1	Franja	55.6
	UPAU	20.6	UPAU	35.0			UPAU	39.3	UPAU	30.5
	JUI	20.0	JUI	19.2						
Engineering	Franja	28.5	Franja	22.7	Franja	24.1	Franja	24.9	Franja	30.2
	UPAU	28.4	UPAU	44.8	UPAU	41.6	UPAU	47.9	UPAU	30.3
Pharmacy	Franja	42.5	Franja	39.9	Franja	45.0	Franja	56.2	Franja	69.1
	UPAU	21.8	UPAU	33.8	UPAU	35.1	UPAU	26.1	UPAU	18.9

Data for the 1988 elections in the Economics college are unavailable.
Sources: Somos, October 10, 1988, and November 28, 1990.

(1987, 1988, 1989, and 1990). In 1990, Franja Morada promoted an aggressive campaign nationwide that attacked the education policy of the Menem administration. Moreover, it began to give greater emphasis to subjects previously advocated by UPAU, such as student services and cooperatives. This shift paid off by year's end when Franja Morada gained control of eight of the UNBA's schools, leaving to UPAU only engineering and veterinary science. Of the remaining three schools, the socialists took exact sciences, the Trotskyites got philosophy, and the independents won in agronomy. In 1991, Franja Morada won in seven of the thirteen schools. These elections marked a serious setback for UPAU, which was unable to consolidate its early achievements. That year the seats of the FUBA were distributed as follows: Franja Morada, 52; UPAU, 8; Menemists, 3; Independents of the Left, 7; Socialists, 3; and Independents of the Right, 3.

What is the importance of student elections? By themselves, they do not count for much, as the funds administered by student councils are meager. Their importance rests on two related factors. First, students who want to pursue a political career find in university politics a vehicle to further their ambitions. It is not by chance that many student leaders have become prominent politicians, particularly in the UCR and the Intransigent party. A second crucial aspect is the political message that elections carry with them. Since 1983, Argentine students have often been in the forefront of political debate and have forced political parties to confront issues that they had preferred to avoid or neglect. Almost invariably, Franja Morada, UPAU, JUP, and JPI have promoted important internal debates within the parties to which they are affiliated. Although the old guard of traditional parties (particularly the Peronists) have resented the intrusion of student leaders into party politics, there is little doubt that those leaders have been instrumental in updating the political discourse and in focusing attention on such issues as human rights, environmental problems, civil liberties, and the inefficiency of basic services provided by the government. In sum, students have been an important political actor in the process of democratic consolidation. Their rejection of violence and outspoken support for the democratic process, regardless of the political standing, have enhanced their status within the Argentine society.

EPILOGUE

The first two editions of this book were written during the periods of the Argentine Revolution and the Process of National Reorganization. Each book ended on a pessimistic note, the revised edition saying that:

At least since 1955, and many would say since 1930, instability has been the dominant feature of the political system, and there is no readily apparent reason to believe that this will not continue to be the case. . . . At present there is no individual, nor political party, nor organized group of any sort, that is truly acceptable both to the leaders of the armed forces and to the general public. In the absence of such an individual, or party, or group, the only realistic possibility is the continuance of political chaos."

Thirteen years later, there may be some room for cautious optimism. In 1983, both Raúl Alfonsín and the Radical Civic Union were clearly acceptable to the general public, although not to the armed forces; but the economic disaster of the Proceso, its total lack of concern for human rights, and the humiliating defeat in the war with Great Britain made the acceptance of the armed forces unnecessary—at least for the time being.

Almost a decade after leaving power, the armed forces remain very much in disrepute. It is quite unlikely that any appreciable civilian support could be found for still another military coup. At the time of the military rebellions in the late 1980s the general public demonstrated its overwhelming support for democratic rule. The attempted military coup in 1990 was quickly put down by loyal forces, and the leaders of the coup attempt were imprisoned.

Unfortunately, this does not mean that the armed forces have retired, permanently, to their barracks. Many, perhaps most, officers believe they won a war that saved the Argentine way of life, only to be castigated by those they saved. The sharp decline in the military budget and in salaries has meant that in some instances military training has all but disappeared, and that lower-ranking officers and NCOs have been forced to obtain part-time jobs. Also alarming is the fact that a great many NCOs took an active role in the abortive coup of 1990. The politicization of noncoms can hardly bode well for the future.

Although the military as an institution seems to have no appeal to the general public, this is not universally true of individual officers, now in retirement. In the 1991 gubernatorial election in Tucumán retired General Antonio Bussi, who had been governor of the province during the Proceso, was very narrowly defeated by Peronism; in fact, Bussi obtained more votes than the Peronist victor, but lost as a result of a new election law that allows parties to nominate more than one candidate. In the 1991 Buenos Aires gubernatorial election retired Colonel Aldo Rico, who twice led military rebellions, came in third with more than 530,000 votes, more even than the UCD candidate.

In 1989 President Alfonsín was able to transfer the presidential sash to his elected successor. This was the first time *in more than half a century* that one civilian president was able to succeed another. And although there has been opposition to some of the policies of the Alfonsín and Menem administrations, there has been near-universal consensus that these have been legitimate governments entitled to remain in office until the end of their term. The question today is how long Argentines will be willing to accord legitimacy to administrations that seem unable to prevent a continuing deterioration of their standard of living.

NOTES

1. Robert Potash, "Alfonsín's Argentina in Historical Perspective," University of Massachusetts at Amherst, Latin American Studies Program, Occasional Paper 21, 1988, p. 24.

2. World Bank, *Argentina: Social Sectors in Crisis* (Washington, DC: World Bank, 1988), p. 11.

3. Ibid., p. 12.

4. Fundación de Investigaciones Económicas Latinoamericanas (FIEL), *El fracaso del estadismo* (Buenos Aires: Sudamericana-Planeta, 1987), p. 156.

5. World Bank, *Argentina: Social Sectors*, p. 11.

6. Secretary of State for University Affairs, José Luis de Imaz, quoted by Cristini Bonasegna in "Argentine Universities Face a New Challenge: Coping with Greater Autonomy," *Chronicle of Higher Education* (October 4, 1989), p. A44.

7. World Bank, *Argentina: Social Sectors*, p. 11.

8. Richard J. Walter, *Student Politics in Argentina* (New York: Basic Books, 1968), p. 50.

9. Carlos L. Yegros Doria, "La reforma universitaria hoy," in *Universidad y estudiantes*, ed. Juan Osvaldo Inglese and Carlos L. Yegros Doria (Buenos Aires: Ediciones Libera, 1965), p. 72.

10. Alberto Ciria and Horacio Sanguinetti, *Universidad y estudiantes* (Buenos Aires: Depalma, 1962), p. 56.

11. David Nasatir, "University Experience and Political Unrest of Students in Buenos Aires," *Comparative Education Review* 18, no. 2 (June 1966): 274.

12. Ibid.

13. Ibid., pp. 274–75.

14. Ibid., p. 227.

15. Juan Osvaldo Inglese, "El poder socializador de las instituciones educativas argentinas," *Aportes* 5 (July 1967): 86.

16. Ronald J. Newton, "Students and the Political System of the University of Buenos Aires," *Journal of Interamerican Studies* 7, no. 4 (October 1966): 648.

17. Richard G. Walter, *Student Politics in Argentina* (New York: Basic Books, 1968), p. 60.

18. Ibid., p. 139.

19. Ibid., p. 182.

20. Ibid., p. 164.

21. David Rock, *Argentina, 1516–1987: From Spanish Colonization to Alfonsín* (Berkeley: University of California Press, 1987), p. 350.

22. William Smith, *Authoritarianism and the Crisis of the Argentine Political Economy* (Stanford, CA: Stanford University Press, 1989), pp. 139–40.

23. Franja Morada was in the beginning dominated by anarchists and socialists, but it came under Radical control after 1969 (Mario Toer, ed., *El movimiento estudiantil de Perón a Alfonsín* 2 [Buenos Aires: Centro Editor de América Latina, 1988], p. 162).

24. James H. Street, "The Reality of Power and the Poverty of Economic Doctrine," in *Latin America's Economic Development*, ed. James L. Dietz and James H. Street (Boulder, CO: Lynne Rienner, 1987), p. 20.

25. Ibid., p. 21.

26. Potash, "Alfonsín's Argentina In Historical Perspective," p. 24.

27. Toer, *El movimiento estudiantil*, p. 216.

28. Edward Gibson, "Democracy and the New Electoral Right in Argentina," *Journal of Interamerican Studies and World Affairs* 32, no. 3 (1990), p. 201.

29. Ibid., pp. 201–2.

30. Oscar Jiménez Peña, interview, in *Plural*, no. 10/11, July 1988, p. 172.

Bibliography

Aduriz, Joaquín. "Religión." In *Argentina: 1930–1960*. Buenos Aires: Editorial Sur, 1961.

Alende, Oscar. *Entretelones de la trampa*. Buenos Aires: Santiago Rueda Editor, 1964.

Alexander, Robert J. *Organized Labor in Latin America*. New York: Free Press, 1965.

———. *The Perón Era*. New York: Columbia University Press, 1951.

Anderson, Charles. *Politics and Economic Change in Latin America*. Princeton, NJ: Van Nostrand, 1967.

Argentine National Commission on the Disappeared. *Nunca Más*. New York: Farrar Straus Giroux, 1986.

Baily, Samuel L. *Labor, Nationalism and Politics in Argentina*. New Brunswick, NJ: Rutgers University Press, 1967.

Bonasegna, Cristini. "Argentine Universities Face a New Challenge: Coping with Greater Autonomy." *Chronicle of Higher Education*, October 4, 1989.

Burns, Jimmy. *The Land That Lost Its Heroes*. London: Bloomsbury, 1987.

Canitrot, Adolfo. "Discipline as the Central Objective of Economic Policy: An Essay on the Economic Programme of the Argentine Government since 1976." *World Development* 8 (1980).

Cantón, Darío. *Military Interventions in Argentina: 1900–1906*. Working Paper no. 39. Buenos Aires: Centro de Investigaciones Sociales, 1967.

———. *El Parlamento Argentino en épocas de cambio: 1890, 1916 y 1946*. Buenos Aires: Editorial de Instituto, 1965.

Ciria, Alberto, and Horacio Sanguinetti. *Universidad y estudiantes*. Buenos Aires: Depalma, 1962.

Colombo, Ariel. "El Partido Demócrata Cristiano: una interpretación de su proyecto político." *Plural*, no. 10–11, 1988.

Comisión Nacional de Difusión del Plan de Desarrollo. *La UCRI, Palanca del Desarrollo Nacional y Justicia Social*. Buenos Aires: Ediciones UCRI, 1961.

Concatti, Rolando. *Nuestra opción por el Peronismo*. Mendoza: Publicaciones del Movimiento Sacerdotes para el Tercer Mundo, 1972.

D'Abate, Juan Carlos. "Trade Unions and Peronism." In *Juan Perón and the Reshaping of Argentina*, edited by Federick Turner and José Enrique Miguens. Pittsburgh, PA: University of Pittsburgh Press, 1983.

Díaz Alejandro, Carlos F. *Essays on the Economic History of the Argentine Republic.* New Haven, CT: Yale University Press, 1970.

Dietz, James L., and James H. Street, eds. *Latin America's Economic Development.* Boulder, CO: Lynne Rienner, 1987.

Di Tella, Torcuato. "La situación argentina: fin de la integración y comienzo de la coexistencia." *Cuadernos Americanos* 124, no. 5 (September–October 1962).

Dodson, Michael. "Priests and Peronism: Radical Clergy in Argentine Politics." *Latin American Perspectives* 1, no. 3 (Fall 1974).

Donghi, Tulio Halperín. "Crónico del período." In *Argentina: 1930–1960.* Buenos Aires: Editorial Sur, 1961.

Drake, Paul, and Patricio Silva, eds. *Elections and Democratization in Latin America.* San Diego, CA: Center for Iberian and Latin American Studies, University of California Press, 1986.

Dunne, Peter Masten, S.J., "Church and State in Argentina." *Review of Politics* 7, no. 4 (October 1945).

Estevez, Luis Adolfo. *¿Liberalismo o nacionalismo?* Buenos Aires: Editorial Difusión, 1941.

Fanelli, José María, and Omar Chisari. "Restricciones al crecimiento y distribución del ingreso: el caso argentino." Paper presented at the Fifteenth Latin American Studies Association Congress, Miami, December 3–6, 1989.

Fayt, Carlos. "El Fenómeno Peronista." *Aportes* 1 (July 1966).

Filippo, Virgilio. *El Plan Quinquenal, Perón y los Comunistas.* Buenos Aires: El Ateneo, 1948.

Fillol, Tomás Roberto. *Social Factors in Economic Development: The Argentine Case.* Cambridge, MA: MIT Press, 1961.

Fontana, Andrés. "Armed Forces and Neoconservative Ideology: State Shrinking in Argentina, 1976–1981." In *State Shrinking*, edited by William Glade. Austin: University of Texas Press, 1988.

Frondizi, Arturo. *La Argentina. ¿Es un pais subdesarrollado?* Buenos Aires: Ediciones CEN, 1964.

Fundación de Investigaciones Económicas Latinoamericanas. *El fracaso del estadismo.* Buenos Aires: Sudamericana-Planeta, 1987.

Gallo, Ezequiel, and Silvia Sigal. "La formación de los partidos políticos contemporáneos: la UCR (1890–1916)." In *Argentina, sociedad de masas*, edited by Torcuato Di Tella, Gino Germani, and Jorge Graciarena. Buenos Aires: Editorial Universitaria de Buenos Aires, 1965.

Garosino, Alberto M. "Radiografía militar del golpe." *Confirmado* 1, no. 12 (July 23, 1965).

Gerassi, Marysa. "Argentine Nationalism of the Right." *Studies in Comparative International Development* 1, no. 12 (1965).

Germani, Gino. *Authoritarianism, Fascism, and National Populism.* New Brunswick, NJ: Transaction Books, 1978.

———. "El surgimiento del Peronismo: el rol de los obreros y de los imigrantes internos." *Desarrollo Económico* 13 (1973).

Gibson, Edward. "Democracy and the New Electoral Right in Argentina." *Journal of Interamerican Studies and World Affairs* 32, no. 3 (1990).

Goldwert, Marvin. *Democracy, Militarism and Nationalism in Argentina, 1930–1966.* Austin: University of Texas Press, 1972.

González Esteves, Luis, and Ignacio Llorente. "Elecciones y preferencias políticas en la Capital Federal." In *La Argentina electoral.* Buenos Aires: Editorial Sudamericana, 1985.

Grondona, Mariano. "Las Cuatro Salidas," *Primera Plana* 5, no. 220 (March 14, 1967).

Guardo, Ricardo C. *Horas difíciles.* Buenos Aires: A. Peña Lillo, 1963.

Guglialmelli, Juan Enrique. *120 días en el gobierno.* Buenos Aires: Edición del Autor, 1971.

Hodges, Donald C. *Argentina, 1943–1976: The National Revolution and Resistance.* Albuquerque: University of New Mexico Press, 1976.

Hutchinson, Paul. "Argentina's Church Struggle Grows More Severe." *Christian Century* 72, no. 21 (May 25, 1955).

Iavicoli, N. E. "La interrelación del desarrollo y la seguridad en el estado moderno." *Temas Militares* 1, no. 2 (January–February 1967).

Imaz, José Luis de. *Los que mandan (Those Who Rule).* Albany: State University of New York Press, 1970.

———. "Los que mandan: las fuerzas armadas en Argentina." *América Latina* 7, no. 4 (October–December, 1964).

Inglese, Juan Osvaldo. "El poder socializador de las instituciones educativas argentinas." *Aportes* 5 (July 1967).

———, and Carlos L. Yegros Doria. *Universidad y estudiantes.* Buenos Aires: Ediciones Libera, 1965.

Inter-American Development Bank. *Economic and Social Progress in Latin America.* Washington, DC: Inter-American Development Bank, 1981.

James, Daniel. "The Peronist Left, 1955–1975." *Journal of Latin American Studies* 8, no. 2 (November 1976).

Kennedy, John J. *Catholicism, Nationalism and Democracy in Argentina.* Notre Dame, IN: University of Notre Dame Press, 1958.

Kohl, James, and John Litt. *Urban Guerrilla Warfare in Latin America.* Cambridge, MA: MIT Press, 1974.

Lewis, Paul. *The Crisis of Argentine Capitalism.* Chapel Hill: University of North Carolina Press, 1990.

Lieuwen, Edwin. *Arms and Politics in Latin America.* New York: Praeger, 1960.

———. *Generals vs. Presidents: Neomilitarism in Latin America.* New York: Praeger, 1964.

Luna, Félix. "José Félix Uriburu." In *Presidentes Argentinos.* Buenos Aires: Companía Fabril Editora, 1961.

McGuire, James. "Union Political Tactics and Democratic Consolidation in Alfonsín's Argentina, 1983–1989." *Latin American Research Review* 27, no. 1, 1992.

Mecham, J. Lloyd. *Church and State in Latin America*, rev. ed. Chapel Hill: University of North Carolina Press, 1966.

Mignone, Emilio. *Iglesia y Dictadura.* Buenos Aires: EPN, 1987.

The Military Balance. London: Institute for Strategic Studies, 1967.

Military Junta. "Proceso de Reorganización Nacional." Buenos Aires: Congreso de la Nación, Oficina de Información Parlamentaria, 1976.

Mora y Araujo, Manuel. "The Nature of the Alfonsín Coalition." In *Elections and Democratization in Latin America*, edited by Paul Drake and Patricio Silva. San Diego: Center for Iberian and Latin American Studies, University of California Press, 1986.

Mora y Araujo, Manuel, et al. *Investigación sobre la economía informal: area sociopolítica*. Buenos Aires: IDEC, 1987.

Mustapic, Ana María, and Matteo Goretti. "Un congreso unánime: la práctica de la cohabitación bajo el gobierno de Alfonsín." Series Documentos de Trabajo. Buenos Aires: Instituto Torcuato Di Tella, 1990.

Nasatir, David. "University Experience and Political Unrest of Students in Buenos Aires." *Comparative Education Review* 18, no. 2 (June 1966).

Newton, Ronald J. "Students and the Political System of the University of Buenos Aires." *Journal of Interamerican Studies* 7, no. 4 (October 1966).

O'Donnell, Guillermo. "Tensions in the Bureaucratic-Authoritarian State and the Question of Democracy." In *The New Authoritarianism in Latin America*, edited by David Collier. Princeton, NJ: Princeton University Press, 1979.

Orona, Juan. *La Logia Militar que derrocó a Castillo*. Buenos Aires: N.p., 1966.

———. *La Revolución del 6 de Septiembre*. Buenos Aires: N.p., 1966.

Osiris Villegas, Guillermo. *Políticas y estratégias para el desarrollo y la seguridad nacional*. Buenos Aires: Editorial Pleamar, 1969.

Owen, Frank. *Perón: His Rise and Fall*. London: Cresset, 1957.

Palomino, Héctor. "Reflecciones sobre la evolución de las clases medias en la Argentina." *El Bimestre*, no. 43 (1989).

Parera, Ricardo. *Democracia Cristiana en la Argentina*. Buenos Aires: Editorial Nahuel, 1967.

Payne, James L. *Labor and Politics in Peru: The System of Political Bargaining*. New Haven, CT: Yale University Press, 1965.

———. *Patterns of Conflict in Colombia*. New Haven; CT: Yale University Press, 1968.

Peralta Ramos, Monica. *The Political Economy of Argentina*. Boulder; CO: Westview Press, 1992.

———, and Carlos Waisman, eds. *From Military Rule to Liberal Democracy in Argentina*. Boulder, CO: Westview Press, 1987.

Poneman, Daniel. *Argentina: Democracy on Trial*. New York: Paragon, 1987.

Potash, Robert. "Alfonsín's Argentina in Historical Perspective." University of Massachusetts at Amherst, Latin American Studies Program, Occasional Paper 21, 1988.

———. *The Army and Politics in Argentina, 1928–1945: Yrigoyen to Perón* (Stanford, CA: Stanford University Press, 1969).

———. *The Impact of Professionalism on the Twentieth-Century Argentine Military*. Amherst: University of Massachusetts, Program in Latin American Studies, 1977.

Ranis, Peter. "Parties, Politics and Peronism." Ph.D. diss., New York University, 1965.

Rennie, Ysabel. *The Argentine Republic*. New York: Macmillan, 1954.

Riz, Liliana de. "Alfonsín's Argentina: Renewal Parties and Congress." (Mimeo, July 1988).

————, and Catalina Smulovitz. "Los actores frente al cambio institutcional." (mimeo, CEDES, 1988)

Rock, David. *Argentina, 1516–1987: From Spanish Colonization to Alfonsín*. Berkeley: University of California Press, 1987.

————. "Political Movements in Argentina." In *From Military Rule to Liberal Democracy in Argentina*, edited by Monica Peralta Ramos and Carlos Waisman. Boulder, CO: Westview Press, 1987.

————. *Politics in Argentina, 1890–1930: The Rise and Fall of Radicalism*. London: Cambridge University Press, 1975.

Rowe, James. "Argentina's Restless Military." *AUFS Reports* 11, no. 2 (May 1964).

————. "Onganía's Argentina: The First Four Months." *AUFS Reports* 12, no. 8 (November 1966).

Sacerdotes para el Tercer Mundo: crónica, documentos, reflexión. Buenos Aires: Publicaciones del Movimiento, 1970.

Saravia, José Manuel. *Hacia la salida*. Buenos Aires: Emecé, 1968.

Scott, Robert E. "Political Parties and Policy-Making in Latin America." In *Political Parties and Political Development*, edited by Myron Weiner and Joseph LaPalombara. Princeton, NJ: Princeton University Press, 1966.

Silverman, Bertram. "Labor Ideology and Economic Development in the Peronist Epoch." *Studies in Comparative International Development* 4, no. 11 (1968–69).

Smith, Peter. "Los radicales argentinos y la defensa de los intereses ganderos, 1916–1930." *Desarrollo Económico* 7, no. 25 (April–June 1967).

Smith, William. *Authoritarianism and the Crisis of the Argentine Political Economy*. Stanford, CA: Stanford University Press, 1989.

————. "Democracy and Distributional Conflict in Argentina: Constraints on Macroeconomic Policymaking during the Alfonsín Government." In *Latin American and Caribbean Contemporary Record*, vol. 8, 1988–89, edited by James Malloy and Eduardo Gamarra. New York: Holmes and Meier, forthcoming.

Snow, Peter G. "The Class Basis of Argentine Political Parties." *American Political Science Review* 63, no. 1 (March 1969).

Springer, Philip. "Disunity and Disorder: Factional Politics in the Argentine Military." In *The Military Intervenes: Case Studies in Political Development*, edited by Henry Bienen. New York: Russell Sage Foundation, 1968.

Stepan, Alfred. *Rethinking Military Politics: Brazil and the Southern Cone*. Princeton, NJ: Princeton University Press, 1988.

Street, James H. "The Reality of Power and the Poverty of Economic Doctrine." In *Latin America's Economic Development*, edited by James L. Dietz and James H. Street. Boulder, CO: Lynne Rienner, 1987.

Timerman, Jacobo. *Prisoner without a Name, Cell without a Number*. New York: Alfred A. Knopf, 1981.

Toer, Mario, ed. *El movimiento estudiantil de Perón a Alfonsín*. Buenos Aires: Centro Editor de América Latina, 1988.

Torre, Juan Carlos. "Entre la economía y la política. Los dilemas de la transición democrática en América Latina." Unpublished paper, Instituto Torcuato Di Tella, Buenos Aires.

Troncoso, Oscar A. *Los nacionalistas argentinas*. Buenos Aires: Ediciones S.A.G.A., 1957.

United Nations. Economic Commision for Latin America. *Economic Development and Income Distribution in Argentina*. New York: United Nations, 1969.

Villareal, Juan. "Changes in Argentine Society: The Heritage of the Dictatorship." In *From Military Rule to Liberal Democracy in Argentina*, edited by Monica Peralta Ramos and Carlos Waisman. Boulder, CO: Westview Press, 1987.

Waisman, Carlos. *Reversal of Development in Argentina: Postwar Counterrevolutionary Policies and Their Structural Consequences*. Princeton, NJ: Princeton University Press, 1987.

Walter, Richard J. *Student Politics in Argentina*. New York: Basic Books, 1968.

Weiner, Myron, and Joseph La Palombra. "The Impact of Parties on Political Development." In *Political Parties and Political Development*, edited by Myron Weiner and Joseph La Palombara. Princeton, NJ: Princeton University Press, 1966.

World Bank. *Argentina: Reforms for Price Stability and Growth*. Washington, DC: World Bank, 1990.

———. *Argentina: Social Sectors in Crisis*. Washington, DC: World Bank, 1988.

———. *World Tables*. Washington, DC: World Bank, 1989).

Yegros Doria, Carlos L. "La reforma universitaria hoy." In *Universidad y Estudiantes*, edited by Juan Osvaldo Inglese and Carlos L. Yegros Doria. Buenos Aires: Ediciones Libera, 1965.

Zalduendo, Eduardo. *Geografía electoral de la Argentina*. Buenos Aires: Ediciones Ancora, 1958.

Zuccotti, Juan Carlos. *La emigración argentina contemporánea*. Buenos Aires: Plus Ultra, 1986.

Index

ABOUT THE AUTHORS

PETER G. SNOW is professor of political science at the University of Iowa in Iowa City.

LUIGI MANZETTI is an assistant professor of political science at Southern Methodist University in Dallas.